YOUR LAWYER
ON A
SHORT LEASH

A SURVIVOR'S GUIDE TO DEALING WITH LAWYERS

By

NyC lawyer specializing in TK

Avi Azrieli, Esq.

© 1997
$16.95

Bridge Street Books
Irvington-on-Hudson, New York

Library of Congress Cataloging-in-Publication Data

Azrieli, Avraham.
   Your lawyer on a short leash : a survivor's guide to dealing with lawyers / by
Avraham Azrieli.
     p. cm.
   ISBN 1–57105–036–1
    1. Attorney and client—United States—Popular works. 2. Practice of law—
United States—Popular works. I. Title.
   KF311.Z9A97   1997
   340'.023'73—dc20   96-42170
                                                                 CIP

Manufactured in the United States of America

In Memory of
Daniel S. Hofer, Esq.

CONTENTS

Acknowledgments xi
About the Author xiii
Note to the Reader xv
Introduction: The Problem With Lawyers and What You
             Can Do About It xvii

PART I
EVASIVE TACTICS FOR THE LAWYER-WEARY:
DO YOU REALLY NEED A LAWYER?

Chapter 1 • Do You Really Need a Lawyer? 3

       Situations in Which You Definitely Need a
          Lawyer / 3
       Situations in Which You May Not Need a
          Lawyer / 6
       Hire a Lawyer for a One-Hour
          Consultation / 10

Chapter 2 • Things You Can Do Without a Lawyer 15

       Guess Who's Coming to Dinner? / 15
       Self-Help: Solving Legal Problems Without a
          Lawyer / 16
       Nonlawyer Legal Services / 17
       Computer Software as a Virtual Lawyer / 25
       Small Claims Court: A World Without
          Lawyers / 25

Chapter 3 • Poor Man's Lawyers: Legal Representation
         Without Cost 31

       The Government May Pay for Your
          Lawyer / 31

Contingent-Fee Arrangements / 37
Pro Bono Counsel / 37
Legal Aid Society and Other Public Legal
    Services / 40

PART II
HUNTING FOR A GOOD LAWYER:
A FIELD DAY IN THE LAND OF LAWYERS

Chapter 4 • **Planning the Hunt: What Type of Lawyer
Do You Need?**   **45**

A Stallion, a Leopard, a Fox, or a Rabbit? / 46
Going to Court: What Is Litigation? / 49
Essential Character Traits / 60
Personality and Demeanor / 61
Expensive or Cheap—Can You Afford It? / 62
Convenience of Location and Hours: Is It
    Really Important? / 63
Safety in Numbers: Advantages in Hiring a
    Large Firm / 64

Chapter 5 • **Hunting for the Right Lawyer**   **69**

The Seven Most Effective Lawyer-Hunting
    Tools / 69
Searching for a Lawyer in a Foreign
    Country / 86

Chapter 6 • **A Day's Catch in Your Basket: Interviewing
Lawyers and Verifying Their Claims to Fame**   **91**

Check Your Prey's Rap Sheet: Nothing Less
    Than an Untainted Record of Integrity / 92
Eye Contact With Your Prey: Interviewing
    the Candidate Lawyers / 95

Chapter 7 • **Dissecting Your Prey: Selecting the Best Lawyer
Among the Front Runners**   **103**

Analyzing the Information: Immediate
    Dropouts / 113

Investigating Former Clients'
Satisfaction / 117
The Beauty "Contest" / 119
Preparing to Negotiate the Terms of
Endearment / 120

PART III
THE ART OF SUCCESSFUL NEGOTIATIONS: FEE AGREEMENT AND LAWYERS' MOTIVATION

Chapter 8 • **Your Lawyer on a Short Leash: Provisions That Foster Respect and Encourage Results**   **125**

Why Should You and the Lawyer Sign an
Engagement Letter? / 125
Techniques for Effective Negotiations With
Lawyers / 126
The Engagement Letter as a Binding
Agreement/ 127
Sample Engagement Letter: Table of
Contents / 128
General / 129
Obligations and Warranties / 130
Service to Entrepreneur/Business Owner
(When Applicable) / 132
Scope of Representation and Desired
Results / 133

Chapter 9 • **Provisions for Estimated Budgets, Referral Fees and Advance Retainers**   **139**

Estimated Budget: The Best Way to Keep the
Shirt on Your Back / 140
Division of Fees With Other Lawyers / 144
Payment of Advance Retainer / 145

Chapter 10 • **It's the Money, Stupid! How to Negotiate a Fee Arrangement That Will Motivate Your Lawyer**   **149**

Method of Calculating the Fee: What Is a
"Reasonable" Fee? / 149

Monthly Retainer: The Long-Term
   Relationship / 153
Hourly Rate Fee: Dancing With Wolves / 154
Contingent Fee in a Lawsuit: Traps, Trips,
   and Trepidations / 156
Contingent Fee in Business Transactions:
   Dangerous Liaisons / 162
Fixed Fee: The Way to Get Quick
   Results / 164
Combination Fee: Another Way to Get
   Results / 167
Expenses and Disbursements / 168
Method of Billing and Payments / 171
Unauthorized Actions by Lawyer: Offset
   Against Fees / 172

Chapter 11 • **Kramer v. Kramer: How to Protect Your
                Interests When Breaking Up With Your Lawyer   175**

Termination of the Representation: The
   Newlywed Syndrome—Why Talk About It
   Now? / 175
Termination by Client / 176
Termination by Lawyer / 177
The Final Bill / 178
Restrictions on Fee-Collection Measures / 179
Dispute Resolution / 182

Chapter 12 • **The Power of Attorney: A Beast Without a
                Muzzle   185**

When Is a Power of Attorney
   Necessary? / 185
Preventing Unauthorized Use of the Power
   of Attorney / 186
Revoking the Power of Attorney / 186
Dealing With Unauthorized Actions / 188

PART IV
STICK AND CARROT: THE FEED AND CARE
OF YOUR HARDWORKING LAWYER

Chapter 13 • All in the Family: The Lawyer's Duty to
Keep Secrets   193

    The Attorney-Client Privilege / 193
    The Privilege Under the Work-Product
      Doctrine / 196
    Criminal Activity May Pierce the Lawyer's
      Duty of Secrecy / 197
    The Lawyer's Legal Obligation to Report
      Criminal Conspiracies / 199
    How to Avoid Accidental Waiver of the
      Attorney-Client Privilege / 200
    The Lawyer's Liability for Disclosure of
      Client's Secrets / 203
    What to Do When Your Protected Documents
      Fall Into the Wrong Hands / 204

Chapter 14 • House Training and Feeding Habits: How to
Get the Most Out of Your Lawyer Without
Raising Your Voice   207

    Who's in Charge? / 207
    Anything for a Bloody Bone / 208
    A Client and a Gentleman (or Lady) / 209
    The Toyota Supply System / 209
    Curbing Your Lawyer's Militancy / 210

Chapter 15 • What Do Lawyers Lie About?   217

    Trust Me, I'm a Lawyer! / 217
    Lawyer's Lies May Not Give Basis to a
      Malpractice Claim / 218
    How to Avoid Lawyers' Lies? / 219

Inflated Bills: Padding Time and
    Expenses / 220
Breast Beating and Rainmaking / 223
Hiding Errors and Other Mishaps / 225
Law Firms' Internal Politics / 227

Chapter 16 • **The Savvy Client's Tool Kit**   229

Train Your Lawyer to Communicate / 229
The Sum of All Fears: How to Avoid
    Unexpected Cost Increases / 232
Being There / 233
The Art of Nonadversarial Supervision /235

Chapter 17 • **Sex, Lies and Videotape: Your Lawyer as a
Mate, Date, or Business Partner**   241

Be a Professional Client / 241
Sexual Involvement With Your Lawyer / 242
Doing Business With Your Lawyer / 243

Chapter 18 • **Cats and Milk, Lawyers and Money**   245

Your Lawyer Is Not a Government-Insured
    Bank / 245
Ethics Rules Governing Clients' Money / 246
Screwed-Up Escrow Accounts / 247
Lawyers as Part-Time Money Managers (and
    other Bedtime Horror Stories) / 249
How to Control Your Legal Costs and Keep
    Your Lawyer Happy / 251
How to Audit Your Lawyer's Bill / 252
Amicable Discussions of Excessive
    Charges / 257
Avoiding "Piecemeal" Cost Increases / 258

**Conclusion: A Final Word on Lawyers
and Used-Car Dealers**

Final Note: Lawyers and Used-Car Dealers   263
Appendix A: Sample Engagement Letter   265
Appendix B: Sample General Power of Attorney   279

ACKNOWLEDGMENTS

I wish to express my gratitude to the many friends and colleagues who gave me their helpful comments and insights throughout the process of writing this book. Though they are too numerous to mention by name, they will no doubt recognize their respective contributions. In addition, I thank Heike Fenton, publisher, Esther Gueft, former vice-president, and the wonderful staff at Bridge Street Books, for their enthusiastic embrace of this project. Barbara Bustos, my devoted secretary at Davis, Polk & Wardwell, is acknowledged for her tireless clerical help. Special thanks are due to my wife, Fiona, for the many nights she spent reading the manuscript in its various stages and for her moral and intellectual support.

ABOUT THE AUTHOR

Avraham (Avi) Azrieli practices law in New York City and has served a wide variety of clients while associated with major corporate law firms, including Baker & Botts (1994–1996) and Davis, Polk & Wardwell (1991–1994). He clerked with a federal district court in Maryland (1990–1991) and with the Supreme Court of Israel in Jerusalem (1988–1989). Mr. Azrieli served as an officer in the Israeli Defense Forces, Intelligence Corps (1980–1984) and holds law degrees from Bar Ilan University in Tel Aviv and Columbia Law School in New York City, and a certificate from the Hague Academy of International Law in The Hague. His publications include "Dispute Resolution Under the U.S.-Canada Free Trade Agreement" (*American Review of International Arbitration,* 1990) and "A Framework for Middle East Free Trade Zone" (*St. John's Law Review,* 1993).

NOTE TO THE READER

A word of caution: This guide will make you a savvy consumer of legal services, enabling you to obtain legal services on a level ground with the lawyers you hire. However, this guide is not a substitute for legal advice and representation, but rather a wise companion while you find the best lawyer, negotiate a fair and motivational fee arrangement with that lawyer, and supervise your lawyer's work and effectiveness. Under no circumstances should you try to pull your own ailing tooth or, similarly, try to be your own lawyer when confronted with a legal situation. At a minimum, you should briefly consult with a lawyer, and this guide will convert that otherwise painful experience into a satisfying and productive one.

INTRODUCTION

THE PROBLEM WITH LAWYERS AND WHAT YOU CAN DO ABOUT IT

Why did I write this book?

Sometime in the next year or two you will probably need a lawyer. You may need a real-estate lawyer to help you buy a new home, a trust and estate lawyer to draft a will, a business lawyer to negotiate the purchase of franchise rights from a national restaurant chain, or a divorce lawyer to help you untangle an unhappy situation. Whatever legal problem you may face, you *will* need a good lawyer, and this book will guide you through a treacherous road: Selecting the best lawyer for your needs (good lawyers do exist!), striking a fair fee arrangement that will motivate your lawyer, and working together with the lawyer to achieve the best results.

What propelled me to sit down and write this book was a phone call from a friend, Ernest, who read to me over the phone a letter he received from his lawyer. We have all heard horror stories involving lawyers, mostly about lawyers who failed to deliver the promised service while not failing to demand an exaggerated fee. But this one hit close to home, and after Ernest had finished reading the lawyer's letter to me, I knew I had to sit down to write. Every page of this book was written with Ernest's experience on my mind, and with the firm belief that good lawyers do exist, can be found by educated consumers, and do provide effective legal representation at a fair price.

Ernest's rogue lawyer: Could it happen to you?

Ernest's grandfather, a successful merchant, died at the age of ninety-three. He left a will, bequeathing his house and land—valued at over

$500,000—to his six grandchildren, among them Ernest. The will designated Ernest's uncle, a lawyer himself, as the executor of the estate. The uncle sent copies of the will to all the grandchildren (including the uncle's own children), but in a letter accompanying the will mentioned that, two years before dying, their grandfather had given him—the uncle—the house and land as a gift. Therefore, the estate was worthless and the generous will practically meaningless.

After futile attempts to obtain an explanation from the uncle as to the circumstances of the alleged "gift," Ernest and his sister decided to seek legal help. Ernest's father knew a "good" lawyer in the town where the house and land were located, and a meeting was scheduled. The lawyer listened to the story and agreed to take on the case. The lawyer further explained that the suit should be filed immediately and that he would start collecting evidence as soon as possible, demanding relevant documents and interviewing potential witnesses in order to find the true circumstances of the "gift"—specifically, whether the grandfather, who had suffered two strokes before his death, understood what he was doing. The lawyer asked for a $10,000 advance on legal fees so that he could start working on the case immediately. Ernest and his sister paid the $10,000, and the lawyer filed a two-page claim and obtained a temporary court lien on the disputed property.

A year later, after no news had come from the lawyer, Ernest called him to inquire about the case and about the content of the evidence that had been collected so far. To Ernest's dismay, the lawyer told him that nothing had been done. "I'm still waiting for the court to issue a trial date," the lawyer said. It turned out that, besides the initial filing of a two-page complaint with the court, the lawyer had done practically nothing.

After discussing the situation with several friends, Ernest wrote to his lawyer to express concern over the passage of time, which could damage his claim as potential witnesses passed away, bank records were discarded, and other evidence became unavailable. Ernest also mentioned that the lawyer himself had indicated during the initial meeting that he would begin discovery of evidence as soon as a claim was filed and that there was no need to wait for a trial date. Ernest reminded his lawyer that the substantial advance paid on account of legal fees had been demanded by the lawyer precisely because of the urgent and extensive discovery required by such a claim.

The lawyer's reply letter, which Ernest read to me over the phone, went like this:

Dear Ernest:

I received your letter dated May 21, 1994. I am deeply insulted by it, and hereby inform you that I no longer wish to represent you. If you do not notify me in writing within 10 days of the name of your new lawyer, I will inform the court that I have withdrawn from the representation in your case and consider myself free of any obligation thereunder.

I will refrain from expressing all my thoughts, but at the minimum would say that your letter was completely out of line. Who gave you the right to criticize my work? I manage my cases the way I think right, and I do not need advice from you or from anyone else. I only took your case as a favor to your father, who is an old friend of mine. I owe you nothing, and you should be grateful that I agreed to take your case. It was my decision not to proceed with discovery but rather wait to receive a trial date, and if my judgment is not good enough for you, you can find yourself another lawyer. And I also resent your comment about the fees, which I have already earned in full.

Sincerely,

John Smith
Attorney-at-Law

The above letter was not only rude, but also grossly unethical, for several reasons. First, Ernest's lawyer attacked his client in an attempt to cover up his own negligence in allowing so much time to pass without starting discovery of evidence through the use of readily available procedure. Second, the lawyer failed to respect his client's instructions in handling the case and failed to serve the client as best as he could. It is completely irrelevant that Ernest's father had recommended the lawyer and that they were friends. Once a lawyer-client relationship is formed, the lawyer is professionally obligated to do his best for the client, nothing less. Third, the lawyer resigned from the case without his client's consent, before a substitute lawyer was found and in the absence of any serious and unavoidable reasons for the resignation. Fourth, the lawyer was deceitful in his letter because discovery always starts as soon as a suit is filed—long before a trial date is scheduled—and the lawyer had collected a large sum as an advance on fees for that very reason. Lastly, and most outrageously, the lawyer's letter was plainly obnoxious. A lawyer who fails to treat a client respectfully (even if the client had been so unwise as to pay a substantial advance on fees before worthy service has been provided) violates the cardinal rule of the service industry: The client is always right.

Will this book save you from legal misfortune?

My advice to Ernest was to immediately dismiss his lawyer and look for a new lawyer—an honest, diligent lawyer with proven experience in litigation involving wills and estates. When Ernest asked me how to go about finding such a wonderful lawyer, I gave him a short list of searching tools, at the same time jotting the list down on a yellow pad. I used that same list a few months later when I wrote Chapter 5 of this book: "Hunting for the Right Lawyer: The Seven Most Effective Lawyer-Hunting Tools."

This book was born to save you from Ernest's fate, not by making you avoid lawyers but by assisting you in finding the best lawyer for your needs. Chapter 2: "Things You Can Do Without a Lawyer" is a useful source in a few simple situations, provided you are comfortable handling them without a lawyer. But this book is not intended to help you be your own lawyer. A good lawyer will be greatly valuable to you whenever you encounter a legal problem. Lawyers are a fact of life that virtually every one of us encounters, in situations such as getting married, buying a house, writing a will, divorcing, selling a house, getting remarried, buying another house, being laid off, starting up a business, taking in a business partner, dealing with a supplier's bankruptcy, selling a business, setting up a living trust, or dying. Most of the foregoing occasions can be less painful with the help of a good lawyer, and this book paves the safe route to finding and using such a good lawyer.

Is this book different from other books?

There are other books available in the market that will be useful to you in dealing with legal issues and with lawyers. One such book is The *ABA Family Legal Guide*, which is published by the American Bar Association. Other books include Dorothy Leeds' classic work *Smart Questions to Ask Your Lawyer*, and Dennis M. Powers' *Legal Street Smart*. However, this book is the first to offer a complete, step-by-step guide to searching for and selecting a good lawyer, negotiating a motivational fee arrangement, supervising the lawyer's work, figuring out the bills and dealing with the many issues that are bound to come up during a lawyer-client relationship.

This book is not intended to teach you the law, but rather to empower you, as a consumer of legal services, by providing you with a problem-solving guide that, while avoiding abstract discussions of lawyers' ills and clients' tribulations, includes examples, anecdotes, and background discussions that demonstrate why choosing the wrong lawyer can be dangerous to your health and wealth, and how you can protect yourself when dealing with lawyers.

Is this book easy to use?

To make this book user-friendly, I chose a simple, chronological structure that will provide you with easy-to-find solutions to practical problems and challenges as you tackle them, from the time you realize that you may need a lawyer to the time you no longer wish to employ one. The detailed table of contents should serve you as a road map. Also, each chapter is written as an independent source of advice, so that you can go directly to a specific subject and find the answer you need without having to review other, unrelated pages while looking for a specific solution. The questions this book will help you answer are:

- Do you really need a lawyer, or can you manage without one?
- Where can you find free legal representation?
- What type of a lawyer do you need?
- Where can you find a good and honest lawyer?
- How do you choose between several recommended lawyers?
- How do you verify a lawyer's claim to fame?
- How do you question former clients about the lawyer?
- What is an *Engagement Letter* and how do you negotiate it?
- Should you sign a power-of-attorney?
- How can you negotiate a fair and motivating fee arrangement?
- Should you tell your lawyer all your dirty secrets?
- How can you monitor your lawyer's work?
- Should you be personally involved in the case/contract negotiations?
- How can you keep down your legal expenses?

Is this a "lawyer-bashing" book?

After reading an early draft of this book, a friend (who is not a lawyer) suggested I publish the book under a pseudonym to avoid the wrath of my fellow lawyers. I thought then, and I still think, that he was wrong. This book is not a frontal attack on all lawyers. Rather, it is a preemptive attack directed solely against dishonest, negligent, and incompetent lawyers who, by virtue of their unconscionable practices, give a bad reputation to a profession that is, by and large, populated by honest, hard-working lawyers who are fiercely devoted to their clients and to the law. This book was written for the mutual benefit of those good lawyers and their clients.

When reading this book, you will notice that many of the cases described took place in the courts of New York, and that the ethics rules cited are also mostly from New York. There are several reasons for this. First, I am a New York lawyer and feel most comfortable discussing examples from the environment in which I practice. Second, New York's ethics rules are based on model rules issued by the American Bar Association. Generally, similar rules would apply in your state, and the examples of unethical behavior by New York lawyers are not, by any means, unique to New York. And last, to paraphrase Frank Sinatra's signature song, if you can make it (that is, use a lawyer) in New York, you can make it . . . *anywhere.*

Is this book really for you?

According to a survey published by the *New York Law Journal* on June 12, 1995, lawyers in the United States collected $106.5 billion from their clients in 1994. Applying that number to the estimated 800,000 practicing lawyers in the United States, each of them collected, on average, about $135,000. Are you one of their clients? The Federal Bureau of Labor, in statistics published by *The New York Times* on June 11, 1995, indicated that approximately 70% of the population used lawyers in the last five years. In other words, a majority of Americans use lawyers at least once every five years, and spend thousands or even tens of thousands of dollars on legal bills.

Should you make the effort?

There is no law forcing you to become an *informed* consumer. Not every fiancé reads Teddy Lenderman's *The Complete Idiot's Guide to Perfect Weddings* (or Renee Newman's *The Diamond Ring Buying Guide*). Not every expecting parent reads Eisenberg, Murkoff & Hathaway's *What to Expect When You're Expecting.* Not every candidate for bypass surgery calls the Joint Commission on Accreditation of Healthcare Organizations for each hospital's "report card." (It's 708–916–5800, if you're interested.) Not every car buyer reviews *Car & Driver*'s latest test-drive report before buying a car. And not every spendthrift shopper keeps a copy of Mark Green's *The Consumer Bible* on his nightstand. But every consumer who makes the effort to become educated before spending large amounts of money on products or on services will benefit greatly, as proven by the success of each of the above bestsellers. Similarly, not all those in need of a lawyer will buy and read a book about finding good lawyers and using them effectively. But many will, and they are the intended beneficiaries of this book.

Avi Azrieli
New York, March 1997

PART I

EVASIVE TACTICS FOR THE LAWYER-WEARY: DO YOU REALLY NEED A LAWYER?

CHAPTER 1

DO YOU REALLY NEED A LAWYER?

To answer this question, you must carefully define the reasons why you are considering hiring a lawyer, and weigh the financial risks at stake against the probable cost of hiring a good lawyer. In some situations, you may want to consult a trustworthy lawyer (whom you'll find by taking the steps described in the following chapters) so that you can better assess whether you need to actually hire a lawyer to represent you in the matter. This chapter will take you through the process of assessing your situation and making the right choices—so you don't lose your case *and* your shirt.

SITUATIONS IN WHICH YOU DEFINITELY NEED A LAWYER

A Classic Case of Liability: Get Help!

Your wife arranged a birthday party for your seven-year-old daughter. As the weather forecast had predicted a storm, the party was taking place inside the greenhouse, which was built at the far end of the back-yard. You were in your study, on the telephone, when the window behind you lit up and an explosive thunderclap sounded. You swiveled in your chair and looked through the window at the balloon-decorated greenhouse to see the seventy-foot Swedish pine, which your grandfather had planted, part from its trunk and collapse on the greenhouse. You rushed out of your study, leaving an important Japanese client on

3

hold, and hurried through the library, the dining room, the breakfast room, the kitchen, the storage room, and the rear porch while horrible images passed through your mind—children trapped under metal beams, glass slivers stuck in blood-soaked T-shirts, hysterical housewives moaning over their slurping infants, your wife and daughter buried under the ruins. . . .

But, to your great relief, you find that the children had stepped out of the greenhouse a moment earlier to launch one of the birthday gifts—a pair of small, freshwater fish in a transparent plastic bag—into the fish pond outside. Their mothers had hurried after them to the pond when the newly released fish quickly and viciously chewed up all seven goldfish and bit one girl's pinky. One mother, however, was screaming, and soon enough you find out that her son, who was more interested in birthday cake than fish, had stayed behind in the greenhouse and was now buried under a mound of glass and metal—and an old Swedish pine.

Now, a day later, as you stand in your backyard watching two restless piranhas swim about in the fishpond, your wife appears on the rear porch, red-eyed and runny-nosed. She tells you that the boy's mother called to say that the boy will live, though scarred, and that her lawyer will be in touch very soon. Then your wife hands you a Federal Express package. You rip open the package to find a letter from a downtown lawyer offering his sincere condolences for the misfortune of having such an awful accident occur on your property, and suggesting that you stop by for a free consultation. In a fit of rage you tear up the letter and throw the pieces into the pond, where they are summarily attacked by the piranhas. Then you go to your wood-paneled study and dial the number of your family lawyer.

Were you right to tear up the letter? Yes, because a lawyer who has the time to chase clients by following up on brief news reports is either unemployed, inexperienced, or just looking to earn a quick buck from a person in trouble.

Were you right to call a lawyer whom you know and trust? Absolutely, because you definitely need a lawyer, and the sooner the better. When someone is injured while on your property, you are liable for any negligence that led to the injury, and should not wait until a lawsuit is filed. Even if you have insurance, the damages might exceed the coverage under the policy, and the injured plaintiff may go after your personal property (not to mention the higher insurance premiums you will have to pay!).

The lawyer you hire to defend you against a probable lawsuit should immediately proceed to investigate the scene of the accident, interview witnesses, and collect evidence to show that the injury was not the result of your negligence. In this example, your lawyer should look for evidence that the greenhouse was properly constructed, that the Swedish pine was healthy and unlikely to topple—except for that one-in-a-million chance of an exceptionally strong lightning bolt—and that you had taken all reasonable steps to prevent such an accident.

Are You in a Financial Danger Zone?

You really *do* need a lawyer if you know (or have a strong gut feeling) that you are in financial danger, or that you are confronted with a situation that requires professional legal knowledge so that your financial or personal interests are properly protected. For example, consultation with a lawyer is needed when:

- A person has been seriously injured while on your property, while driving in your car, or otherwise can claim that you were responsible for his or her injury.

- You or one of your immediate family members came out of the hospital in worse shape than going in, and there is a reason to suspect malpractice.

- You have been accused of a crime and a conviction may result in incarceration, a large fine, or a criminal record.

- You have been sued or threatened with a lawsuit for an amount you consider substantial, or that is in connection with property or a right which has significant value to you.

- You are considering a substantial financial investment, such as forming a partnership, joining a real estate investment syndicate, or becoming a major shareholder in a private or public corporation.

- You are confronted with a serious tax problem involving income or capital gain in connection with your business investments, or you are being audited by the IRS for taking questionable business deductions, for example, the cost of your daughter's piano lessons.

- You contemplate starting or expanding your business, entering into a commercial lease, hiring employees, purchasing a franchise, forming a partnership, or . . . bribing a public official to obtain business.

- You wish to write a will and plan your estate.
- You are buying or selling your house or business.
- You are thinking about a divorce while your spouse talks about a second honeymoon.
- You are thinking about remarrying your ex-wife or ex-husband.

Potential Risks and Gains in Various Situations

No list could include all possible situations that life may throw at you. Your need for legal help may vary from mere advice on a passing legal matter to the need for representation in a small business transaction or defense in a fatal negligence case. But the previous list of hypothetical situations should assist you in weighing your need against the cost of legal services. These situations would always fall into the following categories:

- You are confronted by a lawyer, or by someone who is represented by a lawyer.
- You plan to confront someone who you know will be represented by a lawyer.
- Your property, personal freedom, or family is threatened by a government agency, a powerful corporation, or an individual.
- You are contemplating, or have begun negotiating, a substantial financial transaction that involves signing a contract.

The need for a lawyer is not always apparent. It is important that you define for yourself what are the facts that make you think you need legal help. Sometimes the necessity is obvious, sometimes it is not, and sometimes you could do with hiring the less costly services of an expert nonlawyer. And finally, more often than not, you feel that only a trustworthy lawyer, even if this is not her specialty, will be able to tell you whether you do, or do not, need a lawyer. The following discussion will tell you how to find such a lawyer (and pay for one hour of her time).

SITUATIONS IN WHICH YOU MAY NOT NEED A LAWYER

Not every situation that involves a legal problem necessitates hiring a lawyer. Common sense and a pragmatic approach, together with a brief consultation, can solve some disputes. Good advice from a nonlawyer professional can help you deal with other situations. And, in some matters, city, state, and federal agencies will provide you with a wide variety of services for which lawyers would charge steep fees.

The $100,000 Window Bars: A Classic Case of Wasting Money on Lawyers

On March 17, 1987, the tenants of a ninth-floor cooperative apartment on West 36th Street in New York hired a lawyer to fight the building co-op board over the $909 cost of installing child-guard window bars on the apartment's thirty-two windows. Seven years later, on March 23, 1994, an article in the *Wall Street Journal*, bearing the headline "Ever Heard the One About Lawyers and Window Bars?," described how the modest $909 dispute had become a tale of absurd lawyering in which neither the co-op board nor the tenants could claim victory.

The legal question was whether, under a New York law that required installation of window bars in all apartments in which children under the age of ten lived, the cost of the window bars should be borne by the tenants of the specific apartment in which the children lived or by the co-op board and thus distributed among all of the building's tenants. The building, which had been a zipper factory before its conversion to a residential co-op of loft apartments, hired a law firm to collect the $909 cost of installation from the ninth-floor tenants, whose third child was one month old.

First, settlement negotiations took place, as learned lawyers for both sides communicated with each other to no avail. The co-op board's legal bills had by now surmounted the $909 cost of the window bars; however, the board considered the issue a matter of principle, and a lawsuit had commenced. The board's lawyers filed a complaint, the tenants' lawyers filed a response and a counterclaim against the co-op board. The board's lawyers then filed an answer to the tenants' response and a response to the tenants' counterclaim. Thereafter, the lawyers on both sides spent many hours researching the law and drafting various memoranda and briefs, which were then reviewed, edited, and redrafted by other, more senior lawyers. Various court motions were also prepared and filed, and in the course of time, new lawyers had to spend time reviewing the many documents already produced so that they could substitute for lawyers who left or went on vacation.

Finally, on January 26, 1989, New York Civil Court Judge Richard Lane issued his decision that "logic and substantial justice as well as lease provision" tipped the scales of justice in favor of the co-op board and ordered the tenants to pay the $909. Additionally, under the co-op by-laws, the tenants had to reimburse the co-op for its legal expenses, and they now faced a total bill in the tens of thousands of dollars. They did the only reasonable thing: They instructed their lawyers to continue the war by appealing Judge Lane's decision.

Industrious as always, the board's lawyers promptly dealt with the appeal by conducting intensive research, drafting a comprehensive reply, and even rehearsing the oral arguments to sharpen their skills before the actual performance in court. However, their efforts were in vain, for in May 1990 the court overturned Judge Lane's decision and ordered that the cost of the window bars should be borne by the board and not by the individual tenants who had young children.

With the new decision in hand, lawyers for the board convened and reconvened, did more research, and concluded that, even though the original $909 dispute seemed marginal, there was a greater motive to continue fighting: the legal fees, which the losing side was supposed to pay. Thus another appeal was drafted, reviewed, edited, and filed, to which the tenants' lawyers responded. Then, in February 1991, four years after the legal fight had begun, the higher appeals court reversed the lower appeals court and reinstated Judge Lane's decision in favor of the co-op board.

As the appeals process had been exhausted with respect to the $909 cost of the window bars, the tenants' lawyers turned to fight against the board's claim for reimbursement of its lawyers' fees. After a lengthy legal battle to decide which of the three courts had jurisdiction to determine lawyers' fees, the court appointed a referee.

The co-op lawyers prepared and filed with the referee a detailed claim for all legal bills and expenses, including a $1,500 charge for preparing the bill itself, and a special $5,000 bonus fee for as-yet unbilled work. Throughout the following year, new lawyers' bills for "collection of previous fees" amounted to more than $12,000.

In July 1993, the referee issued his final report to the court: "The parties and their attorneys demonstrated a lack of common sense and a lack of practicality and allowed a claim for $909 to escalate into an attorneys' fee claim exceeding $70,000." He ordered that the tenants, who had lost the original dispute, should pay "only" $30,000 of the co-op board's legal expenses and that the board would have to sustain the unreasonable remainder of $43,000.

In response to the decision, the *Wall Street Journal* quoted the co-op lawyer as saying, "I think the expenditures here were appropriate and were kept to a minimum. . . . Every step of the way [our clients] had an idea of what was going on. . . . There were no surprises in this case."

Don't Let Lawyers Manipulate You Into Fighting Over Nonsense

In the window bars case, while lawyers clocked in hundreds of hours of billable time and four courts issued lengthy decisions, a one-month-old baby grew up and entered the second grade. The foolish dispute left both parties poorer, but no doubt wiser. As to the lawyers, they obviously have a different, more philosophical view. After all, they made more than $100,000. If anyone had made a mistake, it was their clients.

Not true! A good lawyer would have dissuaded the co-op board from filing a lawsuit to begin with because the cost of the window bars was too small to merit litigation. The building was relatively small, the members of the co-op board were neighbors living next door to the tenants who had a child, and the whole matter should have been settled over coffee and cookies, probably by splitting the cost in some manner. Even if personal animosity had already settled in, they could have hired lawyers for the single purpose of negotiating a settlement, or hired a mediator through one of the many mediation services available. The lawyers violated their clients' trust by letting them spend on legal representation an amount greater than the financial risk involved in the dispute: Even if the board would have had to pay for the installation of window bars in several other apartments in the building, the amount of money would have been negligible compared to the cost of the litigation.

Don't Hire a Lawyer When There Is No Financial Risk

Unless you have money to spare without care, never hire a lawyer to deal with a negligible financial gain or risk. Stay away from legal disputes, keep things in proportion, and do not get involved with lawyers unless you have to. And when you do, choose a lawyer wisely after reading the relevant chapters of this book, and ask the lawyer for advice on how to deal rationally and economically with the situation. Hiring a lawyer should be viewed as "preventive medicine," rather than as a weapon to be wielded in a fight over "principles." Unless, again, you do not mind throwing your money into the wind. Examples of situations in which you can do without a lawyer are:

- You have been sued in small claims court.
- You received an undeserved parking ticket.
- Your mechanic overcharged you.
- Your doctor prescribed headache medicine for what your mother is all but convinced must be a malignant brain tumor (you may want a second opinion from a physician, not a lawyer).
- Your neighbor is making too much noise with his new Harley-Davidson.
- Your son did not make the school baseball team.
- You lent money to a friend, and she did not repay.

If you lend money to a friend, consider it a gift, unless you want to lose both money and friend. In all the other situations, exercise great caution before hiring a lawyer to represent you. If you seriously believe that a lawyer could help you, find one you can trust (using the hunting tools provided later in this book). Remember that using lawyers without proper precautions may be as risky as stepping into a bottomless financial pit. Do it only if it's necessary, not just because you want to get back at someone, or because "it's a matter of principle." An exception to this rule is the rare case in which you believe that the wrong done to you is also done to others, and you conclude that your case bears great public interest. In such a case, do not fight it yourself. There are many organizations that employ lawyers to fight for public causes, the best known among them is the NAACP. One of those organizations may take your case and fight it to victory. To find the right organization, first look in your local phone directory, which normally lists all major organizations. Also, you should call a local judge, the district attorney's office, and visit the local library.

HIRE A LAWYER FOR A ONE-HOUR CONSULTATION

Modern times have, to some extent, legitimized living together as a prelude to traditional marriage. Similarly, a one-hour consultation with a potential lawyer is a perfect prelude to hiring one to represent you in a substantial case. After all, it is probably easier emotionally and cheaper financially to get a divorce than to fire your lawyer, so you should get your feet wet first before you commit to a long-term relationship. A preliminary consultation gives you that chance. How should you go about it?

The Trap of Free Consultations

You and your wife fly to New York City on a Friday night to celebrate your tenth wedding anniversary. You arrive at the hotel where your travel agent had made reservations and tell the concierge to rush things as you have a pair of tickets for a Broadway show. You are taken to a fabulous suite on the 58th floor, where champagne and flowers await you. A moment later the front desk calls up to say that your limousine is waiting. On your way down, the elevator gets stuck, and by the time it is manually lowered to the lobby twenty minutes have passed. Your wife makes a great effort not to scream, and you run across the lobby to the waiting limousine. As you get in, you hear the concierge yell at the chauffeur: "Step on it! They're late!"

Going down Seventh Avenue at high speed, the limousine hits a deep pothole and a tire blows loudly. The driver struggles in vain to regain control, the limousine spins, slides, jumps the sidewalk, and sails through plateglass windows into the nonsmoking section of a four-star Italian restaurant.

The following morning, you and your wife share a room with a view at St. Vincent's Hospital, stitched, bandaged, and molded into casts. A large TV perched on a shelf across the room displays the bespectacled face of a lawyer who offers a free one-hour consultation to "all persons injured in any way by anybody anywhere anytime!" You immediately reach for the phone next to your bed because you'd like to know who's going to pay for your injuries, pain, suffering, and spoiled plans. Should you sue the travel agent who reserved the hotel accommodations and the limo? The hotel for its defective elevator and a concierge who tells limo drivers to "Step on it"? The speeding limo driver? New York City, which failed to fix the hole in the road? The contractor who paved the road? The maker of the tire that exploded? The Italian restaurant that refused to call an ambulance unless you ordered dinner first?

Insist on Paying for a Consultation

Responding to a TV, radio, or newspaper offer for a "free consulta-tion" with a lawyer will not only cause you to waste time but may put you at risk for hiring an unqualified lawyer and bringing upon yourself great financial loss. All you know about that lawyer on TV is that she has enough money to pay for an expensive commercial. You know noth-ing about her credentials, experience, expertise, reputation, or honesty. Also, when you call the number on the screen, in most cases you will not talk to a lawyer but to an assistant, whose job is not to help you (which he is not capable of doing anyway) but to "screen" callers like your, to determine if there is any money to be made by luring them into the office.

Especially in the case of an accident, a person who responds to a "free consultation" offer is confused and needs an authoritive helping hand. The person who will answer your call is trained to give you an illusory feeling of security, to convince you that you are in good hands, and to make you come into the office for consultation and sign a re-tainer—a binding agreement under which you hire that lawyer to handle your case for a certain fee.

Most likely, you will be told that "there is no fee unless we get you money!" But the fine print will ensure that the lawyer's expenses be paid by you regardless of the outcome and, most important, that you can not change your mind and fire the lawyer without paying her "for her time." Lawyer's time costs between $100 and $500 per hour, de-pending on location and specialty. Therefore, that last condition practi-cally locks you into the relationship because, even if you realized that you hired the wrong lawyer, you could not hire a better lawyer: Firing the first lawyer would cost too much.

You should consult a lawyer before making any important financial or legal decisions. But, as in anything else in life, there is no free meal. Lawyers sell their time, and if you need time with a lawyer, you must be willing to pay for it. Free consultation is not a form of charity. Rather, it is a way for lawyers to lure potential clients into the office and sign them up as moneymaking clients. Lawyers do not dispense valuable legal advice for free. Even if you actually speak directly to a lawyer and not his "screening" clerk during your free consultation, you will receive only the most superficial legal advice until you've fallen prey to signing a retainer. Remember that a free consultation is time spent by the lawyer with the sole purpose of trying to assess your case *from the lawyer's point of view*, and not with your needs and interests first on the lawyer's mind.

You should, therefore, actively look for a good lawyer for advice, not on TV, but by using the hunting tools provided later in this book. Once you find a good lawyer, get the legal advice you need by insisting on meeting the lawyer herself and paying for her time at an agreed-upon hourly rate, so that your needs take top priority.

To find a good lawyer for a paid consultation, follow the steps provided in Chapter 5, "Hunting for the Right Lawyer." Even if all you need is brief, concise advice about a limited problem, it is worth while to spend some time finding the best lawyer you can. You should consider a lawyer to be a continuing source of advice and help, and after you find a lawyer you can trust, she should always be available to help you, or to refer you to a legal specialist who can.

CHAPTER 2

THINGS YOU CAN DO WITHOUT A LAWYER

When trying to decide whether you do or don't need a lawyer, consider whether you are comfortable with the idea of taking care of the challenge by yourself or with the help of a "nonlawyer" expert. Nevertheless, if the situation presents any risk to your financial or personal wellbeing you should *always* consult a lawyer. This chapter will help you handle certain legal needs without spending big money on lawyers.

GUESS WHO'S COMING TO DINNER?

You own a small bakery in Manhattan's Little Italy. During a Thanksgiving dinner with your family and employees, your daughter informs you that she's in love and wants to marry Anzio, a "tourist" who works in your bakery in exchange for food and shelter until he can return to his village in Sicily. After you've yelled at your wife, made your daughter cry, and threatened to send Anzio back to Sicily, your initial rage gives way to recognition that your daughter's chances of finding a better match are slim—an adjective that could not be used to describe her. You agree to the marriage on condition that Anzio become a legal immigrant. How can you find out Anzio's chances of becoming a legal immigrant?

Most people in your position would go to an immigration lawyer they've heard about from a friend or a newspaper advertisement, pay a hefty advance, and hope the lawyer would do his job quickly. However, with some diligence, many immigration matters can be handled less expensively, with only limited involvement of a lawyer. In the case of

15

Anzio, who is a tourist marrying an American citizen, the procedure should be relatively simple, unless Anzio has engaged in illegal activities or is subject to deportation. In the case of marriage, the Immigration and Naturalization Service has local offices where you can obtain the handful of forms required to be filled out and filed, together with the marriage certificate and the appropriate fee.

Because Anzio is working illegally, you worry about possible complications and want to have assurances that Anzio can become a "legal" immigrant before you allow the marriage to proceed. However, instead of paying thousands of dollars to a lawyer to represent you throughout the long process, the matter (as in most immigration matters) can be solved by meeting a lawyer for a one-hour consultation, for a fee normally not more than $150. During the consultation you should ask the lawyer questions from a list you have prepared in advance, and you should have all the facts pertinent to the case readily available. The lawyer should explain to you the status of the immigrant, specify the correct procedure and forms, and describe to you all other documents that should be prepared and enclosed with the forms. The actual work—filling out the forms, preparing a statement, and collecting other personal documents—can all be done by you and your family, thus you will spend perhaps $150 instead of several thousand.

SELF-HELP: SOLVING LEGAL PROBLEMS WITHOUT A LAWYER

Dealing with some government and judicial agencies, such as the Internal Revenue Service, the U.S. Copyright Office, the Traffic Court, or the local probate court (for probation of wills and estates), can often be done through a brief consultation with a lawyer and independent filing of all the required forms.

Other situations that usually do not require hiring a lawyer include small financial disputes with a landlord, an accountant, a physician, or a maid, or any other dispute over a bill or deficient service in which the amount involved is not substantial. In most cases you can solve the dispute by communicating with the other party and trying to reach an amicable solution. This also applies to negotiating a simple residential lease agreement, resolving a warranty dispute with an appliance manufacturer, or even a dispute under a new-automobile "lemon law," which in many cases can be dealt with successfully without the help of a lawyer.

Even if you cannot resolve the matter yourself, the use of a lawyer should be limited to consultation and, possibly, having the lawyer send a letter to the other party reciting your rights under the law. A short consultation and the writing of a letter should not cost more than the one-hour rate for the lawyer's time, whereas the cost of retaining the lawyer to represent you in the dispute can quickly exceed the financial risk involved.

In the case of a documented debt owed to you, such as rent unpaid by your tenant, a bill unpaid by a customer, or a bouncing check, when the amount is too small to engage a lawyer, you may use other avenues to try to recover the loss. One avenue is the small claims court, which is discussed later in this chapter. Another low-cost avenue is the Better Business Bureau, which offers a small-loss-recovery program through arbitration. After conducting an investigation, the Better Business Bureau will issue a report, which you should immediately send to the trade association relevant to your business, to the state attorney general's office, to the Federal Trade Commission, to the National Consumer League, and to other associations, organizations and agencies that will either take action on your behalf or at least make the debtor's wrong deeds known to others. In many cases, the debtor will feel the pressure and try to settle the case with you by paying at least some of the amount owed.

NONLAWYER LEGAL SERVICES

Nonlawyer legal services can be found in the yellow pages, on the bulletin board in the local court, or in the classified section of a local newspaper or law journal. They offer low-cost assistance in legal matters, as an alternative to using a lawyer. It is the fastest-growing segment of the legal business and includes services performed by form-fillers, trained paralegal, and other licensed professionals (for example, accountants, real estate brokers, mortgage brokers, and insurance agents) who intrude on lawyers' turf by offering low-cost quality services.

Are Lawyers Correct in Warning You Against Nonlawyer Experts?

Lawyers view nonlawyer services as a threat to the legal profession. The American Bar Association Commission on Non-Lawyer Practice issued an interim report on May 18, 1994, which discussed the proliferation of self-help form preparers, legal technicians, and trained paralegals, who all operate in the territories bordering on the legal profession. The Commission's report, "Non-Lawyer Practice in the United States," is the summary of a 12,000-page record that includes the testimony of 337 witnesses given during nine hearings around the country in 1993 and early 1994.

In many states, laws have been passed to limit the unauthorized practice of law. Florida and Ohio, for example, enforce severe restrictions on nonlawyer practice, while California encourages such low-cost services.

In an article entitled "So What Is a Lawyer, Anyway?" (*National Law Journal*, June 21, 1993), writer Randall Sanborn raises the issue of "trained paralegal and untrained lay persons" or "legal technicians," who "look, walk, and talk like lawyers." According to Sanborn, the legal profession is divided between those who believe that no one except lawyers should be allowed to give any advice on legal matters, and those such as Professor Deborah L. Rhode of Stanford Law School, who, as Sanborn reports, argues that such restrictions are "anachronistic," and who points out that "there's no clear boundary between services that lawyers can perform and those that specialists can perform." The ABA Commission, despite its support for restrictions on nonlawyer services, also agrees that "some non-lawyer practice meets legal needs that are not now being met by lawyers."

As a consumer of legal services, you should be aware of the difference between trained paralegals or other licensed professionals, and form-fillers—who have no training or supervision whatsoever. However, by exercising proper discretion, you can find affordable nonlawyer assistance to help in understanding regulations, filling out the correct forms, and sailing through a quasi-legal process in relative safety.

Examples for Proper Use of Nonlawyer Experts

The following are examples that demonstrate situations in which a nonlawyer expert could substitute (cheaply!) for a lawyer and even provide some expertise and assistance that a lawyer might not be able to offer.

Bouncing Checks and Evasive Debtors

In cases of bouncing checks from customers or tenants, or other documented and undisputable debts, you can pursue the evading debtor by using a collection agency. Such agencies normally charge only a percentage of the amount recovered.

Unpaid Judgments

If you already hold a judgment against your debtor—for example, if you won a case against a delinquent tenant in small claims court—and your opponent does not pay the judgment, you should file the judgment with the clerk of the court and request the court to "attach" the debtor's property by placing a "lien." A lien or attachment operates similarly to a home mortgage: If your debtor does not pay you the debt or a judgment, you are entitled to have the debtor's property sold by the local sheriff and take the proceeds from the sale as repayment. The procedure for creating a lien is usually very simple, and the court clerk should be able to instruct you on how to fill out the proper form. In many jurisdictions such a lien is created automatically as soon as a judgment is recorded, without the need for a separate court order.

After obtaining a lien, you should pursue the enforcement of that lien by filing an authenticated copy at the local banks, real estate record office, department of motor vehicles, your debtor's major customers, and any other cash source. In general, a lien can be placed on the debtor's wages, bank account, personal property, real estate property, automobile, and almost any other financial and proprietary interest. Hiring a collection agency for a commission fee could save you some of the legwork without any out-of-pocket expense.

Purchasing a New Home or Office

When you purchase a residence or an office, a knowledgeable real estate broker could save you part or all of the legal fees. Many real estate brokers offer assistance, not only in locating an appropriate home for your needs, but also in preparing for the closing.

Some licensed real estate brokers operate as "buyer's brokers," which means they represent the buyer only, from the beginning of the search, through negotiating the price and terms of the purchase agreement, until the closing.

Whether he is a "buyer's" or a "seller's" broker, an experienced real estate broker can assist you in dealing with title search, documentation of your financial records for mortgage purposes, getting title insurance, and preparing for the closing. A real estate broker can also review the purchase agreement on your behalf, explain to you the different provisions under the agreement, point out provisions that are detrimental to you in any way, and even negotiate on your behalf with the other side to improve the conditions of the deal for you. Often, a real estate broker can offer much more knowledge and understanding of the various aspects of a real estate transaction than any lawyer. In such case, if you engage a lawyer, his role would be limited to reviewing only the purely legal aspects of the transaction, therefore spending less time on the matter (and costing less money).

Looking for a Good Mortgage

With the proliferation of mortgage banks and the confusing variations on rates, length of repayment, and other marketing devices used by mortgage banks, you may find it difficult to make an intelligent choice of a specific bank and type of mortgage without help. A professional who can help you in the process of purchasing a home is the mortgage broker. Though a relatively new phenomenon, licensed mortgage brokers now operate in many states and offer a comprehensive service that covers all aspects of shopping and applying for a mortgage, getting a commitment from the bank, and closing on the loan.

Mortgage brokers not only explain to you the various options and shop on your behalf for the most attractive deal, but also prepare the necessary documentation to overcome any difficulty in getting your application approved by the bank. Experienced mortgage brokers have the know-how to deal with most of the legal issues involved in your mortgage process and in closing the purchase of your home or office. A mortgage broker's fee is paid upon closing of both the purchase of the real estate and the mortgage. Though the fee is calculated as a percentage of the mortgage, and can sometimes be high, mortgage brokers develop many skills in order to bring real estate transactions to conclusion and earn their fee. Therefore, a mortgage broker is motivated to assist you in issues which, in the past, only a real estate lawyer would have done—for a hefty fee.

Filing Insurance Claims

In cases of loss or damage to insured property (a break-in, for example, or a car accident with no physical injury), or even in cases of devastating financial ruin (such as a house fire), your insurance agent may be able to obtain full compensation for you without the help of a lawyer. Though insurance agents are agents of the insurance company, market forces dictate that their motivation lie with your interests rather than those of the insurance company. You are the ultimate consumer of various policies, such as automobile, home owner's, professional liability, and medical insurance. The agent knows that pleasing you is in his best interest, and he will fight on your behalf "against" the insurance company.

A good insurance agent will be able to fill out all the necessary forms to file a claim with the insurance company, advise you on what documentation you need to prove your damages, advise you on the maximum amount of coverage (which should not be exceeded in your claim in order to avoid reduction in your coverage), and advise you on how to properly state the cause of the damages to best position yourself for complete recovery of your financial damages. He will also negotiate aggressively on your behalf until you get all that is entitled to you.

Mediation and Arbitration of Small Business Disputes

When you find yourself involved in a small dispute with a business colleague, the first step should be to convince your opponent to agree on ways to save legal fees by avoiding lawyers and courts. Such "procedural" agreements with the other party can be extremely beneficial to both sides.

In every major city across the United States, the last few years have seen a dramatic increase in the number of private companies offering mediation and arbitration services. Such services are the best way to avoid disproportionate legal expenses and to reach a quick and reasonable resolution.

You should first locate a service that suits your goals. If you believe a settlement is possible and trust your opponent's good-faith desire to resolve the dispute, mediation is your best bet. Mediation services specialize in investigating the facts underlying the dispute and mediating between the opposing parties until a settlement is reached. If you believe such a goal is achievable, look for a mediation service by calling the local bar association, small business organization, or the clerk of the local court.

If you do not think a settlement is attainable, try to convince the other party to submit to arbitration. In arbitration, unlike mediation, the parties submit themselves to the judgment of the arbitrator, who investigates the facts, interviews the parties and other witnesses, and issues an "award." The arbitrator's award cannot be appealed and constitutes a final judgment against the losing party. The American Arbitration Association, which has branches in every large city across the nation, should be your first call. Other services also exist, including "private courts," which operate in a similar but more efficient way than the public courts.

What's wrong with going to court? In most cases, mediation and arbitration can take place without the involvement of lawyers. Even if there is a need for a lawyer due to the complexity of the facts and the applicable law, you will save substantially on legal fees by submitting to mediation or arbitration. Unlike the long process of adjudicating a case through the courts, arbitration proceedings offer limited discovery, no jury trials, no lengthy briefs, and most important, no appeals. That is why fighting a case through the courts can take five to ten years, whereas arbitration generally takes only a few months.

Occasionally, you can save even the cost of mediation or arbitration services if you can convince your opponent to submit the case to a referee, chosen by both of you, who would then investigate the facts and issue a decision based on professional investigation. In financial disputes relating to accounts payable, accounts receivable, supplies, employee benefits and severance pay, tax liability, and similar, purely financial disagreements, the professional expertise of an accountant may be utilized to resolve the dispute without involving lawyers.

Incorporating Your Business

When deciding whether to incorporate your business, you should consult your accountant and read one of the many available books and articles on the advantages and disadvantages of running a business as a corporation, partnership, direct proprietorship, or any other form of doing business.

If you decide to incorporate your business, most states allow you to register a corporation without the assistance of a lawyer by purchasing a book on a "do-it-yourself" incorporation kit, or simply by calling your state office of corporations (different department names will be used in different states), to obtain the information about the necessary forms and filing fee. Additional help can be obtained from the local small business bureaus or from the local branch of the federal Small Business Administration.

Being Audited by the IRS, FDIC, EPA, SEC, NSB, FTC, OSHA, ETC.

Businesses today are subject to tens of thousands of federal, state, and local regulations. The federal Occupational Safety and Health Administration, for example, requires businesses to comply with hundreds of regulations regarding workplace safety. As with other agencies, the OSHA inspectors can roam your business at any time uninvited, and shut it down immediately if certain regulations are not being followed.

For businesses and entrepreneurs, the burden is extremely heavy as they try to comply with government regulations, understand the specific requirements for their industry, fill out the reports and periodic forms required to show compliance, and deal with inspectors coming to ensure compliance. Small businesses are especially vulnerable, because they cannot afford to employ a full-time safety officer to ensure compliance with regulations issued by the OSHA.

Other agencies and laws also present a substantial risk of government intervention, fines, and litigation. These include the Environmental Protection Act, the Americans with Disabilities Act, the Civil Rights Act of 1983 (which prescribes forms of affirmative action and requires businesses to advertise available positions to minorities before hiring), the Family Leave Act (which regulates the right of employees to have insurance coverage during family leave), and the Clean Water Act (which sets rules and measures with respect to sewage and waste from production facilities).

Sailing safely through this ocean of government regulations, or dealing with a government audit, despite the complexity and agony involved, does not necessarily require the costly services of a lawyer. Specialty consulting firms commonly provide large and small businesses effective assistance in complying with government regulations on the environment, employment, and safety. Using consultants can prevent or minimize the problem, save you the cost of hiring an employee to deal with the problem, and may prevent a government audit or a lawsuit from happening, thus saving you the need to hire a lawyer for a hefty fee.

Even when government inspectors are already at the gate, the adversarial attitude is not always the wise choice. An experienced and reputable consultant will not only have the expertise but also an established relationship with agency officials. He will be able to assist you with compliance, with correcting past problems, with reducing fines, and with getting the government inspectors off your back.

To locate a consultant with a specialty in environmental, employment, safety, or any other government regulations, your first call should be to the trade association relevant to your business (or your local small business club). Another source of information on available consultants would be National Small Business United, in Washington, D.C. You could also call a business colleague in the same line of business as yourself, or even call, possibly anonymously, the government agency whose regulations you are dealing with and ask for a short list of recommended private consultants whom the agency recognizes.

Divorcing Amicably

In most jurisdictions, filing for an uncontested divorce with the local court is a straightforward procedure that requires the filing of one form and payment of a set filing fee. Many companies offer "self-help" in this area. For example, DocuPro, based in Taunton, Massachusetts, which has seventy offices throughout New England, will help you fill out official uncontested divorce papers, as well as wills, immigration papers, prenuptial agreements, and many other legal documents that do not require the assistance of a lawyer. Of course, if there are complications or disagreements that make the forms inapplicable or problematic, you should consult a lawyer until you fully comprehend the issues involved.

COMPUTER SOFTWARE AS A VIRTUAL LAWYER

Quicken Family Lawyer (Parsons Technology, Inc./Intuit Co., 800–223–6925) is one of several popular products that offer computer-literate users a way to produce legal documents without the help of a lawyer. The programs provide you with a long list of predrafted documents that require a minimal amount of adaptation to make them legally binding, such as wills, premarital agreements, general powers of attorney (see Chapter 13), healthcare proxies, loan documents and various notices, form letters, and simple agreements. *Small Business Legal Pro* is a new CD-ROM that offers searchable text from four legal books by Nolo Press (800–992–6656 or www.nolo.com): *The Legal Guide for Starting and Running a Small Business, Tax Savvy for Small Business, The Employer's Legal Handbook,* and *Everybody's Guide to Small Claims Court.*

As with software that provides medical advice or auto-repair instructions, using legal software can be both exciting and hazardous. A good lawyer is not merely a guardian of legal forms, and the advantage of using a "real" lawyer, as opposed to computer software, lies in the understanding, knowledge, and experience a lawyer provides even in the simplest situations. Therefore, the use of legal software should be limited, as is the case with any legal self-help, to situations in which you are certain of your understanding of all the aspects of your status and are certain that no risk exists to your financial or personal wellbeing. On the other hand, a brief consultation with a lawyer may provide you with enough understanding so that you could do the rest yourself sitting in front of your computer screen filling in names, addresses, and other basic information onto the predrafted forms.

SMALL CLAIMS COURT: A WORLD WITHOUT LAWYERS

There is one place, right around the corner, where justice can be sought (and maybe even found) without the involvement of lawyers, without escalating costs, without complicated proceeding, and within a reasonable period of time. That place is the small claims court.

What Is the Small Claims Court?

In every county across the nation, you can find a small claims court, which exists to resolve disputes over monetary amounts usually not exceeding two or three thousand dollars, exclusive of interest and costs. The jurisdiction of the small claims court requires the defendant to be a resident, or have a place of business or employment, within the county. A small claims court operates under simplified rules of practice and procedure, and uses standard forms for instituting claims. The simplicity of the process facilitates access to the small claims court for people without legal training. Most small claims courts hold evening hearings at least once a week.

The small claims court is intended to "constitute a simple, informal and inexpensive procedure for the prompt determination of small claims in accordance with the rules and principles of substantive law" (New York City Civil Court Act, § 1802).

Filing Your Claim in Small Claims Court

A case in the small claims court is initiated by filing a straightforward form, which can be obtained from the clerk of the court, with any evidence you have to the merit of your claim. There will be a minimal filing fee (normally less than $10), plus the cost of mailing a copy of your claim to the defendant. There is no cumbersome procedure of service of summons or pleading. The suit commences by mailing of your "statement of cause of action" to the defendant by the clerk of the court by ordinary first-class mail or certified mail with return receipt. After a certain period of time, if the mailing has not been returned as undelivered, the defendant is presumed to have received your notice of claim.

State laws uniformly require the clerk of the small claims court to furnish you with forms and advice throughout the process of adjudicating your claim. At the clerk's office, you should be able to obtain a pamphlet explaining all the terms and procedures, including the rules for adjournment, counterclaim, jury trial availability, subpoenas of witnesses and evidence, availability of arbitration, collection, liability for any fees, procedures for garnishing (placing a lien on) the debtor's assets, availability of prejudgment court orders for production of evidence or for restraining the defendant from certain actions, availability of punitive damages, and the procedure for filing a notification of judgment with the appropriate state or local professional licensing authority in cases of demonstrated fraud or illegality.

Proceeding in Small Claims Court

You have no reason to fear filing a claim with and appearing before the small claims judge. You will find that the court procedure is informal and simple. The hearing before the judge, and the process of arguing and submitting evidence, requires no legal training. The judge will explain to you the more complicated rules, if such apply to your case, regarding privileged communications with lawyers or doctors by the defendant, personal transactions, or communications with a nondeceased or mentally ill person.

You can establish a prima facie right against your defendant by producing a copy of a bill or invoice, or itemized estimates for services you performed, or any document that shows the existence of the debt. After that, your case is presumed to be valid unless your opponent files a defense and brings his own evidence, which will be considered by the judge, who will then issue a decision.

Can a Lawyer Represent You in Small Claims Court?

In most small claims court cases, lawyers are prohibited from appearing on behalf of either you or the defendant. The only exception is a defendant corporation, in which case a lawyer is allowed to appear in the absence of a qualified corporate officer.

Although you may not be represented by a lawyer in small claims court, most judges will allow a friend (who does not have to be a lawyer) to assist you and speak for you, if you are able to convince the judge that, due to age or mental or physical disability, the just resolution of the dispute would be better facilitated by such representation.

Available Remedies in Small Claims Court

The judge in a small claims court has wide discretion to give orders that will achieve substantial justice between the parties. In doing so, the judge may set terms and conditions to the judgment and may order the defendant to perform or to refrain from certain actions. The judge may also—with or without your request—conclude that the defendant's actions were fraudulent or illegal and refer the matter to the attorney general for criminal investigation.

Normally, jury trials are not available in small claims court, and filing your claim constitutes waiver of your right to a jury trial, although you may reacquire such right if the case is transferred to a regular court. The defendant, however, may demand a jury trial if there are issues of fact to determine.

A monetary judgment of the small claims court has the same effect as a judgment by any other court and can be collected by using a lien and a sheriff's sale. (See the discussion on page 17 about enforcing unpaid judgments without hiring a lawyer.)

Additionally, small claims courts in most states have unique powers to enforce their judgments, including the authority to:

- suspend driver's license and automobile registration (if the claim is connected to the ownership or operation of a car);
- revoke, suspend, or deny renewal of business licenses or permits;
- refer a defendant's case to the attorney general for investigation and prosecution with respect to fraud or illegal business practices;
- impose a penalty equal to three times the amount of unpaid judgments;
- require a defendant to pay the plaintiff's attorney's fees, if a lawyer was consulted by the plaintiff (for example, New York City Civil Court Act, § 1811.)

Can You Appeal Small Claims Court Judgments?

When you file your claim in the small claims court, you are deemed to have waived your right to appeal the judgment, except on the grounds that "substantial justice has not been done between the parties according to the rules and principles of substantive law" (New York City Civil Court Act, § 1807). However, the judgment is a "res judicata" (final justice) only with respect to the amount claimed and does not prevent a new suit in another court for the same cause of action but for a different amount. In other words, though you waive your right of appeal, the small claims court decision is not a final adjudication of the facts and may not be used as evidence in other cases involving the same facts.

Whom Can You Sue in Small Claims Court?

As an individual, you may sue any defendant in the small claims court. However, the clerk of the court has the authority to dismiss your claim if he determines that the claim is filed for purposes of oppression or harassment, for example, when the claim has already been filed and rejected in another judicial forum. Also, corporations are normally prevented from filing a claim with the small claims court. This limitation often applies to claims by insurance companies on behalf of policy-holders.

Suing a Corporation in Small Claims Court

It is generally less advantageous to sue a corporation (as opposed to an individual) in small claims court. Unlike an individual defendant, your corporate defendant has the right to send a lawyer to defend it in a small claims court. Normally, when confronting a defendant who is represented by a lawyer, you should also be represented by a lawyer in the proceedings, and that is prohibited in small claims court. Therefore, the small claims court may not be the appropriate venue for bringing a lawsuit against a corporation.

CHAPTER 3

POOR MAN'S LAWYERS: LEGAL REPRESENTATION WITHOUT COST

If you need a lawyer but cannot afford to pay, do not despair! There are several ways to obtain legal representation without cost. In some matters, the government is obligated under the U.S. Constitution to provide you with a lawyer. In other matters, you may be able to find no-cost legal representation through public-interest organizations, local government agencies, or "pro bono" services by private law firms.

THE GOVERNMENT MAY PAY FOR YOUR LAWYER

As a U.S. citizen accused of a crime, you have a constitutional right to effective defense by a lawyer. In other cases, mainly those involving protection of your civil constitutional rights, the government will either appoint a lawyer to represent you, or provide for a method of reimbursement for your lawyer's fees. The following discussion is intended to give you a preliminary understanding of your right to have a lawyer appointed or paid for by the government, for your benefit.

The Constitutional Right to Counsel in Criminal Cases

Amendments IV through VIII to the Constitution of the United States protect against unlawful search, arrest, cruel and unusual punishment, and the deprivation of any other basic rights to life, liberty, and property, without the due process of the law. Specifically, Amendment VI establishes the rules for due process in criminal trials:

In all criminal prosecutions, the accused should enjoy the right to a speedy and public trial by an impartial jury . . . and to be informed of the nature and cause of the accusation, to be confronted with the witnesses against him . . . and to have the assistance of counsel for his defense. . . .

The Bifurcated American Legal System: Two-Pronged Justice or Plain Schizophrenia?

Unlike any other nation in the Western world, the United States has two distinct legal systems working in parallel—the state courts and the federal courts. Criminal prosecution, as in any other legal proceeding, can come from either of these two distinct sources.

First, each state has its own penal code, which is enforced by the state attorney general and local district attorneys, through indictments and trials before the state courts. If either the defendant or the prosecution is not satisfied with the results of the trial, an appeal may be brought before the state appeals court. A second appeal to the highest state court is normally discretionary, as the right to appeal is limited to one appeal. However, if the accused believes her constitutional rights have been violated, she can jump over the wall into the federal court system by filing a "habeas corpus" petition to the federal district court, and possibly take the case all the way up to the U.S. Supreme Court.

Parallel to state laws and state courts, the federal penal system enforces a wide variety of federal crimes, such as drug trafficking, murder of federal officials, certain fraud offenses, and organized crime. Also, federal criminal prosecutions may stem from violations of agency regulations by either corporate or individual defendants, such as laws and regulations relating to securities trading, banking transactions, tax evasion, environmental and waste disposal, and fraud relating to Medicare or welfare. To enforce federal criminal laws, the federal government employs U.S. attorneys throughout the nation, who prosecute cases before federal district courts. Judgments of the federal district courts are appealed to the federal circuit courts of appeal. By special permission ("certiorari"), either the prosecution or the defendant may appeal to the Supreme Court of the United States.

In *Betts v. Brady* (1942) the U.S. Supreme Court ruled that although the Sixth Amendment to the U.S. Constitution guarantees the right to counsel in all federal criminal trials, that right did not extend to defendants in state criminal trials. Until the *Gideon v. Wainwright* decision in

1963, when the Supreme Court reversed itself, the fate of a penniless criminal defendant depended largely upon the court in which the trial took place: In state courts, poor defendants stood trial without a lawyer, defending themselves against an experienced prosecutor. In the federal courts, poor defendants enjoyed the services of a defense lawyer paid by the federal government.

In *Betts v. Brady*, Smith Betts, who had been indicted for robbery in Maryland, asked the Maryland state court to order that the State of Maryland appoint and pay for a lawyer to represent him, because he was too poor to pay a lawyer himself. The Maryland court refused, arguing that Betts had no such right, and that he should defend himself. Betts, who was convicted, filed a petition with the federal court, arguing that the federal Constitution, and the right to a lawyer, applies also in the state courts. Justice Owen J. Roberts penned the Supreme Court's opinion that "the accused was not helpless, but was a man 43 years old of ordinary intelligence and ability to take care of his own interests on trial of that narrow issue [of proving an alibi]." Therefore, the justices of the Supreme Court concluded, "We cannot say that the [Fourteenth] amendment embodies an inexorable command that no trial for any offense, or in any court, be fairly conducted and justice accorded a defendant who is not represented by counsel."

More than twenty years later, on March 18, 1963, the Supreme Court reversed its *Betts v. Brady* decision. In *Gideon v. Wainwright* (which later inspired the movie *Gideon,* starring Henry Fonda), the court issued a decision in favor of Clarence Gideon, who had been convicted in a Florida state court for burglarizing a pool hall, and was refused the assistance of a state-paid lawyer. The Supreme Court, through Justice Hugo L. Black, wrote:

> The Court has made obligatory on the states the Fifth Amendment's command that private property will not be taken for public use without just compensation, the Fourth Amendment's prohibition of unreasonable searches and seizures, and the Eighth Amendment's ban on cruel and unusual punishment. . . . Immunities that are valid as against the federal government by force of the specific pledges of particular amendments have been found to be implicit in the concept of ordered liberty, and thus, through the Fourteenth Amendment, become valid as against the states. . . . We think the Court in *Betts* was wrong, however, in concluding that the Sixth Amendment's guarantee of counsel is not one of these fundamental rights. . . . Florida, supported by two other states, has asked that *Betts v. Brady* be left intact. Twenty-two states . . . argued that *Betts* was an anachronism

when handed down and that it should now be overruled. We agree.

Gideon, who taught himself constitutional law while in jail, won a legal precedent that changed the future for every criminal defendant in the United States. His conviction was reversed, and after a second trial in Florida, in which he was represented by a lawyer, he was acquitted by a jury of his peers.

Whenever you find yourself accused of any crime, whether in a state or federal court, remember your constitutional right to have a competent counsel represent you. If you cannot afford a lawyer, the court is obligated under the Constitution to provide you with competent counsel free of charge. In such a case, you will have a fairly minimal say in choosing the paid-for counsel, because the government has complete discretion in choosing the lawyer for whom it pays.

In some areas of the country, court-appointed criminal-defense lawyers will come from such private not-for-profit organizations as Legal Aid, or from the government-sponsored Public Defender. Also, many lawyers in private practice take on some court-appointed cases.

The fact that your lawyer is paid by the government—which is also (in criminal cases) your opponent, does not create, in and of itself, a conflict of interest. However, during such representation you should be alert to any sign that your lawyer is short on motivation or does not fight aggressively enough for you. If her future appointments—and livelihood—depend on the judge's good will, she might not want to irritate the judge, and may adopt a passive, nonconfrontational attitude at the expense of your defense. However, this risk is minimized, because most courts have a roster from which lawyers are randomly appointed to represent indigent criminal defendants. Such appointments are done by the court clerk without the involvement of the judge.

The Right to Counsel in Civil Rights Cases

Federal civil rights laws provide for court-appointed lawyers when the plaintiff cannot afford one. Therefore, if your case falls within the following categories, or within categories that are not covered in this chapter but may still be of the same nature, you should file a request with the court to appoint a lawyer for you. Such a right is limited, but, surprisingly, many judges view such requests favorably in cases in which they deem the interest of justice best served if the defendant receives a court-appointed lawyer.

Court-Appointed Lawyers in Employment Discrimination Cases

If you believe that you have been discriminated against by your employer (or by a potential employer) because of your age, sex, race, color, religion, or national origin, you may have the right to a court-appointed lawyer to represent you without cost.

Title VII of the Civil Rights Act of 1964 ["Prevention of Unlawful Employment Practices, Civil Action by Commission, Attorney General or Person Aggrieved"], sets criteria for such appointment of a government-paid lawyer "in such circumstances as the court may deem just."

In interpreting the phrase "such circumstances as the court may deem just," courts take several factors into consideration, including:

- *The plaintiff does not have the financial ability to hire a lawyer.* This does not mean the plaintiff must be destitute, but there should be some proof of financial constraints.

- *The efforts made by the plaintiff to hire a private lawyer.* The requirement to show reasonable diligence in seeking a private lawyer is again not strict. The court will consider the availability of experienced lawyers in a certain geographical area, your personal standing and experience in seeking legal help, and the number of potential lawyers you have contacted before requesting the court to appoint a lawyer.

- *The merit of the case.* Because most employment discrimination cases begin with a petition to the Equal Employment Opportunity Commission, a finding by the Commission that you have a reasonable cause of action based on the allegations made is a substantial factor in that respect. Conversely, the fact that the commission found no reasonable cause might be held against your request for a court-appointed counsel.

Other factors that the court might consider in deciding on your request for a court-appointed lawyer is the complexity of your case, your inability to gather facts or present the case on your own, your inability to get assistance and advice from a government agency, and your good-faith attempts to get such help.

Reimbursement of Attorney's Fees in Civil Rights Actions

A defeated party in a lawsuit in the U.S. normally does not have to reimburse the prevailing party for the cost of lawyers' fees, unless such obligation is created by a specific law or agreement. Federal laws have created such exceptional duty in certain civil rights cases, giving the court powers to order the defeated party to pay the winner's legal bills.

Even though reimbursement for lawyer's fees takes place only after the conclusion of trial or settlement, the availability of such reimbursement prompts many lawyers to take such cases in reliance on good prospects of victory and ultimate reimbursement by the defendant. Such an arrangement may be combined with a contingency fee based on the amount of financial compensation won as judgment, and thus may enable you to hire a qualified lawyer without paying any fee unless you win.

The Civil Rights Act of 1964 entitles a successful plaintiff in a case involving discrimination in employment on the grounds of race, color, religion, sex, or national origin to payment of attorneys' fees by the discriminating employer. You should understand, however, that this right does not guarantee you free legal representation, but is limited only to successful cases. Therefore, your lawyer's bills would be paid by your discriminating employer only if you are successful in your lawsuit, and only after a judgment is rendered in your favor. However, many attorneys will take your case for no fee if they believe your case is very strong and that they can safely expect to be paid handsomely after victory. The award of attorneys' fees is limited to "reasonable" fees and is at the discretion of the court. The lawyer will also be compensated for other related costs. Conversely, if you are an employer being sued by an employee for alleged discrimination against the employee, you have an equal right for reimbursement of lawyers' fees by the employee if you prevail in the case and no discrimination is found.

The grant of lawyers' fees is not affected by whether you had an obligation to pay your attorney any fees or not. This makes it possible for you to convince your lawyer that, because you have a good case, no fees will be paid by you whether you win or lose. If you win, the court may grant reasonable fees to your lawyer even though no such obligation existed on your part.

Laws providing for payment of attorneys' fees by the losing party appear also, for example, in Section 718 of the Education Amendment

Act of 1972, providing reasonable attorneys' fees and costs in school desegregation cases and in cases involving the enforcement of voting guarantees under the Fourteenth and Fifteenth Amendments to the U.S. Constitution, as applied by the Civil Rights Act.

CONTINGENT-FEE ARRANGEMENTS

Contingent-fee arrangements exist only when they benefit both client and lawyer. The client does not have to pay out-of-pocket legal fees (and sometimes no expenses), and the lawyer can expect a substantial amount as her share (the contingency) of the expected victory, which will exceed what she would have been paid under an hourly rate arrangement. Obviously, contingent-fee arrangements are feasible only in disputes where a substantial amount of money is sought from a deep-pocket defendant. The subject of contingent-fee arrangements is discussed more fully in Chapter 10. However, it is important to realize that only lawyers who specialize in certain types of cases (such as personal injury, employment discrimination, contested wills and estates, and so forth.) take cases on a contingency basis.

To determine whether your case is appropriate for contingent-fee arrangement, the lawyer will analyze the chances of winning, the approximate amount of judgment if the court rules in your favor, the amount of out-of-pocket expenses needed to bring the case to conclusion, and the expected length of time until conclusion. To predict your future lawyer's train of thought in deciding whether your case is appropriate for contingent-fee arrangement, try to estimate how much money you could possibly win. If it is a substantial amount, you may find a good lawyer willing to take the case on a contingent-fee basis. To find the lawyer, use the "Hunting Tools" listed in Chapter 5.

PRO BONO COUNSEL

Probably the best-kept secret in connection with legal services is that many successful law firms take on cases for no fee at all. The "Am Law 100," the *American Lawyer* magazine's yearly review of the 100 largest firms in America, in 1994 reported that most of the large law firms dedicate more than 10,000 lawyers' hours per year to "pro bono" cases, with some firms dedicating more than 50,000 lawyers' hours during the year. Based on the *American Lawyer* survey, a cautious estimate shows that, across the country, law firms "give away" millions of lawyers' hours every year, serving poor clients without charging any fee. Considering that these law firms normally charge $150 to $500 per lawyer hour, pro bono services are a deep well waiting for you to dip your bucket.

Advantages for Lawyers in Taking Pro Bono Cases

Most people find it surprising that law firms and lawyers—creatures mostly slandered for their greed—take on clients for free. However, despite the lack of fees, pro bono cases offer law firms certain advantages that, at first sight, are hidden from the layman's eye, such as:

- *Lawyers' public image.* First and foremost, law firms take pro bono cases because it's good for their image. In the last ten years, bar associations across the country have mounted major efforts to improve the public image of the legal profession. A primary tool for improving such an image is the creation of available legal representation for people who cannot afford it, thus deflating the claim that greed is the legal profession's sole motive.

- *Networking and prestige.* The involvement in pro bono representation offers lawyers a chance to obtain prestige in bar associations, social and not-for-profit organizations, and the political establishment. Involvement in social activities brings lawyers in touch with businesspeople, corporations, and powerful groups, which could later become profitable, paying clients.

- *Social conscience.* Some lawyers take on pro bono cases to pacify their social conscience. In their youth, these lawyers went to law school to fight for a better society. Even though they ended up fighting for the rich and powerful rather than the underdog, their idealism lost during years of lucrative private practice, many of them still desire such "do-good" feelings. Taking one or two small cases every year without pay is a small price for such nostalgic fulfillment of youthful dreams.

- *Tax breaks.* Taking on pro bono cases also offers a variety of tax advantages. The time and expenses involved in such representation, and other losses involved, can be written off as business expenses, thereby used to offset the profits made serving other clients.

- *Conversion to a fee-generating case.* In many cases, pro bono representation may ultimately be converted into fee-paying representation. Though not apparent at the outset, some legal cases turn, during their lifetime, from one small not-so-promising case into a large and lucrative case, sometimes by converting it into a class action. For example, you have no money to maintain your own telephone line and therefore use the public pay phone on the corner of your street. You notice that out of five phone calls you make every day, at least one quarter disappears without a connection made, thereby forcing you to deposit a second quarter for the same call. You hire a lawyer to represent you pro bono and sue the telephone company for a total of the ten quarters you have lost. Your case, therefore, is worth $2.50. While representing you, your lawyer discovers that every user of any one of 15,000 pay phones across the city experiences the same problem. Your case, which originally was worth only $2.50, is now worth several million dollars because your lawyer requests the court to permit him to represent a class of all people who have used public pay phones in the last five years and lost one out of five quarters. If the court permits such class representation, your lawyer would, in all probability, win a judgment of millions of dollars and a fee based on a percentage of such an amount. Though the potential of your case was not initially apparent to you, by seeking pro bono representation you might encounter a lawyer who possesses the professional training to see the true potential of your case.

Advantages to You in Pro Bono Representation

Your pro bono lawyer has the same obligations and duties toward you as she has toward a paying client. Your lawyer may be the most expensive and prestigious lawyer in town, whose clients pay top fees while you pay nothing. But you deserve quality service, just as any other client, though you pay no fees or expenses, and should expect the best result possible. Also, if you eventually find yourself unhappy with the quality of service given to you, you have the right, as any other client, to sue your lawyers for negligence (malpractice) in their representation of you.

How to Find Pro Bono Counsel

Searching for pro bono counsel differs slightly from searching for paid lawyers. Your primary source of information will be the Committee on Pro Bono Representation of the local bar association, which will give you the names of local attorneys who have expressed willingness to take on such cases. The list of pro bono lawyers may be divided into specialties, and you will have to tell the office of the bar association what type of service you need.

Another source is the local court. You can call the chambers of any judge in the local trial court and request the judge to recommend a pro bono lawyer to represent you. Any judge will have at least a few names to suggest, based on her previous dealings with lawyers in town who are willing to take on such cases as yours for no fee.

Lastly, call every large law firm in the city and ask to speak to the partner in charge of pro bono representation. The partner, or her secretary, will ask you a few questions about your case and will tell you whether it is within the category of cases the firm is willing to consider.

When your search ends and you have located one or several lawyers willing to consider your case, you should interview each of them, as explained in Chapter 6, and proceed to choose between them using the Front Runners' Score Card provided in Chapter 7.

LEGAL AID SOCIETY AND OTHER PUBLIC LEGAL SERVICES

The Legal Aid Society has local branches in almost every city across the nation. It is a not-for-profit organization that employs hundreds of lawyers to serve indigent people in need of legal services. Many Legal Aid lawyers serve as court-appointed criminal defense lawyers. Additionly, most Legal Aid branches have a civil law department that offers representation to indigent people in many types of legal proceedings, including cases relating to family disputes, children's rights, domestic violence, housing, employment, and welfare. Depending on the policy of the local branch, Legal Aid may also assign a lawyer to assist you in small business matters or bankruptcy proceedings.

In addition to the Legal Aid Society, many other organizations offer free legal services to people in need. In many cities and states tax money is budgeted directly to a local agency that operates as a "lawyer for the poor." Such agencies normally are divided into sections that deal with children's rights, spousal abuse, tenant's rights, adoption, and abuse of power by city police or other city agencies.

You can locate the Legal Aid Society or other local not-for-profit legal service organizations in the telephone directory, under "Social Services" or "Legal Services." Additionally, you might call city hall or the mayor's office and ask for the telephone number of the city legal services office. Before making your call, ask yourself "Do I really need a lawyer?" by following the steps described in Chapter 1. Also, be prepared to show some proof that you don't have the financial resources to pay a lawyer yourself. Lack of financial means may be a prerequisite to obtaining free legal services from such organizations, though your word may be sufficient without further documentation.

PART II

HUNTING FOR A GOOD LAWYER:
A FIELD DAY IN THE LAND OF LAWYERS

CHAPTER 4

PLANNING THE HUNT: WHAT TYPE OF LAWYER DO YOU NEED?

If you have been injured in an accident, lawyers are going to hover over you like moths over a candle on a hot summer night. These lawyers may have heard what happened to you from a nurse in the hospital, from hanging around the local police precinct, or from the old lady who lives across the hall. Whatever their source of information may be, they will knock on your door in a dark suit, with a draft lawsuit, a briefcase full of promises, and a power-of-attorney ready to be thumbed. Shut your door in their faces and run for cover! These are not the reliable, experienced, and knowledgeable lawyers you really need.

For a lawyer, the foreplay to client interaction is like the hunting before a feast: The lawyer hunts down the potential client, goes for the kill (a signed Engagement Letter), and sets up the grill. The lawyer is the hunter and you, the client, are the prey. Unless, of course, you arm yourself to the teeth with all the information included in this chapter—your only chance to reverse the traditional roles and make yourself the hunter.

This chapter in no way preaches shooting all lawyers (and/or eating them!). Many lawyers serve their clients honestly, diligently, and loyally, and will do their best to help you. But there are lawyers who operate mean-spiritedly and hunt down the uninformed client to make a quick buck. Therefore, you should search for the lawyer, not the other way around, and when searching for a good lawyer, watch out for the bad ones. You are deep inside the danger zone, and this chapter will give you the attitude and arsenal for survival.

Hunting for the right lawyer should begin only *after* you have analyzed, determined, and written a road map for yourself—the list of requirements and qualifications you expect to find in the right lawyer. You must take into consideration: the lawyer's specialty, his character and demeanor, the expected cost, and the convenience of service. If you cannot afford to pay a lawyer, there are ways to get one for no cost at all, as discussed in Chapter 3 ("Poor Man's Lawyers: Legal Representation Without Cost"). Your choice, however, is much more limited with respect to a court-appointed lawyer.

This chapter takes you step-by-step through your actual search, making full use of the "hunting tools"—all the available sources of information about lawyers who satisfy your requirements.

A STALLION, A LEOPARD, A FOX, OR A RABBIT?

Before you pick up the phone and start calling friends for recommendations, do some planning. Lawyers differ from one another: There are close to one million lawyers in America, and they are not all alike. You should decide whether you need a specialist or a generalist, a litigator or a business counselor, a thinker or a fighter, an expensive "top gun" or a young and restless idealist. Read the following discussion and decide for yourself what suits your needs.

Should You Look for a Specialty Lawyer?

In most cases, yes. If you suffer from chest pain, an eye doctor cannot help you. Similarly, if you want a divorce, a criminal-defense lawyer cannot give you effective representation. In some small matters, such as writing a will or looking at an apartment lease, a generalist will do. But for anything else, get a specialist.

Unlike doctors, lawyers do not have a formal system of specialization. There are no national boards, no required internship periods, no specialty training, no state specialty licensing, and no mandatory exams for specialists. In some states, lawyers are even prohibited from presenting any "certificate of specialty" in one area of the law, because their colleagues fear "unfair" competition. Even in states that allow "specialty diplomas," those diplomas are not based on anything equivalent to the rigorous training in medicine and do not automatically prove expertise or experience.

However, despite the absence of a framed certificate on the wall, most lawyers define themselves as specialists, in one or several areas of the law. They may, indeed, have had long years of practice in that field, have taken courses and even taught, but there is no easy way for you to actually verify a lawyer's claim of specialty. Verifying the lawyer's specialty and competence can only be done with some detective work, as explained below. But first, you should determine *which* is the specialty you require.

What Specialties Are Available?

Beyond the general distinction between criminal and civil matters, lawyers today develop their professional skills in narrow, specific areas of practice in order to offer high-quality legal services to their clients. Legal practice reflects, to a large extent, the applicable areas of modern laws as they have emerged over centuries of evolution. The following is a general list of areas of the law in which lawyers normally specialize.

Criminal Matters

- *White-collar criminal matters,* which include all offenses involving fraud, bribery, embezzlement, and other offenses involving nonviolent financial schemes.
- *All other criminal offenses,* whether violent or not.

Civil Matters

- *Family law,* including prenuptial agreements, divorce, child custody, adoption, wills and trusts, estate division, and, in some instances, issues relating to family-owned businesses.
- *Negligence and injury,* including automobile negligence, intentional mayhem resulting in injury, landlord liability, sidewalk injury. This specialty is sometimes divided into a sub-specialty involving "mass tort," such as plane crashes, chemical and nuclear disasters, asbestos-related illnesses, breast implants, and other product liability.

- *Malpractice litigation*, primarily against physicians and hospitals, which is related to personal injury. Successful lawyers in this field possess substantial and thorough medical knowledge.

- *Bankruptcy*, including representation of individuals or corporations applying for bankruptcy protection, creditors trying to collect from a bankrupt individual or corporation, and management of entities operating under bankruptcy protection.

- *Intellectual property*, including patents, trademarks, trade names, and copyrights related to works of literature, film, music, and software.

- *Employment law*, including employment contracts, retirement packages, employment discrimination, sexual harassment in the workplace, workers' compensation, employers' liability, and work-place safety.

- *Environmental law*, including environmental and waste licensing, disputes with regulatory agencies, environmental litigation and cleanup of contaminated sites.

- *Business law*, which is a broad specialty divided into sub-specialties in small business, corporate governance and corporation management, franchises, business contracts, corporate reorganization, acquisitions and divestitures, partnerships, and resolution of business disputes.

- *Immigration law*, which primarily involves the preparation and processing of various applications before the Immigration and Naturalization Service. Legal work in this field includes: representation of U.S. citizens wishing to sponsor a foreign relative's petition for residency, a U.S. company wishing to bring a foreign employee with unique qualifications to the U.S., foreign students wishing to study and work in the U.S., and political refugees whose safety or freedom are in danger in their own country.

- *Real estate*, including land acquisitions, home and commercial building acquisitions, financing of real estate development, construction projects, and purchase of operational real estate, such as hotels, resorts, country clubs, etc.

- *Securities laws*, including public offerings of shares and debt instruments on a stock exchange, reporting requirements of the Securities and Exchange Commission with respect to the management of public corporations, shareholders' rights, shareholders' class actions, and mergers and acquisitions of publicly-traded companies.

- *Trade law*, including transportation of goods across borders, shipping by air, land, or water, tariff and international trade agreements, letters of credit, and disputes over customs, tariffs, and dumping of subsidized products.

- *Tax law*, including federal, state, and local taxes, tax shelters, retirement plans, and representation during audits and tax disputes.

GOING TO COURT: WHAT IS LITIGATION?

The Process of Litigation

The term litigation encompasses several means of dispute resolution, including court trials, audits and investigations by government agencies, arbitration, and mediation. When you sue someone, or when you are sued by someone, you would need a litigator—a lawyer who specializes in representing parties in legal disputes.

Representation in litigation cases is related to areas of specialty as described above, such as business law, injury, employment, and so forth. However, it is important for you to understand how complex civil and commercial litigation has become and to appreciate how crucial your choice can be. (The following discussion concerns what you can expect in a civil case. Although criminal litigation is in some ways similar to civil litigation, it is governed by very different rules of discovery and procedure, and is concerned with many questions and issues that do not arise in civil litigation. Therefore, if you consult a lawyer in a criminal matter, ask your lawyer to explain the procedural stages and rules that you can expect to encounter and the particular issues involved in your case.) The stages of a civil lawsuit in which your lawyer will represent you are:

- *Initial fact finding*, including interviewing you and other potential witnesses, collecting and reviewing all relevant documents in your possession, forming an opinion about the strength of your case (or defense), and planning a strategy for the legal battle.

- *Discovery*, including service of subpoenas (summonses) for all relevant documents your opponents might have in their possession, taking depositions (questioning of potential witnesses, including hostile witnesses, under oath, in a lawyer's office and in the presence of a court reporter), and providing documents and witnesses to the other side as required by law.

- *Filing of preliminary petitions and requests with the courts (motions)*, including motions to dismiss the case for lack of jurisdiction (the authority of a specific court to hear the case), or for lack of a substantial cause of action, motions for summary judgment (judgment issued before or during the trial because the judge concludes that there is no real issue of fact in dispute), and other preliminary motions regarding difficulties in discovery, summoning of foreign witnesses, and expenses. Note that all the legal issues are normally decided before the trial, so that the jury can concentrate on deciding the true facts of the case.

- *Trial*, including jury selection, opening statements, direct examination of witnesses, presentation of exhibits into evidence, cross-examination of witnesses of the opponent, making objections to the admissibility of evidence, and making closing arguments to the jury.

- *Post-trial motions*, including motions for a new trial, motions to cut down the size of the jury's award of damages, and motions for reimbursement of attorney's fees.

As you can see, trial is a multi-layered operation, requiring a great variety of skills. Trial lawyers are only as good as their thoroughness, attention to detail, and devotion to your case. Big talk, theatrics, and salesmanship often do more harm than good, especially when accompanied by shallow preparation and deficient presentation of the hard evidence. And, beyond the complexity of fighting a legal battle in court, the many stages of litigation—even if represented by a good lawyer, demonstrate how slowly the wheels of justice turn.

In certain types of complex litigation, only a handful of lawyers in your area are likely to have sufficient competence and proven experience in cases similar to yours so that they can give you a fair chance at winning the dispute. Consequently, the more complex and specialized your case is, the more crucial it is that you choose the right lawyer.

Examples of Complex Litigation Cases

The various elements of litigation apply to all types of cases, but each case presents unique problems and challenges to the lawyer, depending on the facts of the case and the specific issues that need to be addressed and proved. The following examples will give you an idea of the differences and complexities involved in several major areas of specialty.

Example 1: A Franchise Dispute

The American entrepreneurial spirit is best proclaimed through the achievements of tens of thousands of American entrepreneurs operating franchise establishments. The first to come to mind is McDonald's, but almost all brand-name chains operate through franchise networks, including fast-food eateries, specialty stores, gas stations, motels, hair salons, and other service franchises. The franchise industry offers entrepreneurs an exceptional way to establish a business by acquiring an already existing "package" that includes a recognized brand name, a reputable and familiar line of products, and existing marketing tools.

Despite the impressive achievements of the franchise industry, statistics show that more than $500 million is lost every year on failed franchise establishments. Purchasing a franchise often involves investing lifetime savings, years of hard and devoted work, and substantial emotional commitment. Consequently, the failure of a franchise business nearly always results in allegations of misrepresentation or other wrongdoing, and finally, in litigation. Disputes between franchisor and franchisee touch on highly complex issues under the franchise agreement, including division of start-up costs, use of trademark and trade names, royalty rates, renewal rights, geographical exclusivity rights, arbitrary termination, and know-how rights. In addition, a franchise dispute may also include general business issues, such as partnership agreements, banking and credit issues, etc.

The stakes in a franchise dispute are extremely high. The franchisor (the company that created the franchise network) normally keeps control over the introduction of new products, national marketing, capital standing, and even termination. As a result, the franchisor has arbitrary powers to limit or even terminate the franchisee (the entrepreneur buying and operating the individual franchise), whose investment of time, money, and soul go up in smoke. Franchisees deal with the arbitrary powers of franchisors by engaging trade associations and business groups, lobbying lawmakers, and hiring consultants. Occasionally, however, a dispute is too complex and too devastating for the entrepreneur-franchisee to be resolved without litigation.

The owner of a franchise network often is also an entrepreneur, who has developed a good idea into an empire. For the franchisor, grave dangers exist in letting the integrity and exclusivity of its franchise ideas be diluted by competitors and disobedient franchisees. The strict rules and procedures created by the franchise agreement and the stream of royalty payments can only be protected through strict compliance by the franchisees, who are given access to the franchisor's trademark, know-how, product, and marketing investment. To you, as a franchisor, allowing your ideas and property to be copied and diluted by competition often presents a risk too great to ignore.

When seeking a lawyer to represent you in a franchise dispute, either as franchisor or franchisee, you need a lawyer who has extensive experience and detailed understanding of the franchise enterprise, including the ability to understand the inherent dangers and damages, and the specific ways of evaluating know-how, reputation, and loss of income. Understanding the franchising business includes understanding the way it operates, tools of marketing and sales, and the procedures by which the franchise operates. The franchise-specialist lawyer must be familiar with the franchisor's operating manuals, must understand the scope of know-how provided to the franchisee, and also must have sensitivity to the personal investments by the individual franchisee. An understanding of external forces, such as local or national depression or recession, alteration of highway routes, changes in people's taste in food or clothing, or a decline in demand for certain services is also necessary.

Representing a franchisor or a franchisee in a trial over a failed franchise establishment involves the presentation of complicated business arrangements to the judge and jury: the structure of the franchise; its intricate financial information, including income stream, royalties, and expenses; and the complex contractual obligations under the franchise agreement. Such representation demands a high level of knowledge and experience, access to sophisticated computers, and creative use of experts. To have a reasonable chance of winning in a franchise dispute, you need a lawyer with years of experience specifically in the field of franchise law and litigation.

Example 2: A Civil Rights Dispute

In 1990 alone, U.S. employers had to defend themselves against 108,000 discrimination claims relating to violations of job applicants' and employees' rights under the various civil rights laws, including, Title VII of the 1964 Civil Rights Act, the Equal Pay Act, the Age Discrimination in Employment Act, and the Americans with Disabilities Act.

The 1991 Civil Rights Act established what amounts to a quota system requiring employers to avoid disparities between the demographic makeup of the company's employee group and that of the population in the area from which the employees are hired. For example, if the population of Smithtown is 60 percent white, 20 percent black, 15 percent Hispanic, and 5 percent Asian, a Smithtown company's work force must include approximately the same percentage of whites, blacks, Hispanics, and Asians. The quota system, otherwise known as "affirmative action," came under attack during the 1994 congressional elections, and is likely to be a central issue in other elections. However, the antidiscrimination elements of the 1991 Act are expected to remain almost intact.

The 1991 Act primarily protects employees against discrimination based on race, gender, national origin, disability, and age. It has presented a great challenge to employers because it does not set clear guidelines, thus creating a vacuum to be filled by endless litigation. For you—as an employee or as an employer—the 1991 Civil Rights Act creates rules governing all stages and aspects of employment, including recruitment, hiring, promotion, salaries, employee training, internal disciplinary procedures, employment privileges and benefits, and firing procedures.

If you are an employee suing your employer (or a former employer) under the 1991 Civil Rights Act, you could recover your actual financial damages (including lost wages), punitive damages (if the jury feels that your employer had been intentionally unfair), and reimbursement for your lawyer's fees. In most cases, the trial will be conducted before a jury, whose verdict could possibly be several times larger than your actual financial damages. Therefore, the choice of an appropriate lawyer is crucial to you and your family's financial future.

As an employer faced by an employee's claim of discriminatory practices, two Supreme Court cases, *Wards Cove Packing Co. v. Antonio* and *Griggs v. Duke Power Co.*, make it much more difficult to prove that your practices are legitimate under the "business necessity" standard or that they are "neutral on their face" because they do not have a discriminatory impact on people belonging to "protected groups" (such as minorities). The courts now place a heavy burden of proof on you as an employer seeking to justify discriminatory practices as a "business necessity." The complexity of the issues involved in discrimination suits, and the ambiguities of the 1991 Act in particular, make it necessary to find a lawyer with great understanding of civil rights laws and litigation.

When seeking a lawyer to represent you in a civil rights dispute (such as employment discrimination), your choice cannot be cautious enough. Defending or proving an employment-discrimination claim involves presentation of statistical and quantitative data regarding the composition of the employer's work force, the population group that is the source for hiring employees, and the practices of similar employers in the region. The lawyer will have to define various job categories, determine the availability of minority employees for hire, explain the company's promotion practices, its over- or under-utilization of certain employees, its assignment of training opportunities, and analyze any affirmative action programs the employer has tried to set up. The presentation of such information to the court and jury involves use of sophisticated computer software and intelligent use of public information sources. It also involves creating a defensible hypothesis to prove or disprove certain claims and theories. Such representation requires a high level of experience and knowledge in the field of employment discrimination, statistics, and business management.

Most lawyers who work in civil rights litigation subspecialize in certain types of discrimination and further define themselves as exclusively "defense counsel" (defending employers sued by employees) or as "plaintiff's counsel" (representing employees claiming discrimination). Your search, and ultimate choice of lawyer, should take this into consideration.

Example 3: Claims Involving Patents, Copyrights, and Artistic Works

In your spare time you like to invent things. You consider yourself an amateur inventor, and several of your inventions have been purchased and produced, though you've never had a big success. A few years back, while helping your daughter with her school work, an idea came to you for making a mechanical pencil with a retractable, always-sharp lead point. The mechanism you invented miraculously works: The pencil never needs to be sharpened.

You promptly asked your longtime friend, a patent lawyer, to register your invention with the U.S. Patent Office in Washington, D.C. After the patent was confirmed, you approached several manufacturers, offering to sell them your invention. A few years later, without any success, you forgot about your innovative pencil. However, when you walked into your favorite general store this morning, you noticed, displayed right there on the counter, a pencil identical to your design, to which you hold an approved patent. You bought one sample and immediately went to see your patent lawyer. Your patent lawyer pulled out the old file, compared the mechanism in the pencil you just bought with the mechanism described in your approved patent, and concluded that there was, indeed, a great similarity between them. He promptly faxed a letter to the maker of these pencils, and a reply came within thirty minutes denying any similarity between your patent and their product's design.

Since the establishment of the Court of Appeals for the Federal Circuit in Washington, D.C., in 1982, and with the availability of computerized data on sales nationally and internationally, damages in patent and other intellectual property claims have risen to billions of dollars each year. As a holder of a registered patent, trademark, copyright, or trade secret, you have a right to demand royalties from any company that sells products identical to your invention or work of art. You have the right to sue the maker of the retractable pencils for a percentage of all sales.

To prove the extent of your damages, your lawyer must obtain extensive financial data from the one or many manufacturers who took advantage of your work without compensating you; review company records and retail numbers, including sales and pricing records, manufacturing costs, materials costs, operating costs, and other expenses of the manufacturer; obtain detailed information about the industry and other competing products; and gain access to government information. To do all that requires a lawyer with knowledge in marketing, manufacturing, cost saving, and interest tables, all of which are complicated calculations that can only be prepared, presented, and explained clearly to the jury by a lawyer with great expertise in such litigation.

For example, your idea might have been used by other manufacturers of similar pencils who copied the idea from the manufacturer who first infringed on your right. To prove this would require investigation overseas and collection of data from sources beyond the reach of anyone but a top-quality legal expert.

In conclusion, if your patent or other intellectual property rights have been infringed upon, you should not settle for an average lawyer, but should find a lawyer who has prosecuted cases relating to similar products and has proven success in winning such cases in a court by obtaining a judgment after a trial (not just a preliminary settlement).

Example 4: A Securities Action

You retired after thirty-five years as a mechanic for the local Chevrolet dealer. Your employment benefits included, in addition to a pension and medical care, a severance pay in an amount equal to your last year's salary. With that large amount of money, you went to the local branch of a well-known New York securities brokerage firm, spent thirty minutes with the investment adviser and decided to follow his advice and invest all the money in the stock of an up-and-coming computer company located in the Silicon Valley. Now, six months later, you call your broker to inquire about the value of your investment, and hear that your investment is now worth only 10 percent of its original value.

After the initial shock, you ask the broker what happened. He explains that the computer company had been, for the last five years, involved in litigation over the rights to use certain technology that is the principal component of its unique product. Apparently, that technology was created by one of the founders of the company who claimed that he was pushed out of the company and that the other partners stole his technology from him. Recently, the company lost its legal battle with the inventor and had to pay him compensation in amounts that left the company almost bankrupt. Naturally, the value of the company stock collapsed.

Your rage is beyond description. You are angry at the broker who failed to inform you that the company was involved in such critical litigation, and you now question the advice he gave you to invest all of your money in one company. The broker, in the middle of an angry exchange, hangs up the phone.

Many investors every year find themselves in your situation. Their investments in stocks, commodities, debt instruments, and other financial products suddenly lose their value and leave them poor and confused. The anticipated profits have gone up in smoke, and the small investor is baffled, his nest egg stomped on by forces beyond his understanding.

Only a lawyer with specialization in securities litigation can understand and explain to you the magnitude of your disaster. Stock and commodities exchanges are controlled by complex rules and mechanics. Commencing and winning an individual or a class-action suit against a company whose stock was traded in the stock market, or against a broker who gave you wrong advice, requires extensive understanding of market manipulations. Every state has laws governing securities trading and securities brokerage, and the whole industry is governed by the federal Securities Act of 1933, the Securities Exchange Act of 1934, and the Commodity Exchange Act.

Every securities lawsuit involves such issues as insider trading, market manipulation, failure to disclose material information, or the falsification of public information to lure investors into purchasing certain stocks. To prove market manipulation, for example, your lawyer must prove that the company and its investment advisors intended to bolster an artificial price for the company stock through dishonest means. Your lawyer will need experts to analyze the history of the market price of the company stock and the actions that the company took to keep the price high.

During the trial your lawyer will present detailed statistical and financial information to prove that the value of the company stock was inflated through the use of fraudulent techniques. There will be issues of compliance with securities regulations, proof of speculation and hedging by insiders, consideration of general economic pressures on the stock market, and an understanding of the computer industry with respect to cost equivalence, inventory, and availability of similar products on the market, and analysis of industry trends in sales and technological innovations. In addition, proving that the value of certain stock was inflated involves a complex mathematical presentation together with analysis of accounting records.

Your suit against the brokerage firm that advised you to buy the stock involves piercing the corporate veil between the broker and the company for which he worked, and proving fraud or negligence in giving you incomplete or wrongful advice. A good securities lawyer will have to develop extensive databases to present hypotheses relating to the stock of the company, show the fraudulent element, establish patterns of manipulative trading in the stock, prove the overall value of the stock you invested in and similar stocks throughout the relevant period of time, and show, in fact, that the company stock was traded in a speculative, arbitrary, or hedging manner. There are only a handful of law firms in the country that can effectively represent a plaintiff or a class of plaintiffs in securities litigation. It is a field that requires an extremely high level of expertise and understanding of financial information. Your choice of a lawyer, therefore, should be made only after extensive research (as explained later in this chapter) and only after the lawyers present to you a solid track record for representing clients in situations similar to yours in which they won large awards for their clients.

Example 5: A Case Regarding Construction Work

It has been your lifelong dream to run your own business. Two years ago you resigned from your position as a maintenance technician at the local milk farm and started your own business doing electric repairs. You distributed business cards and spoke to all of your friends, and after a few months of odd jobs you suddenly received a call from a regional builder offering you the electrical installation job on a project consisting of sixty homes.

After reviewing the plans and consulting with several friends you signed the contract with the builder, took a loan from the local bank, hired two employees, ordered supplies, and started working with the builder. The contract between you included a detailed timetable that was to be the basis for your work in the project and for the payments you were to receive. The homes were built in five-unit groups, and you were to install electrical lines, electrical jacks and switches, lighting fixtures, and certain preparatory equipment for heating and for TV and telephone lines.

Six months into the project, the builder is behind schedule, and you have to stop working and wait. Six months later, the project is completely paralyzed, the builder in bankruptcy, and you are being sued in the local court for creating the delays that led to the ultimate failure of the whole project. The plaintiffs are the buyers of the homes and several banks that financed the project. Liens have been placed on your house and car, and your savings account has been frozen pending resolution of the case. Your passionate pleas to the lawyers representing the buyers and the banks fall on deaf ears, and you fail to convince them that the delays were caused by the builder and not by you. You now decide to hire a lawyer to defend yourself.

Construction projects are awash in legal documents. There are contracts between the builder and the buyers of the units, between the builder and the banks, between the builder and the landowners, between the builder and suppliers, between the builder and subcontractors such as yourself. In addition, there is detailed financial documentation as to payments made and internal memos and correspondence between employees of the builder and all the parties involved. The lawyer you hire to defend you must go through four stages in order to represent you effectively. First, he must gather the relevant data. That will include all the material financial documents, copies of bank statements, analysis of all the financial information, as well as taking of depositions from the builder, his employees, the bank officers, suppliers of the builder, other subcontractors involved in the project, and any other relevant parties. This mountain of information will be compiled and analyzed to assess your contention that the delays were caused by the builder and not by you.

In the second stage, your lawyer will divide all the documents he has gathered and the transcripts of all the depositions and interviews he has taken and index the thousands of documents into all the various subjects and subsubjects that may be relevant to the litigation. In the third stage, your lawyer will hire experts to calculate and analyze the damages suffered by each of the parties.

If your lawyer can show, based on all the material he has collected, that you suffered financial damages because of the behavior of the builder, the bank, or the suppliers to the project, there might be a basis for him to file a counterclaim on your behalf demanding payment of damages to you by the party responsible for the delays. Damages may include direct damages for costs incurred by you in excess of what you have been paid for, costs for any delays or disruptions in other projects on which you worked or could have worked during that time, and lost profits due to damage to your equipment or reputation. Other possible damages include interest you may have paid on loans, salaries paid to your employees, and legal fees spent on your defense.

To effectively defend you against the pending claims, your lawyer must show that other parties were to blame for the delays in the project, that the responsibility for the delays was not yours, that particular, documented actions by other parties actually caused the delays, and that the builder breached his contract with you rather than the reverse. Your lawyer will establish the damages you suffered in the project and in the loss of other business opportunities.

The fourth stage of the presentation will include the actual trial, wherein your lawyer will have to marshal enormous quantities of information and documentation in support of your defense and counterclaim. An experienced specialty lawyer will not only have a thorough understanding of construction projects and financial information but the skill to present this complex information to the jury in language they can understand, avoiding technical jargon and making complex material comprehensible. Graphs, charts, photographs, and even videotapes are now common tools in the courtroom. Litigation over failed construction projects benefits immensely from presentations that clearly explain the relevant financial information, show the actual land or half-constructed buildings, and thus bring an abstract legal issue to life for the jury.

ESSENTIAL CHARACTER TRAITS

After you have familiarized yourself with the different specialties lawyers practice, and have realized the vital importance of hiring a lawyer with the appropriate specialty, you should carefully consider what are the essential character traits you would like to find in your lawyer. However, there are two essential character traits that should be found in any lawyer you hire, whatever specialty he's practicing.

Integrity, Integrity, Integrity!

Never compromise on integrity. A dishonest lawyer can cause you endless harm, which you may not detect until it is irreparable. Such a lawyer may mislead you about the chances of your case, about events and developments during the representation, and, worst of all, may put his interests above yours.

Lawyers are in business to make money, but their business is to serve your interests and protect your rights, including your money. This creates an inherent contradiction, which is successfully resolved only by honest lawyers who put your interests, as the client, ahead of their own financial interests. Therefore, even if the advice they ought to give you from the outset or during the representation will cause them financial loss, such as advice not to sue or advice to settle, they will nevertheless give you such advice because your interest supersedes their own.

Integrity is paramount in your relationship with your lawyer. It should be at the top of your list because a lawyer who lacks integrity cannot represent you effectively. Do not think that because the person you wish to sue is dishonest, your lawyer should be dishonest as well. A lawyer with unflinching integrity has the tools to represent you effectively, including, when needed, to be a hard negotiator, use resourceful tactics, and present a "poker face" when it is called for. The difference is that a dishonest lawyer, even if he is effective in deceiving the opposition, will not hesitate to deceive you as well.

In seeking integrity you should look for evidence of the lawyer's moral behavior, social and professional standing, honesty, and sincerity. You should focus on these elements when questioning people who know him (including former clients, as explained in Chapter 7) and when investigating his representation of clients who have had extensive experience with him, as more fully explained in Chapter 6 under "Interviewing Recommended Lawyers and Verifying Their Claims to Fame." The existence of pending or past malpractice claims against the lawyer is a red flag indicating potential lack of integrity, though not a certain proof of it. The same goes for a history of substance-abuse problems.

Quality and Other Skills

The second indispensable character trait is quality. The lawyer's quality can be judged first by his resume. Did he attend a reputable law school? Did he clerk for a reputable judge? Is he a partner in a prestigious law firm? Who are his clients?

Your lawyer should also have communication skills including the ability to listen, persuade, and advocate a position; poise and negotiation skills; and the ability to act promptly and decisively once a decision is made.

Your checklist should include the character traits of integrity and quality, with the different elements of each category. This checklist will come in handy when you speak with a potential lawyer or when you interview a previous client, friend, or colleague of the lawyer.

PERSONALITY AND DEMEANOR

You are looking for a lawyer, not a friend. Therefore, the lawyer's personality and demeanor should be suitable to your legal needs, not to your personal taste in people. When you try to decide what type of a personality you are looking for in a lawyer, don't imagine a person you are going to like. Having a nice guy for a lawyer can be a benefit if your legal goals are to reach an agreement or compromise with an opponent, but may be a drawback if you need representation in a nasty child-custody fight. Liking your lawyer may feel good, but it should not be anywhere near the top of your priority list of personality traits. Rather, you should look for a lawyer who has the personality and demeanor best suited for the job you need done.

If you plan to divorce and your spouse agrees that divorce is the right thing for both of you, you need a lawyer whose personality is geared toward negotiating a settlement. Such a lawyer should be a pleasant person, easy to deal with and likeable, but with a good understanding of the relevant law and the ability to stand firm for things you view as essential.

On the other hand, if you plan to divorce but your spouse does not know about it and is certain to become enraged, fight tooth and nail over every piece of property, and contest the custody of your children, you need a lawyer who can fight. Such a lawyer may be abrasive, unpleasant to deal with, combative, and insulting in his language, but he may be the best lawyer for you. You might not like him, but your spouse's lawyer will hate him even more than you do.

If you have your own business and you search for a lawyer to give you ongoing business advice for years to come, you need a lawyer who can also be your friend. You should seek a patient lawyer, who is thoughtful, caring, and personable in his demeanor. However, if your business is sued by a former client and the existence of your business is endangered by the lawsuit, you need a lawyer who can fight. That lawyer will not spend time with you, will not give you ongoing advice, will not even care about your business, but will fight. Such a lawyer needs to be quick-witted, slightly impatient, aggressive, and unforgiving. He must be ambitious and competitive—in short, a pain in the neck.

EXPENSIVE OR CHEAP—CAN YOU AFFORD IT?

The cost of legal services should be determined by you, not by the lawyer you choose. And the approximate cost of the legal representation should be determined by you before you even begin your search.

Determining the cost should be based, first of all, on your financial ability. Do you have the money to pay your lawyer a lump-sum retainer at the beginning of the representation, as well as the money to pay monthly bills for the hours your lawyer will spend representing you? Hourly rates vary greatly, but you should expect to pay at least $100 per hour. Therefore, your first decision is: How much am I willing to pay up front, and how much am I willing to spend on the whole case? If the amount you come up with is at or near zero—that is, you do not want to pay anything—you should look only for a lawyer who will take your case on a "contingent-fee" basis.

Whether you need a lawyer for one-time legal advice on a business transaction or for ongoing legal advice to support your business, you will not be able to escape hourly rates. Therefore, you should decide whether you are willing to pay $100 or more. Additionally, you may find a lawyer who is willing to take you on as a client for a monthly retainer, which will enable you to call the lawyer at any time for a brief telephone or face-to-face consultation on a business law matter.

Sometimes your decision as to how much you are willing to spend will be influenced by your perceived chances of winning. A common mistake of consumers of legal services is letting a lawyer convince them that their case is a sure win and that they should feel certain that, on winning the case, a substantial amount of money will fall into their pocket. Such clients are easily lured into signing a hefty fee arrangement and soon find themselves paying out large amounts of money in legal fees based on the lawyer's baseless promises of an ultimate victory. Therefore, you should decide on the amount you are willing to spend without regard to your chances of winning the case. A wise client should decide on the amount assuming he is going to lose the case altogether, and consider looking only for a lawyer who will take the case for a fee based solely on results.

(For a complete discussion of the various fee arrangements for lawyers, and the advantages and disadvantages of all of them, see Chapter 10. For a discussion of the importance of making your lawyer commit to an estimated budget, see Chapter 9.)

CONVENIENCE OF LOCATION AND HOURS: IS IT REALLY IMPORTANT?

When searching for the appropriate lawyer, you must first decide if the type of representation you need requires face-to-face meetings with your attorney. With the popularity and availability of fax machines and telephones, communicating face-to-face has become a thing of the past. No longer do clients spend hours in smoke-filled waiting rooms to discuss a case with a perspiring lawyer. For example, the families of victims in an airplane crash in Ireland are represented by a specialized mass-tort law firm in New York. Thousands of victims injured by a massive chemical disaster in India are represented by a single, high-flying American lawyer before a U.S. court. Hundreds of thousands of investors are represented by a handful of elite New York securities lawyers in many class-action securities lawsuits against brokerage firms and investment banks. Many clients have been, are, and will be served effectively by lawyers whom they will never meet face-to-face.

If you are an entrepreneur seeking a lawyer to advise you on an ongoing basis, you should find a lawyer in your area, whose office is easily accessible in person or via a local telephone call. Similarly, if you are accused of a crime and need a criminal defense lawyer, you should find a lawyer who has had years of practice before the local court where your case is to be prosecuted.

On the other hand, if you are involved in a business dispute with a company located five states away and you believe that a lawsuit is the only avenue available for you to recover your damages, you would most probably have to sue in the jurisdiction in which the defendant's business is located. In such a case, or if you are sued by someone in another state, you should hire a lawyer in the location where the lawsuit will take place. Of course, your first instruction to your lawyer would be to try and move the case to the state where you reside, so that you can hire a local lawyer. But if you have to litigate away from home, hiring your neighborhood lawyer would be a costly mistake.

As a rule, determining whether you need a lawyer in your neighborhood or a lawyer across the country should not be based on convenience. Everyone prefers to deal with someone he knows and can easily meet. But your case may require a specialty that is not offered by any lawyer in your area. Your determination should be based, therefore, on the type of legal representation you need, not on your immediate convenience.

SAFETY IN NUMBERS: ADVANTAGES IN HIRING A LARGE FIRM

There are deep-rooted misconceptions about large law firms, among them the arguments that large law firms serve only large corporations, charge exaggerated fees, and provide impersonal, slow service. Though some large law firms suffer from one or more of the aforementioned ailments, in practice they are really large groups of individual lawyers who serve their different clients under the same roof, sharing word processing, copying, and mailroom facilities. On the other hand, lawyers who practice as members of a large law firm enjoy the reputation and clout of the firm as an institution. Therefore, your search should not exclude lawyers who are partners in large law firms, but rather view such lawyers as individuals practicing within a large law firm. The following discussion will assist you in understanding the unique characteristics of large and small law firms as relevant to your search for the right lawyer.

Individual Lawyers Versus Institutional Law Firms

Each species in nature has its own mode of existence. Snakes live solitary lives, crocodiles bathe as monogamous couples, and hammerhead sharks wander the oceans in large schools. Lawyers, on the other hand, have no set mode of existence. They operate in various ways, either as sole practitioners unattached to any other lawyer, with one partner as a monogamous professional mate, or in small, medium, and large law firms composed of partners (who share profits) and associates (who earn a set salary and work 60-100 hours a week). The primary difference between small and large law firms is the difference between an individual and an institution and their relative suitability to your needs depends on several factors.

Institutions Do Not Disappear

An institutional law firm, by its nature, offers you, as a client, much more safety than an individual lawyer. An institution does not normally disappear, relocate, get suspended from the bar, have a nervous breakdown, quit practice to become an actor, or die.

Many law firms have existed for more than a hundred years and have developed traditions and ethics of practice that protect you as a client. A large law firm has at its lawyers' disposal large libraries, computer databanks, precedents for every type of legal document, and access to all the other lawyers in the firm, who together have accumulated experience thousands of times greater than the experience of any individual lawyer. In addition, large law firms usually enjoy great political clout within the judicial system, and a number of local judges are likely to be former partners of the firm. All these accumulated strengths and resources are at your service when you hire a large firm to represent you.

An Added Layer of Protection

In a large law firm, you normally hire an individual partner, with whom you communicate and who represents you in your case, with the additional support and resources of the whole firm. However, if that individual lawyer is negligent in his representation and his negligence causes you financial loss or damage to your business, you now have a whole law firm to assume liability for your damages, because all partners are responsible for any one partner's actions. Even in states that allow law firms to operate as a "limited liability partnership," which limits mutual liability among partners, most law firms would still take institutional responsibility for one partner's actions in order to protect the firm's reputation. On the other hand, most solo practitioners and small law firms carry malpractice insurance that would also be sufficient to cover losses in most cases.

Many Specialists Under One Roof

Large law firms maintain a departmentalized structure that normally includes litigation (which may be further subdivided into specialties such as securities litigation, labor litigation, copyrights litigation, etc.), corporate, tax, real estate, trusts and estates, and environment. A firm may offer other specialties specific to its location, for example, entertainment law is a common specialty in California, while oil, gas, and energy departments can be found at most large firms in Texas.

For you as a client, a large firm may serve as a "legal supermarket" where all your legal needs can be satisfied under one roof. If you are a business owner, your lawyer could consult with his partners in the firm regarding specialty issues that come up in your business, such as tax, labor, or product-liability matters. On the other hand, an experienced solo practitioner would have established relationships with other specialists for occasional consultations, which may be only slightly more cumbersome than talking to a partner at the same law firm who is only a few offices away.

Are Large Firms More Expensive?

In most cases, yes. Large law firms in New York City, for example, charge their clients an hourly rate of $180 to $500 per hour, depending on the seniority of the individual lawyer working on the case. On the other hand, some sole practitioners who have a unique specialty and strong reputation may charge similar, or even higher rates.

Overall, there are no rules. With today's technology, which offers easy access to data networks, information services, sophisticated communications, and word processing, there is no inherent difference in the quality of service between small and large law firms. Also, large firms are able to negotiate better deals with their suppliers and be self-sufficient with respect to office services, thus eliminating any advantage a smaller firm would have in overhead (the cost of rent, salaries to support staff, etc.). The result is that large law firms that make intelligent use of modern technology can find profit in handling cases for lower fees, and compete effectively with smaller firms while offering a variety of specialties under the same roof.

The advantage in representation by large firms is even greater in cases of a contingent fee or a fee based on results. First of all, because the fee is based on a percentage of the results, there is no cost advantage to a small firm over a large law firm. Second, a large firm has the resources to invest in a case over the long run and could carry the cost for a few years until reaching a jury judgment in your favor. A solo practitioner or a small firm may be hard-pressed to lay out cash for discovery, document production, taking and defending depositions, and hiring expert witnesses. Such cash shortages could provoke a small firm to push you to settle your case in order to get its percentage of the settlement sooner, as opposed to waiting for a larger award after a lengthy trial.

Choose a Lawyer—Not a Law Firm

In conclusion, your primary goal is to find a lawyer—not a law firm—who can best serve your legal needs. There are personal-injury lawyers whose past successes give them endless financial resources to back a good case until a final jury award and payment. Such lawyers, even though they may be solo practitioners, can give you quality service (and perseverance!) to the same extent as a large law firm. Conversely, there are large law firms in which a partner specializing in the law of inheritance, trust, and estate could serve you with as much caring and attention as a small town's Main Street lawyer. All in all, it is the individual lawyer's personality and expertise that should determine your choice, not whether he is a solo practitioner or a senior partner at a 100-year-old New York firm.

CHAPTER 5

HUNTING FOR THE RIGHT LAWYER

Remember *The Deer Hunter,* with Christopher Walken, a bandanna tied around his head, playing Russian roulette? Well, choosing the wrong lawyer for your case is like pulling the trigger at the wrong chamber. To avoid such misfortune, hunting for the right lawyer should be done methodically by using all available hunting tools.

You are about to embark on an exciting, challenging, and possibly rewarding manhunt. This is not a chore, but rather a daring expedition in defiance of the general belief that "all lawyers are evil." There are many good lawyers out there, highly qualified, hardworking, and honest. Among them is the lawyer who is right for you. Find her, and your rewards will be plenty.

THE SEVEN MOST EFFECTIVE LAWYER-HUNTING TOOLS

You should use all possible sources of information in hunting for the right lawyer for your case. In your search, use all available tools. Remember, you are not just looking for a lawyer—you are looking for the *best* lawyer for your case. And the difference between a good lawyer and a good-for-nothing lawyer is the difference between winning and losing your case, your business, your pension, your house, or the custody of your children. The first phase of your research is not complete until you have the names of the five best lawyers for your case. Only then will you proceed to the next chapter in order to choose one of the five front-runners.

To make things clearer, the hunting tools listed below will be demonstrated using the following example.

You are employed as a bookkeeper in a small company that makes baseball caps, which are later sold under different brands and team logos all over the country. When the position of Chief Financial Officer opens, you apply with confidence that your long years of loyal and professional service will get you the promotion. To your dismay, a much junior employee, who is less qualified than you, gets the job. You believe that the only reason for this unfair decision is your age. You are sixty-two, and the person who was hired is thirty-five. A friend tells you that age discrimination by an employer is a violation of federal law and that you could sue your employer and get compensation.

Hunting Tool No. 1: Your List of Requirements

The most essential tool in hunting for a good lawyer is a well-thought-out, written list of requirements. Based on the example, your list of requirements should look like this:

- *Integrity.* You are looking for a lawyer who is praised by everyone as an honest, straightforward person. She does not have any record of malpractice complaints or ethical disciplinary convictions.

- *Quality.* A lawyer who has graduated from a reputable law school, clerked for a known judge, or worked in the district attorney's office, and is described by those who know her as a good communicator who is bright, efficient, and thoughtful. You want a lawyer who has happy (though sophisticated) clients.

- *Specialty and Experience.* A lawyer specializing in labor law and employment discrimination, with specific experience in prosecuting age-discrimination cases on behalf of employees before the Equal Employment Opportunity Commission and the federal courts, with at least three verdicts in favor of her clients for substantial amounts. Because your case is relatively small, you may have to lower your requirements with respect to the number and size of previous court victories. If your case were potentially lucrative, your requirements could be higher. One problem is that in cases of employment discrimination many employers prefer to settle the case before trial. A potential lawyer may boast of winning huge settlements for her clients but will not show them to you, claiming she is obligated to secrecy. This should make you suspicious because the secrecy usually applies only to the size of settlement, and satisfied clients would always be willing to say a good word about their lawyer. Insist on receiving copies of court decisions or on speaking to at least two of the clients whose cases ended with victories.

- *Character: Integrity and quality.* There should be no compromise in this department. If you cannot trust your lawyer, you are better off without her. She may be a good negotiator, poker face and all, but that should not interfere with her integrity toward her client. And don't believe the commonly held belief that an "honest lawyer" is an oxymoron.

- *Personality and Demeanor.* You need a fighter who is aggressive, ambitious, energetic, and uncompromising. Someone who can win, who thinks she can and should correct all the evils in the world—and make a lot of money doing so. She might be terribly irritating, but she'll win your case.

- *Cost.* You have no money to spend. The lawyer for you is one who takes on all her cases for a contingency, success-based fee. Expenses should also be paid only out of the award, if any.

- *Location and Hours.* The lawyer's office should be located nearby, or at least in the nearest big city. If your employer is a national company, seek a nationally known lawyer. Since you do not need ongoing access to routine legal advice, office hours are not important. A case such as yours does not require constant communication with your lawyer, beyond the initial launching and fact-finding stage of the case.

With this list of requirements, as your first tool, you are ready to go hunting. Your search should be methodical, using the seven hunting tools listed. Your search should not end as soon as a friend gives you one lawyer's name. Rather, use these hunting tools to get all the names you can from every possible source, and compile a short list of five front-runners to compete for your case in the manner described in Chapter 7 under the "Beauty Contest."

Hunting Tool No. 2: Referrals From Friends, Lawyers, and Judges

Referrals From Friends

With your list of requirements in hand, you start calling friends. They are the most accessible source for recommendations of good lawyers, though they may not bring the best crop of names. Chat with them about your case, pour your heart out to them about the injustice that was done to you, and gather their sympathy and advice. Unfortunately, only a few of your friends will have a good lawyer to recommend to you but, wishing to help nevertheless, will give you the name of the lawyer who did the closing on their home a few years back, saying: "He's a great guy. He'll do whatever you need because he is a great lawyer."

Stick to your list of requirements. You do not need a "great guy" or "a great lawyer." You need a lawyer who specializes in age-discrimination cases. Therefore, try to rely on those friends with specific knowledge and personal experience. For example, if one of your friends has successfully sued her employer in a similar discrimination case, she would be a good source for referral. Similarly, if one of your friends owns a company and employs people, he could refer you to a lawyer who has served him in similar cases or, better yet, a lawyer who has represented employees against your friend and caused him great distress.

Referrals From Lawyers

Lawyers are knowledgeable about other lawyers' expertise. And because jealousy comes with the legal territory, lawyers know about other lawyers' successes. If you know a lawyer, even if her specialty is completely different from the one you are looking for, she could be a very good source for information on lawyers who specialize in the needed field. Call only those lawyers with whom you have had a previous relationship or who have been highly recommended for their integrity by someone you trust. Again, when you ask for referrals, state your requirements clearly.

When one lawyer refers you to another, ask the lawyer whether he will receive a "referral fee" from the lawyer to whom he is sending you. In many states, a lawyer who refers a case to another lawyer can demand one-third of the fee earned by the other lawyer in that case, even if the referring lawyer did no work on the case. Some states require both lawyers to file a statement with the court in which the case is adjudicated. To determine to what extent you can rely on the warmth of the referral, however, you should find out whether a referral fee is involved. For a complete discussion of referral fees and how you should handle them, see Chapter 9, "Division of Fees With Other Lawyers."

Referrals From Judges

Local judges are probably the best source for referrals. You should feel free to call the chambers of any local judge, whether an elected judge, who may wish to please a voter, or an appointed judge, and present your case briefly to the judge's law clerk. In most cases, the judge will be delighted to help a justice-seeking citizen with a referral to a lawyer the judge trusts. Some judges will go even further and call the lawyer on your behalf asking the lawyer to interview you and consider taking on your case.

The advantages of using a judge as a source for referral is that a judge will not take a referral fee and will have no motive to send you to an inappropriate lawyer. Also, the judge's authority and clout might encourage an expensive lawyer to take your case despite its relatively small size. Additionally, you might not wish your employer to learn about your intention to sue, and if you speak to your friends or to their friends about your intentions, you run the risk of word getting back to your employer. In that respect, a local judge is likely to be the most discreet.

Hunting Tool No. 3: Referral Services

Where Can You Find a Referral Service?

Lawyer-referral services exist in many states, counties, and cities. The American Bar Association lists more than 300 bar-association-sponsored, not-for-profit attorney referral services across the nation. Many other for-profit services also operate across the country. You can find such services listed in your local Yellow Pages or by calling the local bar association. In California alone, nearly eighty different independent referral services operate. According to California bar association statistics, close to one million potential clients call upon referral services each year in search of an appropriate lawyer. In Chicago, the local Bar Association Referral Service gets close to 3,000 calls each month. Other services also report growing numbers of inquiries by individuals or small entrepreneurial companies seeking the name of an appropriate lawyer to represent them. Considering the inadequacy of referral services, these numbers prove how desperate and helpless many legal consumers feel.

Who Benefits From Referral Services?

Referral services offer minimal, occasionally even harmful, information. Referral services pretend to service consumers of legal services, but in truth they benefit the lawyers who have paid a listing fee. Certain attorneys may get preference from the service in the number of clients referred to them, even though they are not better lawyers in any way. The lawyers listed may be required to pay substantial fees and commissions to the referral service and, through it, to the local bar association or whatever organization sponsors the service.

Referral Services Do Not Give You Essential Information

As an ignorant consumer, all you will get from a referral service is the name of a lawyer who claims to have expertise in the field you indicated. Some services will also give you additional information, normally limited to attesting that the lawyer is a member of the local bar in good standing and that the lawyer indicated that she maintains appropriate malpractice insurance. However, referral services do not provide the information you really need, at least initially, to make an informed decision. They do not give any information on the lawyer's actual experience and achievements in the purported area of expertise (except for her own claim of expertise), information about client satisfaction, or a record of client complaints against the lawyer.

Even the minority of services that do keep records of ethical violations by listed members only list actual convictions or disciplinary decisions. This information is very limited, as most disciplinary proceedings take years to resolve, sometimes without any public record. Referral services will fail to give you the information you need and may refer you without warning to a lawyer against whom dozens of complaints are pending in the local bar association.

For-profit referral services have even less incentive to limit their lists to attorneys in good standing or to require attorneys who claim a specialty to provide proof of expertise or formal certification. Such services are motivated to get as many fee-paying attorneys as possible on their lists and to "sell" these listed attorneys to you for a referral fee.

In some states, for-profit referral services are regulated by state law. For example, California Business and Professions Code Section 6155,

"Minimum Standards for a Lawyer Referral Service in California," sets standards for operation of referral services, stating that its goal is to "provide information about lawyers and the availability of legal services which will aid in the selection of a lawyer. . . . " However, Section 6155 does little to achieve that goal, as it does not set any requirements for a minimal information package about a recommended lawyer. Rather, Section 6155 does more to protect lawyers from referral services established by other lawyers to exclude outsiders and keep all incoming cases by "referring" the cases to themselves. This is an example of legislation drafted and passed by lawyers under the pretense of consumer protection when in truth it serves the lawyers themselves.

Therefore, calling a referral service is not much better than choosing a lawyer's name randomly from the local Yellow Pages directory. In both places you will find names of lawyers with their purported areas of specialty. And in both places you will find no useful information to verify the lawyer's capabilities and integrity.

Therefore, if you fail to get a few names from friends, acquaintance lawyers, or judges, do not despair and do not use referral services that fail to provide hard information on the lawyers they recommend. Instead, continue to the next hunting tool recommended below.

Hunting Tool No. 4: Trade Organizations and Union Representatives

With your list of requirements in hand, it is worthwhile to make several calls to the trade organizations in which you are a member and/ or to the local Chamber of Commerce. If you are an entrepreneur in publishing for example, you could call the Writers Guild, the Association of Book Sellers of America, the Association of American Publishers, or other related trade organizations, such as the American Association of Home Businesses. The local Chamber of Commerce will also be able to direct you to trade organizations in your area relevant to your profession or line of business. Similarly, union representatives are well-equipped to direct an employee injured by employment discrimination, or any other physical or personal work place injury, to an adequate lawyer with whom union members have had good experience.

Hunting Tool No. 5: A Visit to the Local Library

Directories

The best-known directory of lawyers is published by, and is known as, *Martindale-Hubbell*. It lists more than 800,000 practicing lawyers in the United States and other countries. The listing is alphabetical by state, and each name—either individually or as a member of a law firm, is followed by a brief biography that includes the undergraduate and law school attended, a brief description of experience, and the lawyer's address and telephone number. *Martindale-Hubbell* is available in most libraries, on-line, or on CD-ROM. Other similar directories are *Counsel Connect*, a subsidiary of American Lawyer Media, L.P., in New York, and *The International Financial Law Review: A Guide to the World's International Business Law Firms* (Josephine Carr, 1993).

Some listings include a ranking of the individual lawyer's reputation, which is based on the opinion of other local lawyers, not clients. The absence of ranking only indicates that the lawyer asked that her rating not appear or that she has not been in practice long enough to earn a reputation. Even though *Martindale-Hubbell* charges a listing fee, it is known to be completely impartial in its information and rating.

Martindale-Hubbell is a vast directory that gives basic background information. It does not provide the disciplinary records of bar associations or courts; it is most useful when you have already obtained the name of a lawyer from a friend or from a news report describing a trial victory. In such a case, *Martindale-Hubbell* provides some professional information about the lawyer and how to contact the lawyer. The biographical information often gives a lawyer's area of practice or specialty, but the listings are very brief and do not include details of achievement. Directories such as *Martindale-Hubbell* are useful to a limited extent as a verification of an individual lawyer's specialty when they list memberships in a specific organization (for example, The Association of Labor Lawyers or the American Association of Immigration Lawyers) that indicate the lawyer's devotion to a certain area of the law. Additionally, some organizations are "invitation only," which attests to the lawyer's prestige (for example, The International Academy of Trial Lawyers). Similarly, the listing may indicate that the lawyer devotes some of her time to teaching in a law school or other professional academy or institution, which is another testimony to her standing in the profession.

Library Search

Local libraries often have listings of local or state-resident lawyers. For example, in California a local listing by city or county can be found in a publication of Parker and Son Publishers, Inc., which includes only the lawyer's name, law firm, address, telephone number, and area of expertise. In the San Diego area, the San Diego Daily Transcript offers a directory of local practicing lawyers with some biographical information. The information in such directories is limited, however, and should only be used to locate an attorney whose name you have already received from someone you trust.

A more useful section of the library is the archives of news reports and magazines. Your search for a successful employment-discrimination lawyer will benefit immensely from browsing through recent newspapers and magazine articles, which some libraries index by computer or by catalog cards. Look for lawyers whose victories in court have been newsworthy. For example, locate an article describing a substantial jury verdict in the local courts, in which a large amount in damages was awarded to an employee in an employment-discrimination lawsuit. The news report will give the name of the winning attorney. Take the name and search through the alphabetical directories to find the lawyer's telephone number. Then call her and schedule a meeting.

Similarly, you could search the legal section of the library for books or law review articles discussing age discrimination in employment. Any librarian will be delighted to help you with such a search. Take down the name of each of the authors of such publications, who will either be a practicing attorney or a law professor, find the telephone number through a telephone or lawyers' directory, and call to ask for a recommendation of an appropriate lawyer.

Hunting Tool No. 6: Lawyers' Ads, Commercials, and 900 Numbers

What's Wrong With Lawyers' Ads?

In TV commercials, all lawyers look the same—respectable, bespectacled, and reputable. But their looks are all you know about them, and even that is forgotten when their face disappears from the screen. Why shouldn't you call their toll-free number and save yourself the hassle of searching through referrals and publications? To answer that, you should first understand how lawyers advertise, and why they consider it one of their best client-hunting tools. If the following discussion looks too lengthy to you, it's because lawyers' advertisements are lawyers' most powerful client-hunting tool. When it comes to lawyers' ads, it is worth your while to understand how they work, and how you can protect yourself from their allure.

Why Do Lawyers Advertise?

Lawyers advertise because they want more business. There is nothing wrong with advertising by professionals and providers of services—including legal services. However, lawyers' ads fail to provide potential clients with any useful information upon which to base their choice of a lawyer.

According to marketing statistics, lawyers' ads produce revenues of $10 for each $1 spent. This ratio stays more or less the same for television commercials, newspaper and magazine ads, and radio spots. A July, 1994 article in the *ABA Journal* ("The Payback," by Daniel B. Kennedy) indicates that lawyers get 50 percent of their business from former clients, 30 percent from other referrals, and 20 percent is generated by active advertising. Another method of marketing is direct mailing to a list of selected potential clients, whom the lawyer then gives follow-up phone calls. Such promotional efforts usually generate up to a 15 percent response. In two examples cited by Kennedy, an Illinois law firm generated $1.6 million by spending $200,000 on TV commercials and a California practitioner generated $120,000 by spending $12,000 on local magazine ads.

As the consumer, you should realize that lawyers' advertisements on TV, on the radio, or in newspapers, are professionally produced marketing tools created by experts whose job is to lure you into making an initial phone call or visit to the lawyer's office. There are studies and statistics as to how the content, size of the letters used, or type of message of a newspaper ad would be most effective in drawing your attention, what frequency of radio and TV commercials is likely to reach you in your car or home, and how repetition of a lawyer's name on the air creates an instinctive name-recognition reaction that increases the chances of your becoming a client when you need a lawyer in the future.

In other words, lawyers' ads are a *lawyer's* hunting weapon, aimed at you as the prey. Whether an advertisement promotes a law firm with many specialties or a single lawyer with a specific specialty, remember that the advertisement was designed only to entice you to make an initial phone call to the lawyer's office. The ad does not contain any useful information regarding the lawyer's actual experience or achievements in the field or any testimony to her clients' satisfaction (or lack of satisfaction). Once you make that first phone call, the other end of the line will be managed by a professional marketing expert who is trained to convince you to come in for an initial meeting. At that point, you have become another catch—one of many who has responded to the advertisement. Your case will be quickly assessed to determine the potential profit for the lawyer and whether it is worthwhile or a waste of time listening to you. Unfortunately, at that point you have already wasted your time.

Can Lawyers Lie on TV?

Yes and no. For example, Opinion No. 661 of the New York State Bar Committee on Professional Ethics states that lawyers' TV or radio commercials may portray fictional situations and fictional characters to dramatize fictional events. Simply put, a lawyer may air a TV commercial in which professional actors portray the respectable lawyer and his happy, newly enriched client. Such an "illustrative" commercial is allowed, as long as the dramatization "is not false or misleading." The committee further stated that such a dramatization of a fictional event is not misleading per se, as long as the fictional event could reasonably occur. Only fictional "client testimonials"—that is, actors playing clients who compliment the lawyer for the excellent services they never really received—are prohibited. The committee left it up to the lawyer to be sensitive enough "to the need to make clear that the presentation is a dramatization and that the actors are not real clients."

The line separating ethical lawyers' ads from misleading ads was correctly described as "hazy" by Professor Linda Morton of King Hall School of Law, University of California, Davis. In her article, "Finding a Suitable Lawyer: Why Consumers Can't Always Get What They Want and What the Legal Profession Should Do About It" (25 *U.C. Davis Law Review*, p. 283), Professor Morton criticizes the confusion created by several Supreme Court cases regarding what types of advertisement lawyers may air under the constitutional right of "free speech" without crossing the line into misleading and false advertisement.

Bar Associations' Attempts to Restrict Informative Advertising

Bar associations make great efforts to restrict lawyers' marketing tools. The excuses for such limitations all stem from the argument that the legal profession is unique and thus individual lawyers should be restrained from "over-commercialized" marketing. Older lawyers with strong practices claim that most forms of advertisement taint the image of the profession, are undignified, and are inherently misleading due to the personal nature of the services lawyers offer. Consumer groups have had little success in freeing up the flow of information about legal services to the consumers. Recently, however, the U.S. Supreme Court, to a limited extent, made such advertising possible based on the constitutional right to "commercial free speech."

The Supreme Court Versus Bar Associations

In cases such as *Bates v. State Bar of Arizona* and *Central Hudson Gas and Electric Corp. v. Public Service Commission of New York*, the Supreme Court allowed lawyers' advertisements when they are not "inherently misleading," which means advertisement that includes "accurate and verifiable facts" but does not include any testimony to the "quality of services" of the advertising lawyer. The advertisement should not "actually mislead" or be "potentially misleading." Needless to say, state bar associations and courts have struggled to interpret these hair-splitting distinctions, leaving the consumer of lawyers' services practically unprotected.

Bar associations across the country consistently try to prevent individual lawyers from advertising useful information. Lawyers are prohibited from proving in their ads that they are experienced, responsive, or affordable. In Florida, for example, a lawyer was sanctioned by professional boards for advertising herself on business cards and in the yellow pages as an attorney and a CPA. This is an example of an attempt to prevent lawyers with unique certifications in related fields (such as accountancy or tax advising) from promoting themselves using such "extra" certifications, which give them a marketing edge over their peers.

Many bar associations maintain this policy despite the fact that such information is useful to potential clients searching for a lawyer with financial skills.

The Florida attorney, enraged by the sanctions, appealed to the Supreme Court of the United States. In its 1994 decision *Ibanez v. Florida Board of Accountancy*, the Supreme Court held that Ms. Ibanez's advertisement was "truthful and not misleading," that her advertisement of her qualifications as a certified public accountant and financial planner was protected by the constitutional right of "free speech," and that her advertisement was helpful to potential consumers of legal services. The Supreme Court further stated that the Florida board failed to show with "sufficient specificity" who was going to be misled or injured by such advertisement. "We have never sustained restrictions on constitutionally protected speech based on a record so bare as the one on which the Board relies here," Justice Ruth Bader Ginsburg wrote.

At the same time that bar associations attempt to prevent members from including helpful information in their advertisement to the public, they also try to prevent individual lawyers from approaching individual persons in need of legal services. Such "direct promotion" is considered to be solicitation, which is prohibited because it has the potential of creating unfair pressure on people in trouble, leading them to make a hasty and uninformed decision to hire an overly aggressive lawyer to assist with pressing legal problems.

In the 1978 Supreme Court case *Ohralik v. Ohio Bar Association*, a lawyer solicited two young accident victims to hire him as their lawyer. He solicited them in the hospital, when it was clear that they were unable to assess their own situation and, furthermore, unable to resist his pressure to hire him for "cost-free" service based on the damages payment he would get for them. Such conduct was considered an unacceptable in-person solicitation. After *Ohralik*, bar associations across the country have tried to prevent their individual members from contacting any individual potential client, even when such circumstances of hospitalization or other incompetency do not exist and even though in many cases it is helpful for potential clients to receive informative professional materials from lawyers whose specialty is relevant to the client's situation.

In *Kentucky Bar Association v. Stewart*, a 1978 case, the Supreme Court of Kentucky reversed sanctions imposed by the Kentucky Bar Association against several members for "unethical and unprofessional conduct" (they had mailed several local real estate agencies promotional letters that included a description of the various services they offered, including claims of high quality and low cost). The court decided that the bar association was wrong in characterizing such promotional efforts as "in-person solicitation." The court held that real estate agencies would benefit from receiving promotional materials from a prestigious law firms informing them of low fees and effective assistance. Of course, such informative promotion could hurt the business of other lawyers whose fees are higher, whose services are less efficient, and who do not make an effort to reach clients in need, but the court considered these protectionist attitudes too harmful for consumers of legal services.

In another move against bar associations' protectionism, recent attempts by the Florida Bar Association to prohibit lawyers from sending promotional materials to personal-injury and wrongful-death clients were held unjustified by the Federal Court of Appeals for the Eleventh Circuit. Circuit Judge Black, in her opinion, held that such attempts by the Florida Bar to limit lawyers' promotional efforts on the assertion of protecting people traumatized by recent injury, or protecting these people's privacy and tranquility, was not a reasonable restriction. In other words, it was an unjustified attempt by the Florida Bar to prevent energetic, consumer-oriented lawyers from engaging in fair competition against other, not-so-energetic lawyers.

Lawyers' "900 Numbers"

A recent phenomenon among legal services is the "900 number," which offers live legal advice over the phone. Such service, limited as it may be, offers consumers who lack knowledge of legal principles access to affordable and valuable information about the legal situations affecting their lives. Within the limitations set by bar associations, such 900 numbers offer advice on a per-minute fee basis. It is a preliminary opportunity to discuss a legal problem and get initial advice without the substantial cost of retaining a lawyer.

Such assistance in identifying the legal problem and advising on how to proceed can offer you direction toward the resolution of your legal problems, without your shelling out a large amount of money. It is a modern-day equivalent to a one-hour consultation with a lawyer, which was recommended above. It is more convenient because it can be done from your living room, but it is somewhat limited because of the anonymity of the lawyer giving the advice.

Each state, and each state bar association, can treat 900 numbers for legal advice differently. Your state may give no protection to you from unscrupulous 900-number operators. In New York, 900 numbers for legal advice were approved by Opinion No. 664 of the New York State Bar Association. The opinion, however, made several limitations on such services: Before any fee is charged to the caller, it required disclosure as to the extent of the advice offered by the service and the limited extent of the attorney-client relationship that is created when the telephone conversation turns to the legal issues.

In New York State, ethics rules also allow lawyers to offer recorded summary legal advice on the "general applicable laws," to be played by an answering machine or a 900 number. The lawyer who gives the advice over the phone, either recorded or during a conversation that is charged per minute through telephone bills, must be competent in the legal area relevant to the discussion and must explain to the caller that the matter requires a check on conflicting interests (whether the lawyer represents any party involved in your legal matter), further legal research, reviewing of relevant documents, interviewing witnesses, and further considerations of related matters—all of which are not possible to do during a single telephone conversation. It is also ethically permissible for lawyers to limit the scope of their services to a client as long as the lawyer explains the limitations and advises the client on the need for further legal assistance.

If you choose to call a 900 number for legal advice, you should be aware of the limitations of such services and make sure that the lawyer with whom you speak follows certain ethics rules. For example, a lawyer's fee may not be in excess of a "reasonable fee." Therefore, if the charge per minute on a 900 number, when multiplied by sixty, is in excess of $100 to $200, the fee you are being charged is excessive. Additionally, such service should not be a promotional service created to lure you, as a potential client, into the law firm that finances the 900-number service. Such a scheme, if not disclosed at the outset of the phone call, is deceitful, and you should terminate the call as soon as the situation becomes clear, for this is an indication that you are dealing with dishonest people.

Should You Respond to Lawyers' Ads?

Newspaper Ads

Lawyers' ads, enticing as they may be for the consumer, offer little or no help in making an informed choice. Take the following (imaginary) newspaper ad:

Employment-Discrimination Specialists:
Smith & Doe
Get the Money You Deserve!
Large and Small Cases!
Speak With Our Senior Partners:
John F. Smith & Jane W. Doe
There is no fee for an initial consultation
Call! Toll Free!
800-SUE THEM
Smith & Doe, Attorneys at Law

Smith and Doe are not necessarily bad lawyers. However, there is no way for you to deduce from their advertisement any evidence regarding the quality of their service. They satisfy your requirement of specialty in employment discrimination, but you do not know how experienced they are or how much success they have had in prosecuting employment-discrimination cases. As far as you know, they may be two young lawyers just out of law school, who decided to become "employment-discrimination specialists," and who deliver newspapers every morning to pay for this advertisement.

TV and Radio Commercials

TV and radio commercials are great hunting tools for a lawyer seeking new clients. But for you, the potential client, these commercials are sharp-toothed traps hiding in the dark forest.

The lawyer on the screen, with his full head of silver hair, shining teeth, and smart spectacles, has enough money to pay for expensive TV commercials, and that is all you know about him. You don't know, whether he can afford to pay for these commercials because he is a great lawyer with a terrific record of victories or because his third wife gave him money to go hunting on TV for his not-so-savvy first client. As discussed above, lawyer advertising can be completely fictitious—and still be ethical. You should not make yourself easy prey.

Answering TV and radio commercials, as with newspaper ads, is an example of laziness. It is equivalent to picking a name from a telephone directory or walking into a lawyer's office after you spotted a sign from across the street. You are much better off researching and collecting recommendations from friends, lawyers, and judges.

Direct Mail

The only type of lawyer's advertisement to which you might consider responding is direct mail. Some law firms, particularly those specializing in specific and narrow areas of the law, may invest in professional marketing research to find potential clients. For example, government-contracts specialists, who specialize in advising companies that supply products and services to the government, would research to find such small or medium-sized entrepreneurial companies that are engaged in selling their products or services to the government. Those specialty lawyers would then create a package in which you, as a potential client, would find a detailed description of their expertise, a schedule of their fees, and sometimes even a short list of clients who will serve as a reference. Such advertising is more informative and helpful and is created with enough attention to justify a follow-up by you to see whether that particular lawyer or law firm could indeed provide you with the needed legal service.

Hunting Tool No. 7: Put Your Own Ad in the Paper

An Unusual Tool That Can Be a Winner

"Reverse advertising" is a rarely used hunting tool—which makes it, in suitable cases, even more effective. It could be the most effective way for you to reverse the traditional roles and make lawyers line up to speak with you. Placing such an ad reverses the traditional roles. A situation is created in which lawyers compete for your attention and trust. It is clear that only the best qualified should apply to get your case. And it is subtly established that you are an informed, sophisticated client who is going to be the dominant party in the lawyer-client relationship.

For example, if your yearly salary after the promotion (which you did not get because of discrimination) would have gone up $150,000, a lawsuit against your discriminating employer could result in a jury verdict of well over $1 million. A victory of that magnitude could only be achieved by a top-gun lawyer, who would earn one-third of the verdict. When your case—and the lawyer's potential contingent fee—is so substantial, many lawyers will be interested in your case.

Posting your own ad may only be effective for large, potentially profitable cases. Also, the most prestigious and successful lawyers may not feel the urge to compete for your case or may be too busy winning cases for their clients to even notice your ad. Therefore, this hunting tool should be used only as a supplement to the other tools.

A Sample Ad

To reach the best lawyer among a notoriously anxious and thirsty crowd, you should place your ad in the local law journal or other publication directed at lawyers. The following is an example of such an ad:

> *Attorney Service Needed*
> Seeking an excellent lawyer for a well-documented, fully-supported plaintiff case of employment/age-discrimination, by a professional with excellent employment history, against a large corporation in the greater Cleveland area. Only highly experienced, highly recommended lawyers please! Include description of previous trial victories and three references (previous clients). Fax information to (123) 123–4567.

SEARCHING FOR A LAWYER IN A FOREIGN COUNTRY

Do You Need a Foreign Lawyer?

With the development of a global marketplace, many companies, including small businesses, find themselves doing business overseas. If your business has never before been active in another country, you may feel intimidated and hesitant in taking the first step. In truth, doing business in other countries is not much different from doing business in your hometown. The basic rules of common sense apply equally in doing business in foreign countries.

In most cases, your first step onto foreign soil, so to speak, will be your search for a foreign lawyer. Hiring an inappropriate or unqualified foreign lawyer can cause as much damage to your business as hiring the wrong lawyer in your own town. The foreign lawyer might neglect to do sufficient research on laws and regulations in his country that apply to your activities, neglect to tell you about the need for government licenses or registration of certain financial activities, or fail to advise you about other business laws applicable to your planned manufacturing or distribution activity in that country. Similarly, incorrect or inadequate advice on tax issues could create tax liabilities that might render the whole venture uneconomical.

How to Search for a Lawyer in a Foreign Country

Searching for a lawyer in a foreign country is not any different than searching for a lawyer in another state within the United States. However, it may require additional effort on your part. Use the same hunting tools as previously described, making any necessary adjustments required by the nature of your foreign-lawyer search.

Referrals are your first and best option. When you seek appropriate referrals, your first source will be other businesspeople or lawyers in other industries, who are not competitive with you and who work on a continuing basis with a lawyer in your target foreign country. Such referrals not only give you names of appropriate lawyers, but can also give you some information about that country's attitude toward foreign businesses (which your business is going to be), and about the working habits of local lawyers in that country.

Because you are not likely to know many people who conduct business in your target country, it may be necessary—and it is perfectly legitimate on your part—to make "cold calls" for references. The term cold calls includes phone calls to people with whom you have no personal experience and who do not know you from any previous business or personal connection. However, before making a cold call, be sure that the person you are calling indeed has experience in doing business or working with a lawyer in the applicable country.

Lastly, you may try contacting a referral service to help you find a lawyer overseas. One such service is Eurolink for Lawyers (44–113–242–2845), located in Leeds, England, which list small to mid-size law firms in 120 cities around the globe. Similarly, the law firm of

Foley & Lardner in Milwaukee operates GlobaLex (414-271-2400), an international legal referral network with speciality in licensing, finance, payment procedure, foreign currency matters, international transportation, foreign customs regulations and international dispute resolution.

If you do not necessarily need legal representation, but rather seek advise on doing business in one or more foreign countries, other referral services could put you in touch with a local CPA firm or a business consultant. For example, HLB International (44-171-334-4783) represents accountants and business advisors in more than 90 countries, specializing in strategic planning, company structures and formation, corporate and personal taxation, commodity taxes, accounting and auditing. Another alternative is CPA Managing Partner Report (800-926-7926), an annual directory of international CPA firms which you could obtain for a per-copy charge or as an annual subscription.

Communicating With Foreign Lawyers

After seeking referrals from several sources, you may find that a certain law firm in that foreign country is repeatedly mentioned. You should continue your search until you have at least three or four names, from which to choose. Chapter 6, which describes the selection process in detail, applies to choosing a foreign lawyer as well. However, there are several differences that should be noted before contacting potential foreign lawyers.

Communicating with a foreign lawyer cannot be done as easily as with local counsel. To select a law firm from among your several referrals, you should fax each firm a short letter, suggesting that you are considering hiring the firm to handle your affairs in that foreign country. Request them to perform an initial check for conflict of interest to see if such representation is at all possible.

Your initial interview of the firm will have to take place on the phone unless you travel frequently to that country. During the first interview, you should ask questions about the lawyer's experience in representing foreign companies; get a clear impression of the lawyer's English-language skills (even if you are fluent in the local language); ask about billing practices, the lawyer's availability to give speedy service, and the firm's ability to provide long-term, diversified legal service for your business. You should also ask specific legal questions to get a definite sence of the lawyer's legal skills and knowledge of relevant law.

When selecting a foreign lawyer, you should consider the unique needs your business has as a foreign operator in that country's local market. In your absence, your lawyer may have to negotiate business transactions on your behalf. She will have to work with you over telephone and fax lines, sometimes during the early hours of the morning due to time zone differences, and she will have to represent you abroad to a greater extent than does your domestic counsel at home. In addition, your lawyer must be capable of comprehending and poised to advise you of any legal or political developments in any foreign country that may have ramifications for your business. Your foreign lawyer must possess substantial legal, political, and business skills.

You do not necessarily need to hire the most prestigious foreign law firm. In some cases, a smaller firm with fewer international clients may be better motivated to prove itself in representing you, as a foreign client, and may treat you with much more respect and energy than a firm that has many other foreign clients. Also, it is often preferable to hire a local firm, and not a branch office of a global firm, to get the most attention and motivation from your foreign lawyer. In many instances, the best choice would be a local lawyer who, at a younger age, spent several years in the United States getting a legal or business education. She can communicate with you as an American, but she also is able to perform on a par with other local lawyers.

CHAPTER 6

A DAY'S CATCH IN YOUR BASKET: INTERVIEWING LAWYERS AND VERIFYING THEIR CLAIMS TO FAME

Do not marry the first lawyer who gets down on his knees to propose. He may be more desperate than he'd like to admit, and you may very well do better waiting for other proposals. If your case is any good, other proposals are bound to come, so keep a cool head and proceed cautiously through the selection process.

By using all the available hunting tools described in the previous chapter, you now hold in your hand a short list of candidates (five is a good number). Each one of these front-runners was recommended to you by someone you can trust, or has won a big case similar to yours. So far, each one satisfies your list of requirements, but each may also have some skeletons in his closet, of which you are not yet aware. These lawyers are all front-runners in the race to win you as a client. How should you select the best lawyer among them?

To make the correct selection, follow these essential steps:

- Check each lawyer's professional record.
- Interview each lawyer face to face, with a list of questions in hand.
- Negotiate a tentative Engagement Letter (including a fee arrangement) with each lawyer.
- Call each lawyer's clients for references.
- Conduct the "beauty contest."

CHECK YOUR PREY'S RAP SHEET: NOTHING LESS THAN AN UNTAINTED RECORD OF INTEGRITY

An initial check of each lawyer's ethical record can save you the time you would otherwise spend meeting and interviewing him. Also, meeting a candidate lawyer without checking his record exposes you to the risk of becoming a victim to his powers of persuasion. Remember, lawyers are advocates—experts in convincing other people of whatever is necessary. When you meet a lawyer who wants you to hire him, he will use every weapon in his arsenal to market himself as the most ethical, devoted, energetic, and get-results lawyer you can find. If you are not experienced in fending off aggressive marketing, any persuasive lawyer, especially one with a questionable ethical history, may be able to overpower you and convince you to sign an Engagement Letter prematurely.

Therefore, before calling a front-runner, check his ethics record. If it's tainted, don't waste your time; erase his name from your list and move to the next name.

Who Polices Lawyers' Misconduct?

State bar associations are the only institutions authorized by law to issue, suspend, or compel forfeiture of a license to practice law. In other words, lawyers' misconduct may only be investigated and punished by . . . other lawyers (unless it is sufficiently egregious and public to warrant criminal prosecution, as well as bar association disciplinary action). This explains the lack of reliable sources of information about an individual lawyer's misconduct.

In general, verifying a lawyer's clean ethical record is a great challenge. Bar associations and local courts are strictly secretive about disclosing a lawyer's record of ethics violations or licensing suspensions. However, you should not waste your time calling a front-runner on your list before you at least try to make sure he is in good professional standing and was never subject to disciplinary sanctions. Even the seemingly elementary requirement of a license to practice law may not exist, as with the New York state prosecutor with five years' experience arguing criminal cases in court, who in 1993 turned out to be a high-school dropout with no legal education nor a license to practice law.

Most Clients' Complaints Remain "Off the Record"

When doing a preliminary check on a lawyer's professional record, you should first distinguish between ethics violations and other problems. Clients' complaints about deficient communications or other disturbing slip-ups by a lawyer are not ethics violations and will not be subject to disciplinary action. For example, if a former client has been frustrated by the lawyer's failure to return phone calls, lack of response to written letters, neglect of various legal actions, or refusal to return documents after termination of service, such complaints do not amount to ethics violations and thus will not result in disciplinary action by the local bar association. As a consequence, such complaints will not appear in any formal record. You can only find out about them by speaking to present or former clients of the lawyer.

Also, your potential lawyer might be . . . crazy. In an opinion issued on July 11, 1989, the Federal Court for the Western District of New York held that the New York Bar Association cannot refuse an application for a license to practice law only on the basis of an aspiring lawyer's mental illness. Furthermore, in reviewing the application, the Bar Association was wrong even to investigate the applicant's mental health. The only line of investigation permitted was to discover any actual misrepresentations or other unethical actions in the applicant's past. The ramifications of that court decision are, obviously, disturbing for a potential, client like yourself, because you may end up hiring one lawyer, only to find out that you have also hired his twenty-seven other personalities.

Disciplinary Proceedings Against Lawyers

In most states, disciplinary proceedings take place behind closed doors, and the public has no way of knowing about such pending complaints. Some states, such as New Jersey, Vermont, and the District of Columbia, allow public access to such proceedings after it has been established that the client's complaint is based on a "probable cause of misconduct." In other states, the existence of such proceedings remains secret until after a formal hearing has concluded that the lawyer should be sanctioned for misconduct. Unfortunately, on average, only 30 percent of the complaints against lawyers ever get an actual hearing. Furthermore, only 10 percent of such complaints lead to sanctions against the accused lawyer.

A 1988 report by HALT, a group active on legal reform issues, found that only 2 percent of 70,000 clients' complaints in California resulted in actual disciplinary action, while 90 percent of these complaints were dismissed at the outset. In 1986, for example, 8,574 complaints were filed by clients against lawyers: The California Bar Association held proceedings against only 192 of those lawyers, of which 185 were actually sanctioned. Worst of all, even in cases in which the lawyer's misconduct had been proven truly unethical, the lawyer's punishment was usually little more than a private, discreet reprimand by his peers and did not become part of the public record.

Considering that these complaints do not even include issues of fees, minor incompetence, and discourteous behavior, such disciplinary proceedings are a poor source of information for the legal consumer. Additionally, clients involved in pending disciplinary action against their lawyers are prohibited by law from disclosing the existence of such a proceeding, which puts yet another constraint on the consumer's chances of finding out about problematic records.

Despite all these drawbacks, it is worthwhile for you, as a potential client, to check with the local bar association as to whether the lawyer who was recommended to you has been found sanctionable in any past disciplinary proceeding. You may not be advised about a pending action, a "minor" slip, or even a serious complaint that ended in a slap on the hand. But you may hear something that will save you from a disastrous choice.

Listings of Lawyers' License Suspensions and Malpractice

A primary source for information about a lawyer's record is the National Discipline Data Bank, a nationwide clearing house for disciplinary information on lawyers, created in 1968 by the American Bar Association's Center for Professional Responsibility to serve local bar associations' reviews of new applicants for licenses to practice law. Even though the National Discipline Data Bank is not open to the public and its hotline is accessible only to state bar associations, a consumer may request information about an individual lawyer's disciplinary record by sending a written request and paying a fee.

Additional information can be found in local law journals, which commonly list decisions by local bar associations' ethics committees against local lawyers. Though these journals are available in any library, they do not normally offer an up-to-date index of such disciplinary cases. Therefore, you would find it a tedious task to search through back issues of the local law journal in search of an individual lawyer's name—which is convenient for a lawyer with a disciplinary record.

A third source of information is a state bar association hotline service. In California, for example, the state bar association operates a telephone service (listed in the Yellow Pages) from which the individual lawyer's state bar I.D. number can be obtained to find out if that lawyer had been the subject of sanctions by the bar. To find out more about the cause of such sanctions, you should call the local state bar association office that manages such proceedings and ask for copies of the record of the proceedings. You may get lucky.

The sources of information discussed here will help you find any licensing suspensions or actual sanctions assessed against the lawyer. However, there is still no way for you to get information about pending complaints that have not yet reached the stage of resolution or about complaints that do not amount to ethics violations.

Because the majority of clients' complaints never reach disciplinary hearing, but rather, are dismissed immediately, no public record exists to assist you in your search. For this reason, interviewing recommended lawyers (before hiring one to handle your case) and questioning their former clients are the most effective methods of gathering information about prospective lawyers.

EYE CONTACT WITH YOUR PREY: INTERVIEWING THE CANDIDATE LAWYERS

The best source of information about an individual lawyer is the lawyer himself. By meeting with the lawyer and asking all the right questions, you can gather all the information you need to select the best lawyer for your case, provided, of course, that you verify the information by asking for copies of court decisions and by talking to satisfied clients. If you give a lawyer the clear impression that you are an informed, sophisticated, and cautious client, he will be truthful in his answers and treat you with the respect and honesty you deserve. If you sense that the lawyer is intimidated by your questions and by your healthy consumer's attitude, you should not hire that lawyer. In general, if the lawyer hesitates or gives vague responses to clear questions, or patronizes you in any way, you should take that as an indication that any professional relationship with this lawyer will ultimately be difficult and frustrating.

The Initial Phone Call

You have made up your mind to hire a lawyer to handle your age-discrimination claim against your employer. You have put together a list of requirements regarding the lawyer's expertise, character, quality, personality, and demeanor, and you have determined the out-of-pocket amount (if any) you are willing to spend on the case. You have come up with the names of five potential lawyers. Now it is time to call and schedule a meeting with each of those five lawyers in order to select the best among them.

When calling the lawyer's office, ask to speak with the lawyer himself. Do not present your case or give detailed information to a secretary or a clerk. If you insist on speaking with the lawyer himself, explaining that you have a case you would like to discuss, he will either take the call or return your call later.

Include these points in your initial telephone conversation:

- Ask the lawyer if he is familiar in any way with your employer (or anyone else you intend to sue or oppose legally). The lawyer you called might, unbeknownst to you, be an acquaintance or even represent the person you intend to sue. At this point in time, you have not yet established an attorney-client relationship, which entitles you to secrecy, and the lawyer has no legal obligation to be discreet. Therefore, do not divulge any additional information to the lawyer until you know that he has no conflict of interest with your case.

- Introduce yourself and present your case in one sentence. Include the basic facts of the case without going into details or giving any names.

- Ask if the lawyer has had experience with similar cases. If you need a lawyer to give you ongoing advice on business issues, ask if the lawyer is familiar with your line of business.

- Schedule a half-hour meeting with the lawyer and offer to pay for his time at his standard rate. If you pay for the lawyer's time, you will get his full attention. Additionally, by paying for his time, you unequivocally establish an attorney-client relationship, and the lawyer is legally obligated to maintain complete secrecy. (An attorney-client relationship may be established even when a lawyer is giving free advice, but payment makes it clearer that such relationship exists.)

- Schedule the meeting at the lawyer's office. Checking out the lawyer's office is part of your selection process, and therefore you should not meet in any other location.

- Be clear that your conversation and the meeting to follow are subject to complete secrecy. Even if, at the conclusion of the initial phone call, you decide that there is no need for you to meet the lawyer, you should still ask for complete secrecy. It is your right.

Meeting Face-to-Face: Your First Impressions

It is extremely important to take careful notes during your meeting with the lawyer. Bring a note pad with you. This will not only make an impression on the lawyer and prevent him from giving "inaccurate" answers, but will also be useful later, when you try to recall the details of the meeting. When arriving at the lawyer's office, look around. The reception area can tell you whether the lawyer is successful and respected or whether he is a loser who shares shabby office space with other losers. You can learn a lot from simple observation, for example:

- Is this a large law firm or a small space shared by lawyers who are not partners?

- Are the equipment, furniture, artwork, and air conditioner modern and well-kept, or old and neglected?

- Is the receptionist courteous and in a good mood? Did he know you were coming? What is his demeanor when he announces your arrival to the lawyer?

The actual meeting should also be observed carefully, keeping these questions in mind:

- Were you kept waiting long beyond the scheduled meeting time?

- Is this the lawyer's own office or is this a bare conference room?

- Is the furniture nice? Is there an up-to-date computer by the desk?

- Are there family pictures or signed photographs with judges and/or civic leaders?

- Is the lawyer pleasant and friendly? Is he courteous to you? (Remember: You are the boss, and you are interviewing him!)
- Is he giving you his undivided attention? Does he take phone calls during your meeting?

Presenting the Facts of Your Case

The meeting should begin with a short presentation of your case, including:

- Your name, employment history, family situation.
- The general cause for a lawsuit (or other need for a lawyer).
- A more detailed description of the relevant events and personalities involved in the matter.
- Your feeling about fairness and how much you personally care about the outcome of the case.

If your need of a lawyer is in the context of a business transaction, your short presentation should include:

- The nature of your business.
- The elements of the business transaction(s) you are considering.
- Names of others involved in the business and their roles, and the names of other lawyers, if any are involved.

During your presentation the lawyer may ask you questions, which you should answer as well as you can. However, make sure to complete your presentation in the planned order, and do not let the lawyer take over the discussion.

The lawyer you hire must be a good listener. If he constantly interrupts your presentation with unnecessary questions, "breast-beating," war stories, or other forms of patronization, this lawyer is not for you.

Also, watch the lawyer while you speak. Is he listening intently or is he jumping in before you finish your sentence? Is he glancing at his watch constantly? Answering his phone? Shuffling through unrelated documents? Or just knuckling the edge of his desk? If he does not really care about you or your case, he's not the best lawyer for you.

The Lawyer's Preliminary Opinion on Your Case

Immediately after you have presented your case (or explained your need for legal service), pose these questions to the lawyer:

- Based on the limited information I've just given you, what is your preliminary legal opinion of my situation?
- What are your projections for the outcome of my case/achieving my goals in the pending business transaction?

The lawyer's response to your first question will give you a clear idea of his knowledge and understanding of the law as it applies to your case. If he becomes impatient or answers too vaguely, he may not be the expert he pretends to be. As to the second question, if the lawyer thinks the case is hopeless or that your entrepreneurial business idea is infertile or infantile, you should end the meeting in a polite manner. Though you should take into consideration the substance of what the lawyer has to say, a clearly evident lack of enthusiasm for your case or business should lead you to remove him from your list.

The "ideal" lawyer should be knowledgeable and positive in his opinion, yet cautious, pointing out strengths and weaknesses. A lawyer who tells you that your case is a "sure win" is either inexperienced or dishonest. No lawyer can predict sure results, and no lawyer knows every element of the applicable law without further legal research. The ideal lawyer's predictions, though optimistic, should also include explanations on the more difficult aspects of the case. His analysis of the applicable law should be presented to you in clear, layman's language, without patronizing you. He should also explain those factual elements are crucial and what type of solid factual evidence would be required to support your allegations.

Listen carefully to the substance of his analysis of your case. Is he trying to impress you with well-spoken commonsensical ideas that do not require real knowledge of the law? Or is he telling you something new about the law and appears to be knowledgeable? Does he admit he does not know everything, and that more research is needed? (Humility is a graceful quality, but incompetency—even if admitted to—is hazardous.)

The same rules apply to a lawyer you interview in search of an ongoing legal adviser for your entrepreneurial business. He should have solid knowledge of your industry, use the correct terms of art, and be familiar with the major players in that business area. He should be familiar with the regulations and laws, both local and federal, that apply to your business, and should sound confident on the issues.

Keeping an Open Ear for Looming Conflicts of Interest

Examples of "Conflict of Interest" Situations

The term "conflict of interest" encompasses several situations in which a lawyer has other interests or motivations that collide in some manner with a particular client's interests. Examples of potential conflicts of interest include:

- *The opposite side is already a client.* This situation is the most common and presents the worst potential for a conflict of interest. In your case, the lawyer you are calling already represents the employer or other party you intend to sue. In less direct situations, the lawyer represents an organization, a union, or another party who has a direct interest in making your lawsuit unsuccessful. In such a situation, the lawyer has an obligation to inform you immediately of such potential conflict of interest and advise you to seek legal advice from another lawyer.

- *The opposite side was a client in the past.* In such a situation, a direct collision of conflicting interests does not necessarily exist, because the lawyer no longer represents the opposing party. However, the lawyer has intimate familiarity with the opposing party's affairs that he is obligated to keep in confidence. In some circumstances, this could enable the former client to demand the court to disqualify your lawyer from representing you in the case. The reason for such disqualification would be that significant information about the former client came to the lawyer's knowledge during such past representation and therefore the former client has "proprietary" rights with respect to such information, including the right to demand that such information not be used against it in the prosecution of your case.

- *The "tabloid-lawyer syndrome."* A phenomenon of modern times is the lawyer who makes more money selling his stories to the tabloids, book publishers, or movie producers than he makes from fees for servicing his client. For example, a lawyer representing a mass-murderer could convert his experience into a book, a series of articles in a tabloid newspaper, a movie, or any combination of the above. The conflict of interest is automatically created when the lawyer does his work representing the client with a view to making future profits from selling a sensational story, whereas the client's interest calls for a low profile. The tabloid lawyer has a distinct interest in converting any representation—especially a trial—into a major media event, for example, by leaking sensational or gruesome details to the press, often to the detriment of the client. Although some states have enacted ethics rules and regulations aimed at preventing such media deals by lawyers, most states allow them, sometimes under the pretense of "raising money for the defense."

Risks in "Conflict of Interest" Situations

The risks to the client who hires a lawyer who has conflicting interests in the case depend on the circumstances and the type of conflict. The following sections present some of the more common risks:

The Lawyer May Be Disqualified Later

Courts frequently deal with requests by parties in litigation to disqualify the lawyer representing the opposite party. In *British Airways v. Port Authority of New York and New Jersey* (1994), the federal District Court for the Eastern District of New York ruled that there is a "per se standard" for disqualifying a law firm that represents one client against another client of the firm, even though that second client is represented by a different law firm in this case. In the above case, the firm representing British Airways against the Port Authority of New York and New Jersey, at the same time represented the Port Authority in another matter, which was completely unrelated. The court held that it was irrelevant that the information the firm had about the Port Authority in the unrelated matter had no bearing on the present case. The court ruled that such a situation requires an immediate disqualification. Any familiarity that the law firm had with the Port Authority could have been used to its disadvantage, and there should be no possibility for such a thing to happen. In other words, a law firm cannot represent one client against another of its own clients under any circumstances.

In *Solow v. W.R. Grace* (1994), the New York State Court of Appeals issued a pro-lawyer decision that limits *British Airways*. In *Solow*, the court affirmed the presumption that a law firm that once represented one client and now represents another client in a substantially related matter breaches the confidence of the first client even if the firm has many lawyers and different lawyers served each client. However, under *Solow*, the presumption can be rebutted if the law firm can show that there was "no reasonable possibility" that confidential information was used against the first client.

In conclusion, the risk that your lawyer will later be disqualified from representing you because he has represented your opponent in a related matter will vary from state to state, and is difficult to assess, given the amount of judicial discretion involved. However, if your direct opponent in the upcoming case is or has been a client of the lawyer you are thinking of hiring, the risk of future disqualification is too great for you to take, and you should not hire this lawyer.

The Lawyer as Your Advocate

A situation that frequently comes up in uncontested divorce cases is the desire of both sides to be represented by the same lawyer. Though dual representation is not prohibited in most states and might save the client legal fees and unnecessary battles with the other party, these situations inherently present a conflict of interest that could hinder the lawyer's wholehearted advocacy of your interests. In all cases, there are significant issues of disagreement, and even though a lawyer may serve you best by helping to resolve such disagreements, the lawyer should be able to represent your interests without hesitation. Resolution of disagreements is often achieved by an emotional communication between the lawyers representing each of the parties. A lawyer is an advocate, which requires him to undertake strong positions in favor of his client, even if fairness might dictate otherwise. Similarly, if the other party has been a client in the past, or is a client in an unrelated matter, the lawyer may find it difficult to advocate your interests without second thoughts.

Don't Make Your Lawyer Choose Between Clients

It is impossible for a lawyer who represents two clients not to prefer one client over the other. Even if the matter in which you wish the lawyer to represent you is completely unrelated to the matters the lawyer handles for the other party, there might still be personal interests on the part of the lawyer relating to future business with the opposing party, or personal feelings toward the other party resulting from past representation. It is better to avoid hiring a lawyer who may have any loyalty toward the party you intend to sue.

Similarly, when hiring a lawyer to provide you with ongoing legal advice, you agree to share with him intimate and confidential information. You do not want to be at risk that the lawyer may be tempted to disclose your secrets to another client whose business may be larger and therefore more lucrative for the lawyer.

Do not put your lawyer in a position of having to chose between you and another client. The lawyer's own sense of fairness may not suffice, and there is no benefit in paying a substantial fee to a lawyer, only to have him judge between you and another client. Therefore, even the slight possibility of conflict of interest is a reason enough not to hire that lawyer. Fortunately, you have several other lawyers on your list of front-runners.

The Lawyer's Personal Beliefs

In situations that raise social or other controversial issues, a lawyer might have strong feelings one way or another. For example, an unmarried pregnant woman wants to have an abortion. She is sued by the biological father, who asks the court to order her not to have the abortion. The woman hires a lawyer who has strong "pro-life" sentiments but is forced, for financial reasons, to take her case. The lawyer may do a good job representing her, but his heart will never be in it, and his representation will never be as devoted and powerful as it should be, due to the internal conflict of interest. Such situations should and can be avoided by inquiring as to whether the lawyer has definite feelings or ideological beliefs that are contradictory to the theme of your case.

Ask About Malpractice and Ethics Violations

Do not feel embarrassed to ask the lawyer about his professional record. It is extremely important for you to hear "from the horse's mouth" that his record is clean. Pertinant questions to ask are:

- Have you ever been sanctioned or reproved by the bar association?
- Are there any pending client complaints against you in any bar, court, or state or federal agency?
- Have you ever been sued by a client for malpractice?

A positive answer to any of these questions will always be followed by an explanation. If the lawyer claims that the matter was resolved in a way that cleared him from wrongdoing, insist on seeing the written documents that confirm the lawyer's version, such as the relevant decision of the Ethics Committee, a court decision on a malpractice case, a settlement, or an apology letter. No client complaint or malpractice lawsuit would be resolved without a formal document of resolution, be it an opinion, decision, judgment, or settlement agreement. You have the right to ask to see such documents; if the lawyer wants you as a client, he will show the documents to you to prove you have no reason to worry. If the document is confidential, the names of the other parties could be blacked out before it is shown to you.

Proven Experience and Record of Victories

Ask the lawyer to summarize for you his experience in the relevant area. The pertinent factors to take note of are:

- Law school and subsequent professional training.
- Teaching in law school or bar association seminars.
- Legal publications in the field.
- Victories in court or through settlements, in cases similar to yours. Ask to see documentation of any settlements, and also ask for the names of the clients and permission to call them for references. Take detailed notes!
- If you need business advice, ask whether he has other clients in your line of business. His answer will help you, on the one hand, to ascertain his expertise and, on the other hand, to determine possible conflicts of interest if he represents your direct competitor.

Work Habits and Frequency of Communication

No lawyer could represent you effectively throughout all stages of a lawsuit without keeping you constantly involved at every stage. Your choice of a good lawyer should be based in part on an informed prediction of the lawyer's attention to communication with clients.

Similarly, if you are looking to retain a lawyer for ongoing business advice, it is essential for you to find out how available he will be to take your calls, to research issues that come up, and to respond to your inquiries quickly. The questions you should ask the candidate lawyer in that respect are:

- How frequently will we meet to discuss my case?
- Do you take calls throughout the day or only during certain hours?
- Do you have a secretary or a law clerk with whom to leave a detailed message?
- Are you usually available to discuss matters on the phone?
- Do you expect to ask the court for extensions of time because of conflicting obligations to other clients?
- Are you often out of town on workdays?
- How will you keep me informed about developments in my case?
- Do you expect to let me participate in strategic decisions in the case or do you require a "free hand" in the management of the case?
- Will I receive copies of all the documents you produce (or receive from the other side) during the representation?

The lawyer's answers to these questions will give you a clear picture of his work habits. You do not want a lawyer who tells you to sit at home and let him take care of everything. Such lack of communication is a sure recipe for disaster. You want to be right behind him at all times, know everything that happens in your case, and receive detailed explanations about the actions he takes on your behalf. The most effective ways of communicating with your lawyer are described in Chapter 15: "The Savvy Client's Tool Kit." At this initial meeting, all you want to know is whether the lawyer would be receptive to the way you intend to supervise his work.

Who Would Work on My Case?

If the lawyer you interview practices on his own, it is assumed that he will be representing you himself without involving other lawyers, unless specifically discussing it with you. But if the lawyer you interview is a partner at a larger law firm, the question becomes relevant.

Law firms are composed of partners, who share the firm's profits, and associates, who have less experience than the partners and are paid a fixed salary. Associates' hours are normally billed to the client at a rate twice or even three times the compensation they actually receive. For example, an associate at any large New York firm is expected to bill a minimum of 2,000 hours per year (which doesn't include the time spent on administrative, marketing, or other work that cannot be billed to a client). Such New York law firms bill associates' time to clients at an average of $250 per hour. On a yearly basis, that amounts to $500,000 in revenues for the law firm, per associate, less an average yearly associate's salary of $120,000, which leaves the law firm an average profit per associate of approximately $380,000, less overhead (expenses for rent, electricity, secretarial support, etc.). As the calculations show, it is more profitable for a law firm to have most of the work done by associates, thus leaving the partners free for "rainmaking," that is, marketing and bringing in more clients.

As a potential client you want to know that your case will be handled by the experienced partner himself, not by an associate you do not know. If, as is customary in large cases, research and preparation will be done by a junior lawyer, you should get a firm assurance that the partner himself is going to run the case every step of the way, write each important brief, argue each motion in court, and represent you in the trial. Most important, make it clear that you are hiring the partner because of his qualifications, and will not agree to being represented by other lawyers in the firm.

A relevant question in this respect is: "Are you (the lawyer) planning to leave this firm, this area, or do you in any way think you might not be able to complete the representation for any reason?" This is important because, in our modern society, people tend to move frequently, and transferring your case to another lawyer midway would cost you money and time and possibly harm your chances of winning.

Malpractice Coverage

When it comes to lawyer malpractice, the general rule applies: Hope for the best, but prepare for the worst. For example, you have a terrific case against your employer. You hire a reputable lawyer, who takes over all the documents you have collected and promises great victories. One year later, to your great dismay, you discover that no lawsuit has yet been filed on your behalf. Your lawyer does not take your calls. You decide to fire him and promptly send him a termination letter.

Soon thereafter, you consult with another lawyer, who advises you that, even though you have a great case, it is not possible to file a lawsuit anymore because the "statute of limitations" time limit has expired. Fuming, you instruct your new lawyer to file a malpractice suit against your former lawyer. Three years later, a jury awards you $1 million in damages. Your joy, however, is short-lived, because it turns out that your former lawyer, being the way he is, has no money or assets from which to collect the judgment against him. He has no malpractice insurance either.

You can prevent something like this from happening by making sure your prospective lawyer has enough malpractice insurance coverage at the time you hire him. If your case is substantial, the damages you could suffer because of the lawyer's malpractice are also substantial. Therefore, do not be satisfied with a simple positive answer, but rather ask to see the malpractice policy itself, write down the name and telephone number of the insurance company, and look for the following details:

- A minimum of $1 million in primary coverage for each case.
- Renewal of coverage should be at least six months away.
- Specialty clause. Most lawyers' malpractice policies are limited to the specialty or expertise specified by the lawyer on the insurance application. For example, an immigration lawyer has no malpractice insurance when he takes on a divorce case. If you need a lawyer to litigate an age-discrimination employment claim, the policy should cover all of these areas of specialty: litigation, labor law, and federal practice.

If a lawyer tries to convince you that there is no need for you to look at his malpractice policy, he most probably does not have one, or his policy reflects a problematic record and is limited in ways the lawyer does not wish you to see. Wish him a good day and leave for your next meeting.

Get a Firm Commitment on Fees and Expenses

The fee arrangement is the most dispute-prone element of a lawyer-client relationship. Your lawyer will agree to represent you because he hopes to make money, not because of your pretty ears. Even if there is great rapport between you, a dispute over the lawyer's fees will make a roomful of good feelings evaporate within seconds. It is, therefore, extremely important to be clear from the outset on the issue of fees.

In response to your question about fees, the lawyer may give you a vague projection, trying to avoid specific numbers. If he is more specific and straightforward, he is exceptional and should get credit for it on your final scorecard. For now, take careful notes!

A whole chapter of this book (Chapter 10) is dedicated to fee negotiating arrangements, but for the purpose of this stage of your search, it is important to distinguish between four primary alternative fee arrangements.

Hourly Rate

An hourly rate is both the most common fee arrangement and the worst one for a client. You will be billed occasionally for the work done by the lawyer, according to the number of hours spent by the lawyer (and his colleagues, employees, etc.) on your case. Unfortunately, the lawyer could bill more hours than he actually spends on your case, and even if truthful, the underlying incentive is to work slowly and spend as much time on your case as possible. It is therefore important to ask:

- What is the hourly rate of each lawyer who will work on the case?
- Will any nonlawyers work on the case (for example, paralegals) and at what rate?
- Will the lawyer's bills include a breakdown of the hours spent on each task?
- Can he give you an estimate, or better, a cap on the maximum hours for your case?

Contingent Fee

If your case is of the type appropriate for a contingent-fee arrangement, such as an employment discrimination or personal injury case with chances for a large judgment of damages, the lawyer may suggest a contingent fee of, for example, one-third of the amount you actually receive as compensation at the end of the trial. Questions to ask with respect to a contingent fee are:

- Will I have to pay anything at all, either fees or expenses, before the trial has ended and a final judgment has been paid by the defendant?
- Which expenses will be added to the fee and when will they become due?
- What happens if I decide to replace the lawyer in the middle of the litigation? Will I owe any fees?
- What percentage will the lawyer charge out of an amount paid through settlement?

Fixed Fee Based on Results

If you want results that are not necessarily measured in numbers, such as winning enforcement of a sales contract or an injunction against infringement on your rights, a fixed fee based on results is probably the best fee arrangement for you. A lawyer who knows he will be paid only if he achieves the desired results will put everything into winning your case.

For example, you own an apartment building, and one of your tenants has failed to pay the rent for over three months. The lease agreement calls for immediate eviction in such a case. When hiring a lawyer to evict your tenant, you should agree with your lawyer on a fixed fee, to be paid only after the tenant has been evicted from the apartment. That way, you have no risk of running legal costs disproportionate to the amount of debt owed, and at the same time, your lawyer has an incentive to save time and achieve the result you want.

Combination Fee

Though relatively new to the world of lawyers, innovative methods of calculating legal fees have been promoted by corporate clients with more leverage over their lawyers. Even though the possibilities are endless, the underlying theme is to combine some form of low hourly rate with a special bonus based on results.

Preliminary Discussion of the Engagement Letter

Most lawyers will ask you to sign an agreement, commonly called an "Engagement Letter" or "Retainer Agreement," setting forth the terms of the lawyer-client relationship and the fee arrangement. But during the initial interview, it is too early to negotiate the details of the Engagement Letter, which will be signed only after the "beauty contest" and the final choice of one lawyer over the other candidates have taken place. Nevertheless, at this point you can ask to receive a copy of the lawyer's standard Engagement Letter, so that you may review it later in private and compare it to the sample Engagement Letters given to you by the other lawyers.

It is important to write down the lawyer's explanations about the fees he expects to collect from you. When he is done, repeat to him what you have written and ask whether your understanding is accurate. Do the same with respect to any other provision of the Engagement Letter to which the lawyer refers specifically as he hands you the blank form. Lastly, ask whether his standard demands are flexible, and whether he would be willing to negotiate some alternatives at a later point, after you have done more research. Whatever his answer is, leave it at that. You are not committing yourself to anything at this point in time, and you should not commence actual fee negotiations until you have decided to hire this lawyer. For now, his commitment to certain expected fees and his blank-form fee Engagement Letter are enough for purposes of comparison with the other lawyers you interview.

Ask for Names of Other Clients as References

Ask the lawyer to give you at least three names of other clients (one of which is a former client) as references. The lawyer may insist on speaking to those clients before giving you their names, which is a legitimate thing to do, as long as they agree to talk to you. Insist on talking to other clients. There is no way around it, and you should not let the lawyer talk you out of it. Be specific in your request by pointing that you would prefer to talk to clients who have been served by the lawyer in a case or matter similar to yours, and that:

- The service has been completed successfully, such as a judgment in a case of employment discrimination on the basis of age.

- The lawyer represented or is currently representing the client in a business negotiation or commercial transaction similar to the one in which you are about to engage.
- The client is not a relative, associate, partner, or in-law of the lawyer.

Do Not Sign Anything Prematurely

Lawyers are, first and foremost, salespersons. They are trained to sell a case to the jury, to sell an argument to the judge, and to sell themselves to a potential client. In representing criminals in court, for example, the lawyer's professional duty is to convince the judge, jury, and media that his client is innocent, even if the lawyer does not believe it himself. Any salesman—including a lawyer—knows that there is no sale until the customer has signed something and feels committed. Leave the lawyer's office without committing yourself. You need time to think, to meet other lawyers, to speak to former clients, and to conduct the "beauty contest." Do not sign anything yet.

When you actually leave, be gracious about leaving without making an immediate decision. Explain that despite the good impression he has made on you, you need time to reflect and consider other lawyers. Mention this book and make him realize that you are an informed and educated client. If that fact intimidates him, he is not for you!

CHAPTER 7

DISSECTING YOUR PREY: SELECTING THE BEST LAWYER AMONG THE FRONT-RUNNERS

ANALYZING THE INFORMATION: IMMEDIATE DROPOUTS

Even if you have only met one lawyer and cannot yet make a comparison, you may decide to drop this lawyer's name from your list of front-runners. After leaving the lawyer's office, your first step is to reflect on the meeting. When doing so, try to make a quick determination whether the lawyer you have just met should be dropped from the race. The factors discussed in this section are sufficient basis for such summary judgment.

Negative Gut Feelings

Listen to your gut feelings. If the overall impression left by the lawyer is clearly negative, or if you have a strong sense that you doubt the lawyer's honesty, integrity, or professional expertise, it is a waste of your time to keep that lawyer on your list.

It is not necessary for you to analyze the reasons for your negative gut feeling, but you may find that it results primarily from the lawyer's inability to listen and respond to your concerns. If such is the case during your first meeting with this lawyer, the lack of respect and communication skills will only become more severe as your lawyer-client relationship progresses. In any event, you should give great weight to your general impression and sense of the lawyer's qualities as a person and as a professional you consider hiring.

Lawyers who give their best performance on the initial meeting with a potential client may fall into one of these character types:

- *The Evasionist.* You cannot get one straight answer from this lawyer. Everything is always "generally speaking, subject to further research, and very similar to another case I had, very interesting, let me tell you. . . ."

- *The Charmer.* Here you are bathed in honey, flattery, and gracious gestures. The lawyer compliments you on your appearance, your sharp mind, your understanding of legal matters, and your good taste in lawyers. This lawyer relies heavily on personal charm to salvage herself from lack of real knowledge and hard work.

- *The Father Figure.* All you are going to hear from this lawyer is that you are in good hands. He will take care of you. And do not bother your little head with questions of law, liability, evidence, or jury selection. Daddy will take care of you.

- *The VIP.* This lawyer is too important and too busy to talk to you right now. She has other, very important clients to meet, bar associations to chair, and politicians to lobby. You should consider yourself lucky that she agreed to take on your case. Just drop off all the relevant documents (and a $5,000 check) with the secretary, and wait for a phone call in a week or two.

- *The Slanderer.* "Who else are you considering to hire as your lawyer? Dan Kollb? He's a racist and a loser. And he cheats his clients on fees. Whatever you do, stay away from Kollb!" This lawyer is determined to get your case by stepping on the bodies of his buddies. Stay away from him.

- *The Bargain Basement Dealer.* "I'm losing money to take your case, believe me, I'm doing you a favor because I know your cousin. Anyway, it'll cost you nothing, what do you have to lose?

- *The White Knight.* "Just jump on the saddle behind me, and let's conquer the world together! There's no time to think, the Barbarians are at the gate!" This lawyer will convince you that she is your only savior in a world full of charlatans and evil spirits.

Of course, all of these characters are no good. If your candidate falls into one of these categories, take him or her off your list. The lawyer might have given you a good show, but gave you no substantive answers, no explanation of the legal issues involved in your case, and nothing on which to judge his or her qualifications as a lawyer. Drop this lawyer immediately!

Other Reasons for a Snap Rejection

Additional reasons that justify dropping the lawyer's name from your list are:

- *Over-pessimism.* The lawyer has a pessimistic opinion about the chances of your case, has no real understanding of the business you are engaged in, or fails to express an opinion about your case because "she needs to do further research." This caveat does not apply when the lawyer is merely being cautious in expressing her opinion about the relevant legal issues, but it applies to a situation in which the lawyer expresses no opinion or shows no real interest or hope for a successful outcome in your case.

- *Conflict of Interest.* The lawyer would have a substantial conflict of interest if she took your case. In that respect, no compromise should be allowed. If the lawyer is closely connected with the person you wish to sue, to a major competitor in the same business, or in any way has interests or a personal agenda that may cause a situation in which your interests will not be first priority for her, you should drop her name from your list.

- *Ethics Violations.* The lawyer admitted to a record of ethics violations or to pending malpractice lawsuits. In that respect, if you have an extremely positive feeling about the lawyer and find her explanations of these negative occurrences satisfactory, you could keep her name on your list, on the condition that you will research the matter and read the relevant court decisions and bar association opinions. Remember that some of the most charming people are compulsive liars, and your sympathy may be greatly misplaced, putting you at risk. Keep her on your list only if you can satisfy yourself through independent sources of information that the lawyer's negative ethics or malpractice record has no bearing whatsoever on her character.

- *Lack of Expertise.* The lawyer has no experience or no record of victories relevant to your case. In this respect, there is no room for compromise. You should not be a guinea pig for the lawyer's desire to specialize in a new field. It is very important for lawyers to gain experience and expertise in new fields of the law, but you are better off if they gain such experience by representing other clients.

- *Obnoxious Attitude.* Arrogance is a dangerous character trait in a person who presumes to give services. If the lawyer explains to you that there is no need for ongoing communication during the representation or that she expects complete and unconditional authority from you to take any steps without a discussion with you, she shows a dangerous attitude and should be dropped from your list. For example, the lawyer tells you there is no need for you to meet or discuss anything until the case goes to trial, that her secretary will communicate with you unless it is absolutely necessary for you to speak to the lawyer personally, that it takes her at least two weeks to return a client's call, that she makes all strategic decisions in her cases without consulting clients, or that you will receive no copies of any documents in the case unless it is absolutely necessary. In summary, a lawyer who shows tendencies not to consult a client during the representation or not to have any desire to communicate with a client, should be dropped from your list.

- *Lack of Involvement.* The lawyer tells you that an associate or a colleague will do most of the work on your case and she will only supervise the work. In this respect, your judgment depends on the circumstances. In a large law firm, this situation is common. However, whether the firm is large or small, if your interest is not going to be fully protected because the lawyer is only a "supervising partner," making the benefit in hiring her minimal, drop that lawyer from your list unless you have assurances that she will at least attend important meetings and be available to speak to you frequently.

- *Lack of Malpractice Coverage.* The lawyer has no malpractice coverage adequate to cover the risk involved in her representation. You should not compromise on this issue. Moreover, a lawyer without malpractice insurance is, most probably, unable to obtain such insurance because of previous malpractice lawsuits. Drop that lawyer from your list.

- *High Cost.* The approximate cost of the representation, as presented to you by the lawyer, exceeds your financial abilities or exceeds the amount you are willing to spend on the case. In this respect, immediate dropout is justified only if the lawyer indicated that there could be no further negotiation of the legal fee.

- *No Reference.* The lawyer refuses to give names of other clients for purposes of reference. There is no reason why a lawyer would not be able to get a few clients to give a good reference to a potential client. The lawyer may claim "client privacy" as the reason. However, for a truly successful lawyer, who maintains adequate relationships with happy clients, there should be at least a few satisfied clients whose matters are not confidential and who should have no reservation about saying a good word about their lawyer.

The Ultimate Gut Quiz

The last, and maybe the most important litmus test, is what your gut feeling tells you. Ask yourself:

- Do I like this lawyer?
- Can this lawyer do the job?
- Does this lawyer care about my case?
- Can I trust this lawyer?

INVESTIGATING FORMER CLIENTS' SATISFACTION

Introducing Yourself

Before calling former clients of the lawyer, you should be certain that the lawyer has spoken to them and told them that you would be calling. You should first introduce yourself and explain the reason for your call, that is, to hear their opinion about the quality of this specific lawyer and her services. There is no need to share with them the facts of your case, but as a courtesy you may indicate the nature of the case. Remember, you are making the call to obtain information, not to divulge information.

You should ask the former client whether he believes that he is in a position to give you a reliable reference for the lawyer. In that respect, ask the client what type of services or representation the lawyer was hired to do and whether such representation had reached a favorable conclusion.

Follow-Up on the Lawyer's Boasting

Your first questions are intended to validate the lawyer's claims of achievement with respect to that individual client. Tell the lawyer's client in a few words what the lawyer has said, that is, that she has won such-and-such a case on behalf of the client and won the client so many dollars in compensation. Listen to the client's answer, whether it is an enthusiastic confirmation, a hesitant confirmation, a qualifying description of a lesser achievement by the lawyer, or a flat-out denunciation of the lawyer.

Did the Lawyer Achieve the Desired Results?

Ask the client to recall the time he hired the lawyer to represent him. Can the client describe his expectations from the lawyer and the results he hoped to achieve in hiring the lawyer? If the client is able to clearly recall that earlier stage, ask the client whether the lawyer actually achieved such desired results.

If the desired results were not achieved, listen to how the client describes the reasons for such wholesale or partial failure. Does the client rehash the lawyer's excuses, or does the client truly believe that the lawyer's failure was due to extenuating circumstances rather than inadequate professional capabilities or lack of devotion to the case?

Warmth of Former Clients' Recommendations

In addition to understanding the details of the relationship between the lawyer and her former client, much can be learned from the tones and nuances chosen by the client when speaking about the lawyer. Is there warmth and trust in the words used by the client to describe the lawyer, or is there a doubtful, cynical undertone to the factual descriptions?

How Responsive Was the Lawyer?

This question refers not only to timing but also to the quality of the lawyer's attention to her clients. How long did it take the lawyer to return a phone call? Did the lawyer respond to questions presented by the client? Was the lawyer a good listener? Did she respond to the real concerns of the clients? Did the lawyer inform the client of the events that took place during the case? Was the lawyer quick to give answers on pressing business questions?

The Lawyer's Integrity and Billing Practices

This is a touchy issue. Many lawyer-client relationships end with disputes over fees and expenses. However, it is also true that some clients are unreasonable in their complaints about the lawyer's billing practices. Therefore, a former client's complaint about the lawyer's integrity with respect to excessive bills should be taken cautiously. The fact that the lawyer had an argument with her client over fees does not necessarily prove that the lawyer was dishonest. Listen carefully to the client's description of the dispute and try to judge whether it is a real indication that the lawyer is dishonest. Keep in mind that most people dislike and distrust lawyers—even people who have never been swindled by one—and most people think lawyers charge too much—even people who have paid relatively low fees in exchange for competent legal service. On the other hand, many people harbor justifiable resentments toward their former lawyers, and if, in your judgment, the person you talk to belongs to this group, drop the lawyer's name from your list.

The Lawyer's Loyalty and Devotion to the Case

It says a lot about a lawyer if a former client walked out of the lawyer's office at the conclusion of his case feeling that the lawyer did his best to provide him top-quality legal representation. Try to question the client about the lawyer's loyalty throughout the relationship, and find out whether the lawyer's devotion to the case was on a par with the client's expectations.

THE "BEAUTY CONTEST"

Now it's time for the front-runners to pace up and down the track before you, show off their great qualities in mind and soul, and let you choose the best one among them.

Comparison Between the Candidates: Front-Runners' Score Card

You have met several lawyers, all able and very interested in your case. They all want you as a client, they all promise you mountains and oceans, and they all claim to have the expertise required to satisfy your legal needs. After meeting with each of them, you called a number of their former clients for references, following the instructions in the previous section, and now you are faced with the final choice.

In order to make an intelligent selection of the best lawyer among the front-runners, you should draw up a "scorecard," as shown on the next page, that records the complete results of your research. While filling in the scorecard, refer to the detailed notes you took when you met each of the lawyers and when you spoke to their former clients. Notice that some scores depend on actual facts (such as the existence of malpractice claims, which should count as 5 points unless it was dismissed with clear and unequivocal exoneration of the lawyer), and some are based on your personal impressions, or those of a former client. Think carefully before grading each lawyer, and consider each grade in the context of the other front-runners so that you don't end up with equal grades when there are unequal qualities.

The lawyer with the highest score is not necessarily the best one for you. However, the numerical scores will force you to make your selection based on merit—not on emotion. In any event, scoring should be done by comparing each lawyer to the other four. It is possible, however, that two or more lawyers will score equally. (Use a pencil so you can change your mind.)

Listen to Your Gut When It's Talking to You

Filling out the front-runners' scorecard should give you a clear picture of how the candidate lawyers compare. If one lawyer's total score is much higher than the others, your choice should be clear. If two or more have close scores, it is time for your gut feeling to play its most important role. Listen to it closely, sleep on it overnight, and make your final choice accordingly.

PREPARING TO NEGOTIATE THE
TERMS OF ENDEARMENT

When you have made your choice, proceed to the next three chapters, which will take you by the hand through the process of negotiating

FRONT-RUNNERS' SCORECARD

Scores: 1-Excellent   2-Very Good   3-Good   4-Fair   5-Poor

	Lawyer A	Lawyer B	Lawyer C	Lawyer D	Lawyer E
Ethics record					
Malpractice claims					
Reputation					
Attentiveness					
Verbal skills					
Interest in your case					
Optimism for results					
Conflict of interest					
Expertise/Specialty					
Record of victories					
Malpractice insured					
Expected cost					
Former clients'					
opinions as to:					
1. Results					
2. Communications					
3. Integrity					
4. Responsiveness					
5. Cost					
6. Loyalty/Devotion					
7. Gen. satisfaction					
Your gut feeling					
Total:					

the terms of your relationship with your new lawyer. Typically, the terms are set forth in an "Engagement Letter" or a similar document that details the elements of the relationship and the agreed fee arrangement. A power of attorney will be signed only if absolutely necessary. A written Engagement Letter is very important as a written set of conditions and obligations defining the terms of your relationship with the lawyer, because even the best choice of a lawyer may turn out later to be a mistake.

Do not notify the other lawyers on your list that you have made your choice, until you have concluded your negotiations with your first-choice lawyer and you are completely satisfied with the fee arrangement and with the lawyer's way of dealing with you during the negotiations. If you are not satisfied, you can still drop her and move to the next lawyer on your list.

Only after an Engagement Letter has been signed (and a power of attorney, if unavoidable), and the representation has begun, should you call the other lawyers, thank them for their time, and inform them that you do not, need their services at this time. You have no obligation to tell them who your chosen lawyer is or any other details regarding your decision-making process or your case.

PART III

THE ART OF SUCCESSFUL NEGOTIATIONS: FEE AGREEMENT AND LAWYERS' MOTIVATION

CHAPTER 8

YOUR LAWYER ON A SHORT LEASH: PROVISIONS THAT FOSTER RESPECT AND ENCOURAGE RESULTS

WHY SHOULD YOU AND THE LAWYER SIGN AN ENGAGEMENT LETTER?

You have searched diligently for the right lawyer by using all available hunting tools. You have interviewed several of the recommended lawyers, called their clients for reference, and filled out a scorecard to compare between them. Finally, you have chosen the best among those front-runners.

After you have made your choice, it is essential that the relationship between you and your new lawyer be defined in writing. Lawyers' professional ethics and work discipline may provide lawyers with the theory of quality and honest service. But an Engagement Letter will provide a more effective and clear set of contractual obligations, which could be enforced in a court of law, on the part of the lawyer. If he fails to do what the Engagement Letter requires him to do for you, you would be able to point out the specific provision in the Engagement Letter which he has violated.

The following sections outline the different elements of the Engagement Letter and includes sample provisions and background information that will assist you in negotiating with your new lawyer. Though the lawyer may present you with a standard Engagement Letter and try to avoid negotiating it with you, you should insist on your right to review and propose changes to the document. It may seem complicated at first, but once you separate each element of the lawyer-client relationship and understand the relevant terms, you will find this an exciting challenge.

An Engagement Letter is a contract that defines the rules of your relationship with your lawyer. Some lawyers will provide you with their own ready-made, standard-form Engagement Letter, which you should compare with the sample provisions given below. Other lawyers will dismiss the idea of an Engagement Letter, claiming that their level of service and loyalty to their client will be exemplary without any written document.

The Engagement Letter is essential because it defines a clear set of rules by which the lawyer must play. It is the most effective disciplinary tool in your arsenal, especially if a misunderstanding occurs between you and the lawyer. A written document of this kind should resolve the dispute quickly and decisively without the need to resort to lengthy arguments. Lawyers worship the written letter of laws and agreements: It is their source of livelihood. Therefore, watching the lawyer twitch and lurch under the weight of each provision in the Engagement Letter will help you understand how valuable a signed Engagement Letter is to you.

TECHNIQUES FOR EFFECTIVE NEGOTIATIONS WITH LAWYERS

Your candidate lawyer may not agree easily to some of the provisions you suggest. That's when some negotiating skills will come in handy. Your first step is to understand each of the provisions by reviewing the samples provided below and the accompanying discussion, which clarifies why each provision is essential for your protection.

Most important, do not treat the lawyer with excessive reverence. The lawyer's primary interest is money. Specifically, your money. All the candidate lawyer can think about is the potential profit for him represented by your case, including the advance retainer, bonus fee, expenses reimbursement, etc. Equally present in the candidate lawyer's mind is the mounting pile of office bills. If you are a business owner in need of ongoing legal advice for your business, a lawyer will do anything to get you on his client list, thus making you a constant income-producing source for years or even decades to come. Remember: This lawyer needs your business! And if he does not, another lawyer, no less qualified, will gladly take you and your business, and will negotiate with you willingly. The lawyer's main goal is to sign you up as a client and get an advance on the fee (or an agreement for contingency if the case is very promising). Now is the time to negotiate a favorable Engagement Letter.

It will be much easier for you to negotiate a favorable Engagement Letter by resolving all issues before discussing the fee arrangement, that is, before the lawyer is certain that you have become his client. Later, after you have agreed on the fee, your negotiating position is much weakened, because you have consented to the element most important to the lawyer.

Generally, you should not commit to the lawyer, even verbally, before concluding all provisions of the Engagement Letter. As long as the relationship has not yet begun, the lawyer, knowing that there are thousands of other competent lawyers eager to get you as a client, will be much more willing to compromise and change provisions in the Engagement Letter in ways that enhance your rights.

Do not underestimate your bargaining powers. As long as the lawyer has not collected any money from you, he will agree to almost anything you suggest in order to get you as a client. Do not retreat from your trenches. Your rights, and the lawyer's duties, as detailed in an Engagement Letter, could become extremely important to you if a future dispute arises between you and the lawyer. A written contract, such as the Engagement Letter, will be your winning card.

THE ENGAGEMENT LETTER AS A BINDING AGREEMENT

The Engagement Letter stands on two legs. First, it creates the foundation for a smooth and effective relationship by way of setting forth the lawyer's obligations for continuing communications and consultations during the representation, your rights as a client to be served with the quality and integrity you deserve, the scope of the representation, the desired results, the rules of termination of representation, and the method of dispute resolution. Second, it defines the method of calculating the fees and expenses to be paid to the lawyer. Together, the two constitute a solid foundation for a healthy lawyer-client relationship.

Depending on local custom and the lawyer's own habits, the lawyer may propose to sign a document with a different title. Whether it is called "Fee Agreement," "Engagement Letter," or "Retainer Agreement," this contract should include all the issues discussed in the following section and include provisions similar to the samples provided. It is important to make sure that such a document is signed by both you and the lawyer, making it a binding agreement.

The following discussion and sample provisions should be reviewed before you begin discussing details with your new lawyer. The sample includes a table of contents showing the structure and provision-titles of the Engagement Letter and a discussion of each provision, including a proposed sample. Sample provisions are reprinted at the end of the book in a format that enables you to copy them for use as the actual Engagement Letter on which your new lawyer would place his signature. (See Appendix A.)

If the lawyer wishes to retype the engagement letter, make a few changes, or use his own standard-form Engagement Letter, be careful and patient while comparing the lawyer's proposed Engagement Letter with your sample, and do not hesitate to request changes ensuring that you are fully protected under the final version.

This sample Engagement Letter is an amalgam of various standard letters used by lawyers in different types of practice and may need tailoring to fit a specific type of representation. To a large extent, it borrows from a proposed set of rules regarding matrimonial practice, which was approved by the Appellate Division of the State of New York and the Administrative Board of the Courts on November 1, 1993. It provides the best protection for the client in every type of representation.

SAMPLE ENGAGEMENT LETTER: TABLE OF CONTENTS

The following is a table of contents for a sample Engagement Letter. The text of each sample provision is provided together with a relevant discussion of the issues concerning that specific sample provision. Use this table of contents as a guide to find the relevant discussion, a process made easy because the title of each section of this and subsequent chapters corresponds to the appropriate title of each provision of the Engagement Letter. (Again, for your convenience, a complete reprint of the sample Engagement Letter is provided as an appendix at the end of the book.)

Table of Contents:

1. General.

2. Obligations and Warranties.

3. *Service to Entrepreneurs and Business Owners (when applicable).*

4. *Scope of Representation and Desired Results.*

5. *Estimated Budget.*

6. *Division of Fees With Other Lawyers.*

7. *Payment of Advance Retainer.*

8. *Method of Calculating the Fee* [choose only one option].

   8.1. *Monthly Retainer.*

   8.2. *Hourly Rate.*

   8.3. *Contingent Fee in a Lawsuit.*

   8.4. *Contingent Fee in Business Transactions.*

   8.5. *Fixed Fee.*

   8.6 *Combination Fee.*

9. *Expenses and Disbursements.*

10. *Method of Billing and Payments.*

11. *Unauthorized Actions by Lawyer: Offset Against Fees.*

12. *Termination and Withdrawal from the Representation.*

   12.1 *Termination by Client.*

   12.2 *Termination by Lawyer.*

13. *The Final Bill.*

14. *Restriction on Fee-Collection Measures.*

15. *Dispute Resolution.*

GENERAL

This provision sets the names of the parties to this Engagement Letter and indicates that this is a binding contract between you and your lawyer.

1. *General.*

This Engagement Letter is hereby entered into by _____ (the "Client") in connection with the representation by _____ (the "Lawyer") in the matter described below. This Engagement Letter constitutes a binding contract between Client and Lawyer, and defines their respective rights and obligations with respect to each other; provided, however, that this Engagement Letter is intended to supplement, rather than replace or detract from, Lawyer's obligations under any applicable rules of ethics and/or professional responsibility, which are hereby incorporated herein.

OBLIGATIONS AND WARRANTIES

This section sets forth the general rules governing the lawyer-client relationship. It gives special attention to the obligations of the lawyer to provide quality service, deals with basic technical matters involved in the relationship, and includes warranties made by the lawyer with respect to the lawyer's qualifications and intentions.

2. *Obligations and Warranties.*

(1)   *Lawyer will be readily available to represent Client's best interests. Lawyer may not refuse to represent Client, or withdraw from the Representation (as this term is defined below), because of Client's personal beliefs, faith, color, sex, national origins, or disability.*

(2)   *Lawyer has the professional qualifications and experience to handle the Representation. Lawyer shall engage in the Representation with good-faith intention to serve Client with courtesy, zeal, loyalty, and confidentiality, and will preserve Client's secrets revealed to Lawyer in the course of the Representation.*

(3)   *Lawyer has negotiated in good faith this Engagement Letter, setting forth the nature of the Representation and the fee and expenses to be paid by the Client.*

(4)   *Client will receive from Lawyer clarifications in writing of any terms or provisions of this Engagement Letter which Client finds confusing, and any amendment to this Engagement Letter will be in writing, signed by both Lawyer and Client after good-faith negotiations between Lawyer and Client.*

(5)   *Lawyer hereby acknowledges that Lawyer reviewed this Engagement Letter with Client, and that Lawyer is satisfied that Client fully understands the provisions included in this Engagement Letter.*

(6)   *No fee, bonus, expense reimbursement, or any other payment, will be required by Lawyer, unless specifically agreed to in this Engagement Letter. No advance retainer is "non-refundable" unless this Engagement Letter specifically so states. Any unearned fee will be refunded to Client if Representation is terminated for any reason.*

(7)   *The Representation, and all related work, will be done by Lawyer personally, unless the identity of other lawyers or support staff has been specified*

in this Engagement Letter, and the cost for such additional persons' work has been so specified and agreed upon.

(8)   If this Engagement Letter includes a provision of budget for the cost of the Representation, lawyer shall provide all the Representation in accordance with such budget.

(9)   Client will be provided with written, itemized bills on a monthly basis, unless no additional costs have been incurred during such month.

(10)   The monthly bills will be reviewed by Client, and Client will notify the Lawyer of any disputed entries. Lawyer will not charge Client for time spent in discussions of such bills, related dispute-resolution proceeding, or any other discussions relating to this Engagement Letter or the relationship between Lawyer and Client.

(11)   Lawyer will inform Client immediately of any developments in the Representation, and of any communication or event otherwise relevant to Client's affairs or to the Representation.

(12)   Lawyer will provide Client with copies of all documents exchanged with other parties during the Representation, including, but not limited to, briefs prepared by Lawyer or received from other parties, correspondence, and court documents.

(13)   Lawyer will consult with Client regarding any development in the Representation. Lawyer will discuss strategy of the Representation, and will not act on any matter without Client's consent. Lawyer will consult with Client before scheduling any meeting, conference, or a trial in the case. Client will have the opportunity to be present at any such event.

(14)   Lawyer will notify Client of any material change in the law that is applicable in any way to the Representation.

(15)   Client will have the sole discretion regarding any settlement.

(16)   Lawyer will notify Client in advance of any unexpected costs or expenses in connection with the Representation.

(17)   Client will provide Lawyer with all necessary information, documents, and any other assistance required to enable Lawyer to provide competent Representation.

(18)   In case of termination of Representation by either Lawyer or Client, outstanding fees or expenses owed to Lawyer shall be paid by Client promptly. If any such fees or expenses are disputed by Client, such dispute shall be resolved in accordance with the relevant provisions of this Engagement Letter. Lawyer will not take any collection actions other than in accordance with the relevant provisions of this Engagement Letter. All of Client's files and documents relating to the Representation, and all other

property or money in which Client has proprietary rights, will be returned to Client promptly after termination of the Representation, and will not be held pending payment of fees or expenses.

(19) *Lawyer will devote best efforts to achieving the desired results of the Representation as defined below.*

(20) *At any time, Client may report to the clerk of the court [or any other authority overseeing lawyers' conduct and discipline] with respect to any suspected unethical conduct by Lawyer.*

(21) *In case of any disagreement between Lawyer and Client, Lawyer will advise Client of the availability of fee-arbitration procedures, as defined below, bar association ethics committee procedure, and malpractice legal action, as the case may be. Lawyer will assist Client in obtaining legal representation by another lawyer in such matters.*

SERVICE TO ENTREPRENEUR/BUSINESS OWNER (WHEN APPLICABLE)

The following provisions should be included in the Engagement Letter, with necessary tailoring to your specific needs, in order to cover special issues involved in the unique relationship between a lawyer and an entrepreneur or a business owner.

3. *Service to Entrepreneurs and Business Owners [when applicable].*

(1) *Lawyer is familiar with Client's line of business, and has knowledge of the laws and regulations applicable to Client's business activities.*

(2) *Lawyer will be available to service Client through telephonic conferences and meetings on short notice, to facilitate Client's needs for ongoing, day-to-day legal advice.*

(3) *Lawyer will notify Client of any scheduled business trips or vacations that will keep Lawyer out of town for more than two days. Lawyer will provide Client with forwarding telephone numbers and other ways of communication. If such communications are impractical, Lawyer will provide Client with a substitute lawyer with equal qualifications to be available for Client's legal needs. Such substitute lawyer's services will be billed to Client by Lawyer (not by the substitute lawyer) and will be paid in the same manner and rates as Lawyer's services are paid for according to this Engagement Letter.*

(4) *Lawyer will notify Client when Client's legal needs are not within Lawyer's areas of expertise, or exceed Lawyer's professional capabilities. Lawyer will, at Client's consent, make the necessary arrangements to obtain*

the services of another lawyer with the needed competence as required. If Lawyer concludes that it would be economically beneficial for Client if Lawyer devotes time to gaining expertise in such new matter, Client will not be billed for such additional time.

(5) *Client will submit to Lawyer's review business contracts and other documents, including government forms and statements. Lawyer will review such documents and provide Client with legal advice in a prompt and speedy manner. When needed, Lawyer will communicate with Client's accountant or other professional advisors.*

SCOPE OF REPRESENTATION AND DESIRED RESULTS

The Importance of Defining Your Expectations

Hiring a lawyer to represent you is equivalent to getting married. You have just made a binding agreement with another person that gives that other person the power and authority to commit you legally in matters related to the representation. The Engagement Letter, even if not accompanied by a signed Power of Attorney (as discussed in Chapter 12: "The Power of Attorney: A Beast Without a Muzzle"), empowers the lawyer to act on your behalf, incur obligations on your behalf, speak in your name, and cost you a lot of money. Just like a spouse. On the other hand, as in marriage, engaging a lawyer can also be mutually beneficial, complementary, pleasurable, and financially productive. The key is good communication, setting clear rules of behavior, and discussing troubling issues without holding back.

The first step in establishing effective communication is to agree on the scope of the representation and the desired results. The definition of the representation should include both an inclusive and exclusive component. The inclusive component defines the scope of the representation and the desired results, while the exclusive component defines the issues that are outside the representation. That way, the limits of the lawyer's authorized representation are clear to both you and the lawyer.

Sample Provisions: Scope of Representation and Desired Results

The examples presented here should serve you in drafting the appropriate language, or in reviewing language drafted by the lawyer, which defines the scope of the representation and the desired results to be achieved by the lawyer on your behalf. The sample provisions apply to different types of representation. If your case does not fall into any of the following categories, reviewing these sample provisions will still give you enough understanding of the essential elements of the provision to enable you to draft a provision that achieves the same goals in your unique circumstances.

Representation in a Personal Injury Claim

4. Scope of Representation and Desired Results.

Client hereby retains, employs, and authorizes Lawyer to represent Client and advise Client in the following matter (the "Representation"): Lawyer will represent Client in prosecuting an action against _____ (the "Defendant"), for money damages, including all forms of compensation, with respect to an accident that occurred on _____ (date), as described in a report filed with _____ and dated _____. Lawyer will pursue any cause of action in connection with the accident against other liable parties, and will advise Client on all matters relating to the accident and to any other ramifications of the accident for Client. Said Representation will include general counseling, preparation and review of all relevant documents, and any other matters directly relating to the Representation.

Lawyer will not take any action on Client's behalf against any members of Client's family. Lawyer will not sign any document on Client's behalf, including, but not limited to, any settlement agreement, without consulting Client.

Representation in Commercial Disputes

4. Scope of Representation and Desired Results.

Client hereby retains, employs, and authorizes Lawyer to represent Client and advise Client in the following matter (the "Representation"): Lawyer will represent Client in connection with a dispute with _____ concerning a contract dated _____. Lawyer will represent Client in settlement negotiations and, if needed, in a lawsuit, and will represent Client in any trial if such is the case. Said Representation will include general counseling, preparation and review of all relevant documents, and any other matters directly relating to the Representation.

Lawyer will not represent Client in any other matters not involving the aforementioned contract unless specifically agreed to.

Representation in Foreclosure Action

4. Scope of Representation and Desired Results.

Client hereby retains, employs, and authorizes Lawyer to represent Client and advise Client in the following matter (the "Representation"): Lawyer will represent Client, in its corporate capacity, in all matters relating to a foreclosure action filed by _____ Bank against Client (the "Action"). Lawyer's representation will include all legal service related to the Action, including devising appropriate defenses and counterclaims, counseling Client on legal means to avoid foreclosure, revocation of the Notice of Default dated _____, and the filing of a Petition under Chapter 11 of the United States Bankruptcy Court, Title 11 USC, if such is deemed necessary. In such case, Lawyer will represent Client, in its corporate capacity, as counsel for the Debtor and Debtor in Possession during the proceedings under Chapter 11, including, but not limited to, court proceedings, interim motions, contested liabilities, and plans of reorganization. Said Representation will include general counseling, preparation and review of all relevant documents, and any other matters directly relating to the Representation.

Lawyer will not represent _____ (Client's sole shareholder) in his individual capacity, or represent Client in its corporate capacity in any other matters other than the matter described herein.

Representation in Business Negotiations

4. Scope of Representation and Desired Results.

Client hereby retains, employs, and authorizes Lawyer to represent Client and advise Client in the following matter (the "Representation"): Lawyer will represent Client in negotiations with _____ with respect to the sale/purchase of _____. Lawyer will accompany and advise Client during all negotiations, advise Client on legal and business issues relevant to the proposed transaction, and will draft relevant documents as needed to finalize the transaction. Said Representation will include general counseling, preparation and review of all relevant documents, and any other matters directly relating to the Representation.

Lawyer will not negotiate independently on behalf of Client, will not sign any agreements on behalf of Client, and will not represent Client in any business transaction other than the matter described herein.

Representation in Purchase of a Home

4. Scope of Representation and Desired Results.

Client hereby retains, employs, and authorizes Lawyer to represent Client and advise Client in the following matter (the "Representation"): Lawyer will represent Client in contract negotiations with respect to the purchase of a residence known as _____ (address). Lawyer will also represent Client in the preparation and filing of all necessary forms required to finalize and close the transaction, and will attend the closing. Said Representation will include general counseling, preparation and review of all relevant documents, and any other matters directly relating to the Representation.

Lawyer will not represent Client in any other purchase of any other property, unless specifically agreed upon in writing. Lawyer is not authorized to make any concessions with respect to price, terms of payments, or other substantive provisions in the sale contract without Client's explicit instructions, and is not authorized to sign any document on behalf of Client.

Representation in Divorce Proceedings

4. Scope of Representation and Desired Results.

Client hereby retains, employs, and authorizes Lawyer to represent Client and advise Client in the following matter (the "Representation"): Lawyer will represent Client in all matters relating to separation and divorce of Client from Client's spouse. Lawyer will advise Client on all legal issues relevant to Client's legal situation, will assist Client in devising the best strategy to achieve an amicable divorce from Client's spouse, will negotiate on behalf of Client in order to reach such goal, and will draft all relevant legal documents and forms relating to the divorce. Said Representation will include general counseling, preparation and review of all relevant documents, and any other matters directly relating to the Representation. The desired result of this Representation is to achieve an amicable (to the extent possible) separation and divorce from Client's spouse and to obtain for Client a monetary settlement that will, at the minimum, enable Client to keep ownership of the house in which Client currently resides, and receive income sufficient to support Client and _____.

Lawyer will not reach any settlement and will not refuse any settlement, without Client's specific authority. Lawyer will not represent Client in any other matters, except that Lawyer should investigate financial and other information in order to establish Client's financial rights and properties subject to such rights.

Representation in Ongoing Business Matters

4. Scope of Representation and Desired Results.

Client hereby retains and employs Lawyer to represent and advise Client in the following matter (the "Representation"): Lawyer will advise and represent Client in all matters pertaining to the Client's Business (known as _____), including the provision of routine legal advice on all legal matters relating thereto, *negotiations with other parties and representation before government agencies, when required. At Client's request, Lawyer will accompany and advise Client during business negotiations, advise Client on legal aspects and concerns relevant to any business activity or transaction, and draft relevant legal documents as needed for the lawful operation of Client's business. Said Representation will include general counseling, preparation and review of all legal documents, and any other matters directly relating to the Representation.*

Lawyer will not negotiate independently on behalf of Client, will not sign any agreements on behalf of Client, and will not represent Client in any business transaction unless specifically authorized by client to do so.

CHAPTER 9

PROVISIONS FOR ESTIMATED BUDGETS, REFERRAL FEES, AND ADVANCE RETAINERS

The relationship between a lawyer and a client almost always involves substantial amounts of money, in many cases amounts greater than anything the client has ever risked before. A conflict between client and lawyer could have devastating ramifications for the client's interests, and in many cases, the client's interests might be held hostage by the lawyer as leverage in demanding extra fees. To prevent this from happening, a well-drafted fee agreement should cover all contingencies and set forth clearly the total fee that the lawyer may demand.

As a client, putting your financial fate in the hands of a lawyer may involve hiring a real estate lawyer to represent you in the purchase of a new home, a divorce lawyer to represent you in the division of property accumulated over thirty years of marriage, or a litigator to represent you in a lawsuit against your employer for unlawful discrimination. The amounts of money at stake in many types of legal representation may be greater than your income over an entire decade of hard work. Therefore, paying a fee to a lawyer for representing you in any of these matters should not be done hastily. The provisions of the Engagement Letter relating to the payment of money are essential to complete the set of obligations as it defines the method of computing the fees you will pay, lists the expenses that the lawyer may charge to you, and provides solutions to all the financial matters involved in the representation.

It is important to remember that you or the lawyer may later decide to terminate the relationship. When you try to terminate the relationship

139

with a lawyer, any dispute over the amount of fees and expenses owed to the lawyer could easily escalate into a lawsuit, including garnishment of your wages, your home, and your business. At such time, the lawyer will be in a powerful position by having learned everything there is to know about your finances and personal affairs and could use such "inside" knowledge against you if you dispute any of her bills. In such case, you would have to hire a new lawyer to represent you against your ex-lawyer.

Therefore, when hiring a lawyer, bear in mind the risks involved. To minimize such risks, all the rules governing the financial aspects of the engagement should be detailed in the Engagement Letter, which should also include means of resolving any future disputes over fees. The following provisions cover all the financial aspects of the relationship between you and the lawyer. (As before, section numbers pertain to the table of contents of the sample Engagement Letter in Appendix A, and appear in the same order.)

ESTIMATED BUDGET: THE BEST WAY TO KEEP THE SHIRT ON YOUR BACK

Preventive Medicine Against Malignant Costs

In the *Wall Street Journal* article "Disney Seeks to Cut Overcharging Firms" (March 3, 1992), Amy Stevens outlined an attempt by the Walt Disney Company to control its legal costs. Disney distributed a ten-page memorandum to all its outside lawyers, numbering about two hundred law firms, in which Disney demanded detailed legal bills, refused to pay general office costs, and required projections for costs on each matter.

Such large companies as Disney have enough economic power to engage in such "disciplinary" and cost-cutting efforts, which are unpopular with lawyers. These efforts represent the widespread sentiment that legal costs have mushroomed unjustifiably. One reason for ever-increasing legal costs is lawyers' attempts to shift their office overhead to clients. Secretarial services, photocopying, weekend and overtime work, and other office costs that traditionally were borne by the lawyer and not by the client are now billed to clients through use of sophisticated computer software that allocates such expenses to each client. For example, in every law firm you will find that no copying machine works unless a client's "charge number" is first entered on the attached keypad. When a lawyer makes a phone call or copies a document, she first keys in the appropriate charge number allocated to each client and then makes the call or the copy. The expense is automatically charged to the client and appears on the client's monthly bill. This process of shifting overhead to clients, sometimes to the extreme of charging clients for office supplies, local transportation, faxes, and food and beverages, is an innovative management technique intended to increase lawyers' profits without increasing the hourly rates or other direct legal fees charged by the lawyer.

Some lawyers argue that this practice is not harmful to the client because, otherwise, the direct legal fees would have to be higher in order to cover general overhead. Because some clients' cases require more copying and other office expenses than others, it would be unfair to make one client share the cost of making another client's copies. On the other hand, the practice enables the lawyer to charge a "premium" on such office expenses, thereby creating "profit centers" in addition to its core legal services, thus making more profits indirectly. These methods also enable law firms to abuse the expense account in more subtle and fraudulent ways.

Engaging in aggressive cost-cutting measures carries the risk of creating an adversarial atmosphere in your relationship with your lawyer. Even though your goal as a client is primarily to control the costs of legal representation, you do not want to sacrifice the quality of the service or imperil the lawyer's devotion to your case. In other words, the quality of the representation should not fall victim to cost-saving efforts. To maintain mutual confidence and preserve your lawyer's devotion to your case, it is important to agree, in advance, on the format of bills and the cost of the legal representation itself and to list associated expenses to be paid by you. Whereas such discussions are perfectly acceptable during negotiations of the Engagement Letter, leaving these issues undecided and then arguing over the charges after they have already appeared in periodic bills may backfire and cost you in the quality of service you receive. The best method, therefore, is to reach a detailed agreement in advance, preferably in the form of a budget followed by detailed provisions on the way fees and expenses are to be calculated.

Should You Ask for a Budget Provision?

How nice it would be to know in advance exactly how much it would cost you to hire a lawyer, go to trial, and win your case. In a business transaction, you'd love to hear: "It will cost you $3,000 to negotiate the purchase agreement and the financing agreement." But in reality you end up with a laundry list of all the things the lawyer believes she will have to do, all the unexpected things that can happen, and that "It will cost you $3,000 plus maybe two or three thousand more if there's more work to do." The solution is to ask the lawyer to present you with a detailed budget, which spells out the legal costs involved in each element of the representation.

How to Make Your Lawyer Commit to a Budget

The decision whether to demand a projected budget depends on the type of legal representation required. However, most legal matters are very easy to analyze, and most lawyers should be able to predict, with relative accuracy, the amount of work needed in the matter. There are almost no "unexpected" issues that may come out of nowhere and require additional work by the lawyer. Nothing should be "unexpected," unless the lawyer lacks the required experience to predict the probable developments in your case.

Whether you hire a lawyer to represent you in a business transaction, real estate purchase, or lawsuit, your lawyer should be experienced enough to predict what needs to be done and the amount of time it would take. It is true that most matters can take different routes, depending on the decisions made by the opposing side. For example, a business transaction that normally would be easy to negotiate might become a complete fiasco because the lawyer on the opposite side is inexperienced, incompetent, or plainly mean (commonly called a "deal breaker"). In such a case, what your lawyer believed would not take more than a day or two of negotiations will end up being a prolonged and time-consuming ordeal.

Nevertheless, lawyers often take the professional risk of running "overtime." Additionally, an intelligently drafted budget can take such risks into consideration and offer a breakdown for additional legal costs resulting from predictable turns of events. However, it is best for the client if some risk is taken by the lawyer in order to give the lawyer strong motivation to keep things from getting bogged down and from wasting time on easily resolved issues.

The existence of a written budget, as part of the Engagement Letter, will assist you in monitoring your legal costs and also assist the lawyer in devoting all her attention to the representation itself, without needing to haggle with you over each bill.

Last, when negotiating with a lawyer over the need for a written budget, take into consideration that most lawyers will react with a definite and well-reasoned rejection. However, your insistence may prove to be beneficial for both you and the lawyer throughout the representation. And, if the lawyer does agree to commit to a budget without argument, there is a fair chance that you are dealing with a decent lawyer.

Sample Provision: Estimated Budget

A budget provision is too specific to appear in a blank form. Therefore, this sample is provided as a model, which you will need to copy and adjust to your specific circumstances. In this example, you have won the right to purchase a franchise from a chain of Italian fast-food restaurants. Your franchise is slated to open in a new mall being built in your area. The lawyer you approach agrees to give you an estimated budget for legal representation in the purchase of the franchise and related issues. The budget should look like this:

5. Estimated Budget.

Lawyer agrees that the following is the estimated total cost of the Representation, including all of Lawyer's services in this matter, which shall not be exceeded except in the event of unforeseeable developments and only if agreed to by Client:

Task:		*Cost for Client*
(i)	*Review of relevant documents (list documents below)*	*$*
(ii)	*Drafting of relevant documents (list documents below)*	*$*
(iii)	*Negotiations with other parties*	*$*
(iv)	*Registration of legal entities and other government filings*	*$*
(v)	*Providing legal advice, including research and draft memos*	*$*
(vi)	*Travel time and other preparatory work not included above*	*$*
(vii)	*Maximum total expenses reimbursements (See Section 9)*	*$*
	Total cost of Representation not to exceed	*$*

DIVISION OF FEES WITH OTHER LAWYERS

The Ethics of Referral Fees

Because fee-paying clients are, for many lawyers, few and far between, there is a common custom of paying a referral fee or a referral commission for client referrals. For example, if your neighbor is a personal injury lawyer and she suggested that you hire a certain lawyer to represent you in your employment discrimination claim against your former employer, she would ask the other lawyer to pay her a referral fee, calculated as a percentage of the fees you end up paying the employment discrimination lawyer, even though she had nothing to do with your case. Naturally, any such referral fee is added or built into the fees you pay, because, as in all other aspects of the lawyer-client relationship, everything comes out of the client's pocket except the lawyer's time.

Ethics rules governing referral fees commonly forbid payment of a referral fee to a nonlawyer, so that if your neighbor was not a lawyer herself, she could not ask for a referral fee from her friend the lawyer. Referral fees are usually restricted to cases in which the person making the reference is a lawyer but does not do any part of the legal work in the case. However, such rules are often bypassed by claiming that some work was done by the referring lawyer and that the division of the legal fees is based on sharing the legal work involved in the presentation. Another limitation imposed by ethics rules on referral fees or other methods of fee-division among lawyers is the ban on sharing legal fees with a lawyer who is not a partner or an associate of the lawyer hired by the client. Exceptions to this rule are:

- The client was informed in advance of the involvement of the other lawyer and of the fact that some of the fees charged would be paid to the second lawyer.

- The second lawyer receives a fee proportionate to work performed by him and shares the representation by signing an appropriate "Retainer Statement."

- The total amount of fees paid by the client do not exceed "reasonable" fees for the services performed.

Lawyers are, therefore, required to inform clients if some fees are to be diverted to another lawyer. Moreover, as a client you have the right to object to such diversion of fees, based on the fact that such fees are in truth added to the amount that constitutes a "reasonable" fee.

Also, you have the right to object to any fees for work you do not require or for work that is not really performed, and to fees for the services of a lawyer other than the one you chose to hire.

Sample Provision: Division of Fees With Other Lawyers

6. Division of Fees With Other Lawyers.

No referral fee, finder's fee, or other commission is paid by Lawyer to any person in connection with this Engagement Letter or with the Representation. No person will have the right to receive or collect from Lawyer any portion of the fees paid to Lawyer by Client without the written consent of Client.

PAYMENT OF ADVANCE RETAINER

Refundable Versus Nonrefundable

Most lawyers will demand an advance retainer—a request which you should consider reasonable. Except in lucrative personal injury cases or other cases based on a contingent fee, any fee structure would work well with the payment of a minimal advance retainer, to be deducted from future accumulation of legal fees. It shows commitment on your part, it gives the lawyer a sense of security that her time is not going to be wasted, and it does not cost you anything because it will be deducted from the first bill.

What worries most clients, and should worry you, is whether you are going to recover any unearned portion of the advance retainer if the representation is terminated prematurely. For example, you hire a lawyer to represent you in a business transaction and pay her an advance retainer of $1,000 on account for future fees. However, the lawyer does very little work for you because the business transaction falls through. In such case, can the lawyer keep the $1,000, or is she required to refund any unearned portion?

How to Avoid Future Disputes

Most states have laws requiring lawyers to refund any unearned fees. For example, New York courts have repeatedly stated that nonrefundable fees are against public policy and should not be allowed, except when such amount is equivalent to "forecast by the attorney of the minimum the client can expect to pay in order for the attorney to represent the client to completion in the contemplated matter" (*Matter of Cooperman*, 187 A.D. 2d 56, 57). That statement was further limited by the New York Court of Appeals to say that the amount kept by the lawyer, out of any advance fee, should not exceed the actual services rendered. As the Court of Appeals said in *Cooperman*, "If special non-refundable retainers are allowed to flourish, clients would be relegated to hostage status in an unwanted fiduciary relationship."

However explicit, the *Cooperman* decision may be interpreted as allowing nonrefundable fees in cases in which the attorney is agreeing to be generally available for advice on a certain matter. Only when the lawyer is contracted to do a specific assignment or to handle a specific matter would the *Cooperman* decision apply. Note that New York courts were the first to issue a relatively clear decision forbidding nonrefundable fees. In other states, the laws are less clear on the matter. In general, if you pay a hefty advance retainer, you may not be able to fire your lawyer for fear she might keep the retainer. And without the money you paid as a retainer, you might lack the funds to hire a new lawyer to handle the matter. To prevent such a "hostage" situation, pay only a minimal advance retainer based on a clear provision in the Engagement Letter requiring immediate refund of any unearned portion of the advance retainer by the lawyer if the representation is terminated.

In order to avoid future disagreements over what part of the advance retainer has already been earned by the lawyer and whether you are entitled to a refund if the representation is terminated prematurely, the provision must be clear in stating that the advance retainer is in no way "nonrefundable," and that any unearned portion should be refunded.

The *Cooperman* decision left behind it a trail of reactions, such as "Non-refundable Fees For Lawyers Banned by New York's Top Courts" (Junda Woo, *Wall Street Journal*, March 18, 1994), and "Fall-out From Fee Decision: Some Arrangements Doomed" (Edward A. Adams, *New York Law Journal*, March 21, 1994: "Both Lester Brickman, a professor at Benjamin N. Cordozo School of Law of Yeshiva University who filed an amicus brief in *Cooperman*, and Stephen Gillers, a professor at New York University School of Law, said the decision requires firms to make explicit what the retainer pays for.") Your Engagement Letter should reflect *Cooperman*'s spirit, and require that the lawyer specify exactly the method of calculating any unrefunded portion she claims to have earned.

Sample Provision: Payment of Advance Retainer

To protect yourself against any disagreements or the unpleasant need to engage a second lawyer in order to sue the first lawyer for any unearned advance fees, your Engagement Letter should include the following provision:

7. Payment of Advance Retainer.

Client shall pay Lawyer an advance retainer (the "Advance Retainer") of $_____, payable upon the signing of this Engagement Letter. Such Advance Retainer shall constitute an advance payment on account of future fees and expenses, as accumulated periodically, and shall be credited to client through a deduction from the first amount of fee billed to Client hereafter. Should the Representation be terminated for any reason, Lawyer shall refund promptly any portion of the Advance Retainer that has not been actually earned prior to such termination or been applied to specific expenses. At such time Lawyer will provide Client with a Final Bill, as provided by this Engagement Letter.

CHAPTER 10

IT'S THE MONEY, STUPID! HOW TO NEGOTIATE A FEE ARRANGEMENT THAT WILL MOTIVATE YOUR LAWYER

This chapter will help you prepare for the most pivotal issue in negotiating with your prospective lawyer: How much money will he make? In preparing for the money talks with your prospective lawyer, remember that a lawyer is, first and foremost, a businessperson. The lawyer will take you on as a client only if it's worth his time. Therefore, the fee arrangement has to be reasonable in size (for both you and the lawyer), motivational for the lawyer (somehow tied to achieving the desired results), and affordable to you (preferably, paid out of money you earn due to the lawyer's success). This chapter outlines the principles of "reasonable" fees, and helps you weigh the advantages and disadvantages of several structures of fee arrangements.

METHOD OF CALCULATING THE FEE: WHAT IS A "REASONABLE" FEE?

Vague Definitions Are Lawyers' Oldest Trick

[A] lawyer shall not enter into an agreement for, charge or collect an illegal or excessive fee.... A fee is excessive when, after a review of the facts, a lawyer of ordinary prudence would be left with a definite and firm conviction that the fee is in excess of a reasonable fee.... (New York State Code of Professional Responsibility, Rule 2-106)

New York, as in most other states, provides in its law books a definition that makes it almost impossible to distinguish between an "excessive," an "unreasonable," or a "reasonable" fee. The factors to be weighed in deciding whether a fee is reasonable include the amount of time involved in the representation, the complexity of the legal issues, the uniqueness of the professional skills required of the lawyer, the need for the lawyer to forego other cases in order to dedicate his time to the case, the customary fee charged by lawyers in the same geographical area for a similar representation, the size of the case in terms of financial risks and chances of winning, time restraints and the nature of the client, the existence of other cases in which the lawyer represents the same client, the experience, reputation, and prestige of the lawyer, and whether the fee is paid in advance, throughout the representation, at completion, or contingent upon results.

You Against All the Lawyers

As a client claiming that the fee charged by your lawyer is excessive, you will have to hire a second lawyer to fight the first lawyer in court or in arbitration and to prove to a judge (who is also a lawyer) that a "reasonable lawyer" (another, imaginary lawyer), after reviewing the facts, "would be left with a definite and firm conviction that the fee is in excess of a reasonable fee." Note the emphasis on "definite and firm conviction." Not just a plain, old, honest conviction, but a conviction that is "definite and firm." This language, which obviously was drafted by lawyers, makes it almost impossible to win a legal battle to prove excessive legal bills. Your only chance, therefore, is to resort to "preventive medicine" by supplementing the law with a clear and straightforward fee provision in your Engagement Letter.

It is important to realize that, when it comes to fees for legal services, most bar association ethics committees produce opinions that send a clear message: The client is always wrong. For example, the Committee on Professional and Judicial Ethics of the Association of the Bar of the City of New York (Opinion No. 1994–9) discussed a case in which a client complained about excessive billing by a law firm. Apparently, that particular law firm delegated full discretion and authority for the preparation of fee bills to a nonlawyer, clerical employee. The committee wrote:

> The determination of fees and the rendition of bills is an important aspect of the fiduciary relationship between attorney and

client, not a mere ministerial task. As E.C. 2–17 counsels, the determination of a proper fee requires consideration of the interests of both client and lawyer. A lawyer should not charge more than a reasonable fee, for excessive cost of legal service would deter non-lawyers from using the legal system to protect their rights and to minimize and resolve disputes. Furthermore, an excessive charge abuses the professional relationship between lawyer and client. . . . It would be imprudent to permit a non-lawyer to have unsupervised and unlimited discretion regarding sensitive matters of judgment such as the propriety of attorney time entries, the propriety of charging for certain legal services, and the reasonableness of the legal fee being charged given that, in effect, the lawyers are the guarantors of the end product's compliance with applicable standards.

After you read through the above statements, which seemingly trumpet the rights of legal consumers, you see that the committee concluded that it is merely "imprudent" for a lawyer "to delegate final billing authority to a non-lawyer. . . ." In plain language, despite all the strong words about clients' rights, when it comes to the preparation of legal bills, the committee left it to lawyers' own discretion and good sense by concluding that such delegation was not prohibited per se.

Why Should the Fee Be Agreed to in Writing?

Opinion No. 1994–9 shows that, despite lip service to the ideas of "reasonable" fee and "fiduciary relationship," lawyers are left to promote their own interests. It is, therefore, your obligation to yourself as a client to negotiate a fee agreement that will protect you from any improper billing practices and will clearly limit excessive fees and, in case of a dispute, prevent the use of unpleasant fee-collection methods by your lawyer. On the other hand, a fee arrangement must also motivate the lawyer to provide you with quality, speedy, and effective service, by tying, as much as possible, the size of the fees to the measure of the lawyer's success in reaching the results you had hoped for in the representation.

Lawyers Are Receptive to Alternative Fee Arrangements

A 1993 survey by Altman Weil Pensa Publications, Inc. gives a comprehensive view of how law firms and clients work together to create alternative fee arrangements that provide profits and savings for both lawyers and clients.

The Altman Weil Pensa survey shows that creative fee arrangements have been initiated both by lawyers and by clients, often jointly. Alternative arrangements are most common in litigation matters, with fixed fees and volume discounts being the most popular. A total of 72.9 percent of law firms indicated that they are "developing alternative billing and pricing alternatives," either at clients' requests or at their own initiative.

The lesson from the Altman Weil Pensa survey is that lawyers are open to alternative fee arrangements, and recognize the necessity of offering different fee arrangements depending on clients' needs and economic visions. Therefore, when your lawyer tells you he will charge you a certain hourly rate for his services, you should feel free to come up with a different fee structure. In most cases you will find that the lawyer is receptive to such suggestions and recognizes the need to be flexible. Your lawyer wants to make money by representing you. As long as the potential for profit exists, you have the upper hand.

A good fee arrangement will also give the lawyer an incentive to reduce legal costs by serving the client in a manner that is speedy, efficient, and tailored to the client's financial means and legal needs. A good fee agreement rewards lawyers for their efficiency, creativity, and investment in higher technology.

Your fee structure should achieve the following primary goals: make costs predictable throughout the representation, require payments only for work that has been done, reward the lawyer for success and for saving time, money, and expenses, and give the lawyer active disincentives to fail, to be slow or to otherwise waste time and money. The fee arrangement should also ensure that the lawyer does not make money if you are not happy.

There are innumerable variations of fee structures for different types of representation. In the following sections, several types of fee arrangements are explored, and sample provisions are supplied. These examples should provide you with enough understanding of the issue, so that you can design, with the help of the lawyer, the appropriate fee structure and draft an effective provision into your Engagement Letter.

MONTHLY RETAINER: THE LONG-TERM RELATIONSHIP

A monthly retainer is an arrangement by which the client pays the lawyer a fixed monthly fee, which is predetermined and covers all services provided by the lawyer to that client during the month. The lawyer, in return, undertakes to be available to answer legal questions and handle any legal representation the client may require, as needed, without charging additional fees.

The Entrepreneur's Best Choice

A retainer paid once a month (a "monthly retainer," not to be confused with the advance retainer) is the best arrangement for an entrepreneur, a small business owner, or an investor who is in constant need of routine legal advice with respect to the day-to-day management of his business or investments.

As a business owner or manager you need frequent access to legal advice. Such constant access may be had by purchasing the lawyer's time "in bulk" through a monthly retainer arrangement. The amount of the monthly retainer should reflect the approximate number of hours the lawyer will spend each month considering the issues you raise and rendering good and speedy advice. The amount of the monthly retainer should also reflect a discount from the lawyer's regular hourly rates, because of the regularity with which the retainer is paid. In other words, lawyers usually discount their hourly rates in consideration for the security of knowing they will be paid, for example, in advance for ten hours per month whether or not such time was actually spent.

The basic assumption underlying a monthly retainer arrangement is that the lawyer is going to be available to answer your legal questions on the phone and conduct research on such issues as needed by you in exchange for a regular, fixed monthly fee for such "free access" to the lawyer, even if you did not actually use the lawyer during the month.

How to Calculate the Monthly Retainer

Normally, the amount of the monthly retainer will at first be based on a rough estimate, to be determined in the manner described above,

by agreement between you and the lawyer before signing an Engagement Letter. However, most lawyers will require that the amount of the
monthly retainer be subject to periodic adjustment based on the amount
of time actually spent on your matters during the first few months of
the representation. Similarly, special projects, such as unexpected contract work, litigation of a lawsuit, or other time-consuming legal matters
will not be covered by the monthly retainer, but rather will be billed
separately in a manner that should be discussed and agreed upon in advance.

Sample Provision: Monthly Retainer

8.1 Monthly Retainer.

*Client will pay Lawyer a monthly retainer (the "Monthly Retainer") of
$_____ every month on the first day of the month. Lawyer will not charge
Client any additional fee for legal services, except for work not included in the
Representation (as such term is defined in Section 4 of this Engagement Letter:
Scope of Representation and Desired Results) and only after such additional fee
has been agreed upon between Lawyer and Client in writing. The amount of
Monthly Retainer will be subject to renegotiation once every twelve months, and
will be based on a tentative hourly rate of $_____ per hour. Any amount of
Monthly Retainer actually paid will be nonrefundable, and will be considered
earned as soon as it was paid.*

HOURLY RATE FEE: DANCING WITH WOLVES

Why Do Lawyers Love Hourly Rate Fees?

Under an hourly rate fee arrangement, you undertake to pay a lawyer,
or a firm of lawyers, a certain amount for each hour spent on your case.
It is the most popular fee arrangement among lawyers because it gives
them all the power: The lawyer determines how much time will be spent
on your case, the lawyer fills in a daily time sheet with numbers no one
can dispute. Worse still, an hourly rate fee is a direct incentive for the
lawyer to take his time: The slower the service the higher the pay.
(This matter is more fully described in Chapter 15: "What Do Lawyers
Lie About?")

For example, in your endeavor to purchase and establish the Italian
fast-food restaurant Tacky Belle of Happy Shoppers Mall, you engage a

lawyer on an hourly rate basis, without a detailed budget. You have no way of estimating the amount of money you will spend on legal fees. The fact that the lawyer charges $150 per hour has almost no relevance to the amount you may ultimately be asked to pay in legal fees. The lawyer may charge you the equivalent of five hours as time spent to research the law on the assessment clause in a franchise agreement, or he may charge you the equivalent of ten hours for the same task, or twenty hours, or forty hours. How can you prove he is lying about the time actually spent? Remember the vague definition of "reasonable" fee?

Without a detailed provision of the Estimated Budget, included as part of the Engagement Letter (see above sample provision on Estimated Budget), which sets forth either the number of hours to be spent on negotiating the franchise agreement, or a set fee for such a task, the lawyer's fees may fluctuate over a wide range, at the complete discretion of the lawyer, without you having any way of gauging the fairness of the bill.

Suppose you receive a bill from your lawyer and the amount of time billed seems excessive to you. If your Engagement Letter provides for an hourly rate fee, the lawyer has every right to collect the amount charged. Could you prove that the lawyer did not spend all that time on the franchise agreement? Who could tell?

In summary, an hourly rate fee should only be agreed to in conjunction with a binding Estimated Budget provision that caps the number of hours the lawyer may charge. Otherwise, there is no way for you to estimate—and later control—how much time (and therefore money) will be charged to your account; and if the charges seem excessive, there is no way for you to prove it. Without this defense, an hourly rate fee arrangement may turn into a bottomless financial pit.

Sample Provision: Hourly Rate Fee (One Lawyer)

8.2. Hourly Rate.

Client will pay lawyer a fee which shall be calculated as follows: for time spent in connection with the Representation, including advice and conferences between Client and Lawyer, client will pay a fee at the rate of $_____ per hour for services actually rendered (with credit for the Advance Retainer paid at the signing of this Engagement Letter). Under no circumstances will Client be charged for time in excess of the maximum set forth in the Estimated Budget provision of this Engagement Letter.

Sample Provision: Hourly Rate Fee (Law Firm)

The following provision should be used when hiring a lawyer who, in turn, employs or shares the work with partners, associates, or others whose work will be billed to the client at various hourly rates:

8.2 Hourly Rate.

Client will pay, for services rendered, the following hourly rates with respect to each of the following persons who performed work in connection with the Representation: Lawyer A: $_____ per hour; Lawyer B: $ _____ per hour; Associate A: $_____ per hour; Associate B: $_____ per hour; Legal Assistants: $_____ per hour; Typist: $_____ per hour. No other person's time will be charged to Client unless agreed to in writing. Client shall not be charged for time spent in excess of the amount(s) set forth in the Estimated Budget provision of this Engagement Letter.

CONTINGENT FEE IN A LAWSUIT: TRAPS, TRIPS, AND TREPIDATIONS

What Is a Contingent Fee?

Contingent fees (sometimes called "contingency fees") are based on an arrangement between a lawyer and a client by which the lawyer will be paid a fee only at the conclusion of the representation, calculated on the basis of a percentage (a "contingent") of the monetary judgment or settlement won for the client.

A contingent-fee arrangement is not always appropriate, depending on the type of case involved. Legal representation in a business transaction, a small business dispute, or other similar matters do not merit contingent-fee arrangements. Filing a lawsuit to recover substantial damages is the classic case for a contingent fee. How do you know whether your case is appropriate for a contingent-fee arrangement?

Two essential criteria determine the justification for a contingent-fee arrangement: the lawsuit must be against a "deep pocket" defendant, and the plaintiff must have a good chance of winning a substantial award of monetary damages. Typically, a contingent fee is appropriate in personal injury cases, large contractual disputes, medical or legal malpractice suits, or product-liability suits (such as the asbestos and breast implant cases). These types of cases always present a good chance to win a substantial dip into the coffers of a "deep pocket" defendant.

Under a contingent fee arrangement, the lawyer does not charge any fee until the case is concluded by the actual payment of damages by the defendant. At that point, when the defendant has actually paid, the lawyer is entitled to keep a certain portion of the winnings, usually up to one-third, and the remainder goes to the client.

The Fairness of Contingent-Fee Arrangements

The American Bar Association's Model Code of Professional Responsibility (EC 5-8 [1980]) requires that "a lawyer, because he is in a better position to evaluate a cause of action, should enter into a Contingency Fee arrangement only in those instances where the arrangement will be beneficial to the client."

Contingent-fee arrangements are not allowed, in most states, in divorce cases or other domestic relations disputes, in which the payment of a contingence would become due to the lawyer upon securing a divorce and winning money in maintenance, support, equitable distribution, or property settlement. Additionally, contingent-fee arrangements are not compatible with representation that does not involve a monetary judgment award at the end of the case, such as a criminal case that will end in either acquittal or conviction. However, most states allow an arrangement by which the lawyer would get a bonus if certain results were achieved, for example, a certain bonus for acquittal, for obtaining a conviction of a lesser offense, and so on. This type of fee is based on results, not on a percentage of a monetary victory, and therefore is more accurately called a "fixed fee," as discussed more fully in the next section.

In general, contingent fees can be beneficial to you as a client because there is no obligation on your part to pay any legal fees out of your own pocket, and legal fees would become due only if the case was won and the lawyer has collected money (as a result of a judgment or a settlement) from your opponent. The contingent fee would never be disproportionate to the size of the amount you are paid by the defendant (which can happen if the lawyer is paid by the hour; hourly rate charges can accumulate during a case to an amount greater than the amount you win in the lawsuit), and therefore creates an incentive to the lawyer to win for you as much money as possible. On the other hand, if your case is a sure win, for example, when your opponent is eager to offer a generous settlement, a contingent-fee arrangement may end up costing you a lot more than a reasonable lawyer's fee. Also, many institutions, including several state legislatures, have been critical of contingent fees, and it seems that there is "No End in Sight in Debate Over Contingency Fees" (Barry J. Nace, *The National Law Journal,* August 1, 1994).

Avoiding Traps in Contingent-Fee Arrangements

Contingent-fee arrangements are more complicated than monthly retainer, hourly-rate fee, or fixed fee. The size of the contingent fee is open to negotiation, and disputes may arise during the representation as to what work is covered by the contingent fee (or requires additional fees), what recoveries are subject to contingent fee, how to calculate the contingent fee in case of an early settlement, and whether you should pay anything if you fire your lawyer midway through the case. Those matters should be resolved through negotiations between you and your lawyer, and should be embodied in the relevant provision in the Engagement Letter. The following sections discuss those matters and propose solutions.

What Recoveries Are Subject to the Contingent Fee?

In such cases as car accidents under no-fault coverage, the insurance company is liable to pay all your medical expenses automatically, and therefore these payments should not be covered by the contingent fee. Only payments made toward lost earnings, and monetary and other damages—including pain and suffering—should be subject to the contingent fee as the "sum recovered" for you by the lawyer.

Negotiating the Rate of the Contingency

What would be the rate of the contingency? In New York, the law requires the lawyer to file with the court a form stating that a contingent fee will be paid and specifying what percentage of the amount recovered in damages will go to the lawyer. New York's Judiciary Law § 474–A, governing contingent-fee awards in medical, dental, or podiatric malpractice actions, establishes at subdivision (2) an incremental formula for calculating fee awards as follows:

- 30% of the first $250,000 of the sum recovered
- 25% of the next $250,000 of the sum recovered
- 20% of the next $500,000 of the sum recovered
- 15% of the next $250,000 of the sum recovered
- 10% of any amount over $1,250,000 of the sum recovered

Other states also set such contingent-fee schedules, commonly limiting the contingent fee to a maximum of one-third of the amount actually recovered.

Variable Rate for an Early Settlement

What would be the rate of the contingent fee in case of settlement before trial? According to some statistics, only 1 percent of civil cases ever reach the stage of a final verdict by judge or jury. All other cases are resolved through settlement or dismissal before or during the trial. Therefore, the Engagement Letter should be clear in stating that no fee is due unless an amount of money has been recovered through the lawyer's representation, and that if the case is resolved by settlement, the lawyer will receive a diminished contingent, correlating to the lawyer's diminished amount of work (compared to the amount of work required for a trial).

What Part of the Lawyer's Work Is Covered by the Fee?

In the case *Red v. County of Nassau* (New York Supreme Court, Nassau County, as reported in *New York Law Journal,* June 17, 1993), a lawyer had successfully obtained a judgment in favor of his client, a plaintiff in a medical malpractice case. After collecting the judgment, the lawyer allegedly demanded an additional fee based on a provision in the New York law allowing for a lawyer to receive amounts in excess of the contingent fee "because of extraordinary circumstances" that merit greater compensation. The court opined that the following items, which appeared on the lawyer's list, should be considered part of the representation and not "extraordinary":

- Interviewing clients
- Obtaining medical records

- Obtaining obstetrical consult
- Filing notice of claims
- Attending hearing
- Drafting summons and complaint
- Drafting bill of particulars
- Filing notice of medical malpractice actions
- Attending preliminary conference
- Attending medical examinations of plaintiffs
- Taking depositions of defendants
- Making motion to compel disclosure and opposing motion to discover confidential records
- Resolving appeal by defendant of confidentiality decision
- Attending physical examination with a client
- Placing case on calendar
- Appearing six times in court, including representation before the administrative judge
- Performing computer and library research on the subject matter of the medical malpractice case
- Trial preparation and witness preparation
- Jury selection
- Trial
- Post-trial assessment of verdict
- Settlement conference
- Additional hearing
- Preparation of judgment
- Preparing alternative judgment

The only task that the court considered to be beyond those lawyer's duties subject to the contingent fee was "respond[ing] to defendant's counter judgment." The judge added, that "[T]his was an ordinary obstetrical malpractice case. The fact that the injuries were devastating and were successfully (and quite ably) pursued by [the lawyer] does not render it extraordinary. To the contrary, [the lawyer] has already been compensated more because of the extent of the injuries, and his success then would have been less had the defendant plaintiff's injuries been less and/or had the case not been as successful even with the same expenditure of time and effort."

This decision illustrates the potential for abuse of contingency fees by lawyers. The fact that an additional judicial proceeding was required, and the corresponding expenditure of time and money on the part of the client, in order to determine that the lawyer was attempting to collect an "unreasonable" fee, makes it all the more important to use the Engagement Letter to avoid falling into this trap.

What Would You Owe if You Fire Your Lawyer Midway?

The contingent-fee arrangement may hold you hostage, if firing your lawyer requires (under the fee arrangement you negotiated) immediate payment of fees by you out of your own pocket. As in the sample contingent-fee provision given below, the fee agreement should specifically provide that, if you decide to replace your lawyer, no fee would be owed by you immediately, and the lawyer's right to a fee would be postponed until the case was resolved through the representation of another lawyer. The fee should be divided proportionally between the lawyers based on the amount of work each performed.

The Final Statement

The New York State Code of Professional Responsibility (Cannon 2, DR 2-106) provides that, when a lawyer is hired on a contingent-fee basis, the lawyer is required to:

> Provide [the] client with a writing stating the method by which the fee is to be determined, including the percentage or percentages that shall accrue to the lawyer in the event of settlement, trial or appeal, litigation and other expense to be deducted from the recovery whether such expenses are to be deducted before or after the contingency is calculated. Upon conclusion of a Contingent Fee matter, the lawyer shall provide the client with a written statement stating the outcome of the matter and if there is a recovery, showing the remittance to the client and the method of its determination.

This requirement should be included in the Engagement Letter, as provided below in the sample final bill provision. Because the above rule appears in the laws of all states, including the ABA Model Code of Professional Responsibility, you have every right to demand that such provision be part of the fee agreement and be followed accordingly.

Sample Provision: Contingent Fee in a Lawsuit

The following sample provisions can be tailored to fit the needs of your case. The blanks left open should be filled in after considering the above issues and negotiating with your lawyer:

8.3   Contingent Fee in a Lawsuit.

Client will pay Lawyer a fee (the "Contingent Fee") to be calculated as a contingent of the amount recovered on Client's behalf in this Representation (the "Sum Recovered"). Lawyer will not demand any additional fee for any work done in connection with this Representation or otherwise, unless such unrelated work and the payment of a fee therefor has been agreed to in writing. In the case of a settlement before the beginning of a trial, the Contingent Fee would be ___% of the Sum Recovered; the Contingent Fee would be ___% with respect to any Sum Recovered during or after a trial. The Contingent Fee will cover all the work done by Lawyer in connection with the claim against _____, and with this Representation. The Sum Recovered which is subject to this Contingent Fee shall not include any reimbursement paid to or on behalf of Client for any medical or other expense sustained by Client. Lawyer's expenses listed below will be deducted from the Sum Recovered and paid to Lawyer before the calculation of the above Contingent Fee.

In the event Client decides to terminate this Representation for any reason prior to the final resolution of the Representation, no Contingent Fee or other will be owed by Client to Lawyer. However, in such case, Lawyer will have the right to receive a reduced Contingent Fee, equivalent to the portion of the legal work performed by Lawyer of the total legal work required to bring the Representation to final conclusion. Such reduced Contingent Fee will not become due unless such final resolution of the suit has taken place in favor of Client, and the Sum Recovered has actually been recovered. The measure of such reduced Contingent Fee will be determined by agreement, between Lawyer and Client, at the time of such termination or, in the event of disagreement, shall be subject to the provisions of this Engagement Letter relating to Dispute Resolution.

CONTINGENT FEE IN BUSINESS TRANSACTIONS: DANGEROUS LIAISONS

Should You Take on Your Lawyer as a Partner?

A contingent fee may also be tailored to fit large business deals, especially when a client can convince the lawyer that a fee based on future profits has the potential to be much greater than a fee paid up front. On the other hand, if that is the case, the client will end up paying the lawyer a much higher fee (in the form of a share in the profits), than an hourly or fixed fee would be. For that reason, a contingent-fee arrangement will be advantageous for you only when the lawyer's contribution to your business venture goes beyond basic legal service and actually adds to the success and profitability of the business.

Contingent fee arrangements for business transactions are most common in the entertainment business. For example, according to *The American Lawyer* (D. M. Osborne, "The Players," December 1994), the Los Angeles law firm of Ziffren, Brittenham & Brana, like other "entertainment boutiques," charges its clients 5 percent of their total earnings from every deal in which the law firm represented the client. The law firm's show-business clients, such as The Rolling Stones, Michael Jackson, Henry Winkler, and others, are willing to pay a "cut" to such specialty entertainment-law boutiques, not only for legal representation but also for their lawyers' access to the sprawling networks of top agents and executives in the entertainment industry.

Where a lawyer offers not only traditional legal services but also serves as a business promoter and a broker, traditional hourly rate fees give way to some form of a contingent fee, making the lawyer a de facto partner of the client. Thus, the lawyer is rewarded for his contribution to the success of the business, and the client knows there will be no legal fees if there is no profit from the business venture.

For you, as a client, such an arrangement could be extremely lucrative, providing that the lawyer indeed has the skill, contacts, and experience to make such contribution to your business success. However, you should only sign your lawyer up as your "business partner" if you are certain that the arrangement leaves you in complete control of your business. Such protection is afforded by the Engagement Letter (see chapter 8, section F, on Obligations and Warranties), which should provide that all business decisions would be made exclusively by you, with the lawyer serving only as your representative, advocate, and advisor.

Sample Provision: Contingent Fee in a Business Transaction

The following sample provisions should be tailored to fit the specific circumstances of your situation. This provision relates closely to the definition of "Representation" in the provision titled: Scope of Representation and Desired Results. Before adopting this arrangement, review the section above that discusses contingent fee arrangements in connection with a lawsuit, which to a large extent applies here, and discuss the different possibilities with the lawyer.

8.4. Contingent Fee in Business Transactions.

Client will pay Lawyer a fee (the "Contingent Fee") to be calculated as a contingent of the amount received by Client in connection with this Representation (the "Sum Recovered"). Lawyer will not demand any additional fee for any work done in connection with this Representation or otherwise, unless such unrelated work and the payment of a fee therefor has been agreed to in writing. The Contingent Fee would be ___% of the Sum Recovered, and be paid out of amounts received by or on behalf of client as each such amount is received. The Contingent Fee will cover all the work done by Lawyer in connection with the Representation. The Sum Recovered which is subject to this Contingent Fee shall not include any reimbursement paid to or on behalf of Client for any professional, medical, travel or other expense sustained by Client. Lawyer's expenses listed below will be deducted from any Sum Recovered and paid to Lawyer before the calculation of the Contingent Fee.

In the event Client decides to terminate this Representation for any reason prior to the final conclusion of the Representation, no Contingent Fee or other fee would be owed by Client to Lawyer. However, in such case, Lawyer would have the right to receive a reduced Contingent Fee, equivalent to the portion of the legal work performed by Lawyer of the total legal work that directly contributed to the successful conclusion of the Representation. Such reduced Contingent Fee would not become due until such final conclusion of the Representation, and until the Sum Recovered has actually been collected by Client. The measure of such reduced Contingent Fee would be determined by agreement, between Lawyer and Client, at the time of such termination or, in the event of disagreement, shall be subject to the provisions of this Engagement Letter relating to Disputes Resolution.

FIXED FEE: THE WAY TO GET QUICK RESULTS

Fixed Fee: Good for Both Lawyers and Clients

The 1993 Altman Weil Pensa survey, mentioned above, found that all of the surveyed law firms sometimes used fixed-fee arrangements, without exception. As a result, fixed-(or flat) fee arrangements were 40 percent more popular than all other fee arrangements.

Fixed-fee arrangements are popular because they benefit both lawyers and clients. The determining factor is whether the lawyer achieved the desired result, rather than how much time the lawyer has spent in the process. A fixed-fee arrangement forces the lawyer to consider and determine, in advance, the amount of work the representation would require, and justify the requested fee. It gives the lawyer a relative assurance that his fee has been stated and accepted as reasonable by the client. It motivates the lawyer to provide speedy service, spend less time per dollar of fee, and accomplish the desired results quickly so that the agreed fee will be paid sooner. A fixed-fee arrangement will also motivate the lawyer to save on expenses, which are commonly included in the fixed fee. Thus, the client enjoys effective service, quick results, and no risk of inflated legal fees or expenses. Lastly, fixed-fee arrangements help the client determine at the outset whether the desired results are worth the fee demanded by the lawyer.

When Is a Fixed Fee Appropriate?

A fixed-fee arrangement should only be negotiated for representation in specific and well-defined tasks, such as handling of the purchase of a home, representation in a lawsuit (either as a defendant or a plaintiff), representation in a criminal trial, incorporation of a business, or in divorce or separation proceedings.

Because the agreed-upon fixed fee will be paid only after the legal task has been successfully completed, your lawyer will be highly motivated to get the job done efficiently. The fixed fee should include all expenses, reimbursements, and any other related fees, and should be paid only at the completion of the representation. Payment in advance (except for a relatively modest advance retainer) would defeat the motivational aspect of such an arrangement.

A fixed-fee arrangement will work well even when the task involved is complicated or has many components. For example, the New York law firm LeBoeuf, Lamb, Lieby & MacRae has, according to a report by *The American Lawyer* (John E. Morris, "Two Pioneers Make a Fixed-Fee Work," December 1993), engaged one of its clients, Aluminum Company of America, (ALCOA) on an unusually comprehensive fixed fee arrangement. As reported, LeBoeuf will represent ALCOA in all of the litigation cases in which it is involved (more than 500 such cases across the country) for a period of three years. For its services, LeBoeuf will charge a fixed fee (thought to be between $6 and $7 million per year), open an office in Pittsburgh, hire several former Aluminum Company in-house lawyers and several support staff members, and hire local counsel in any litigation in other jurisdictions, as needed. The flat fee will include all expenses and fees and would save ALCOA 25 percent of its litigation expenses, while LeBoeuf carries the risk of spending more time on the cases than it originally anticipated.

Such agreements between law firms and corporate clients shift the risk of unexpected legal costs to the lawyers, but at the same time, these agreements assure the lawyers of constant and predictable fees and minimize the risk (for the lawyers) that the client-build an in-house legal department, leaving the outside lawyers without work.

Conflicts of Interest in Fixed-Fee Arrangements

Last, when considering a fixed-fee arrangement you must determine whether there is potential for a conflict of interest between you and the lawyer.

For example, in *Winkler v. Keane* (Court of Appeals for the 2d Circuit, 1993) a fee agreement between a criminal defendant and his lawyer provided for an additional fee in case the defendant was acquitted or otherwise found not guilty with respect to certain felonies. In *Winkler*, the plaintiff argued that a conflict of interest existed because the lawyer's strategy in the case was motivated by the desire to earn the bonus. According to the client's complaint, by way of a plea agreement the lawyer achieved an acquittal on the severe offenses that were the subject of the "bonus" fee, but at the same time purportedly caused his client's conviction on the lesser offense. Such a strategy may not have been the most beneficial for the client if there had otherwise been a fair chance to reach a complete acquittal. However, the court found that, in this particular case, there was insufficient proof that the lawyer's representation was deficient or otherwise affected by the alleged conflict of interest.

When considering a fixed-fee arrangement you must take into consideration all the facts involved in the representation and make sure that your lawyer, in his rush to earn the fee, does not cut corners in ways contrary to your interests. Such a risk, however, can be mitigated through proper provisions in the Engagement Letter and by following the advice detailed later in the chapters dealing with the effective use and supervision of your lawyer.

Sample Provision: Fixed Fee

8.5. Fixed Fee

Client will pay Lawyer $ _____ as complete and total fee for all of Lawyer's services involved in the Representation. Such fee shall be paid at the completion of the Representation, and shall include any and all expenses, reimbursements, and fees involved in this Representation. Lawyer will not demand any additional fees or expenses for services relating to this Representation.

COMBINATION FEE: ANOTHER WAY TO GET RESULTS

The Elements of Creating a Seamless Combination

In some cases, none of the traditional fee arrangements discussed above will satisfy both lawyer and client. The client may consider an hourly rate fee to be a bottomless pit, leaving the client without control over the cost of legal services and the lawyer without the incentive to complete the representation quickly and efficiently. The lawyer may consider a contingent fee economically unjustified, either because the case is not strong enough or because the lawyer does not have the financial means to invest years of work without getting paid until judgment is rendered and collected. A fixed fee, on the other hand, may not be adequate in a case in which it is hard to predict the amount of time and expense involved. And lastly, even in a case where a large amount of damages may eventually be paid, a contingent fee arrangement might not be adequate for the lawyer representing the defendant, or for a lawyer representing the plaintiff if the case is expected to be very difficult to win.

When the common types of fee arrangements are inadequate, some creativity is called for in constructing a combination fee arrangement that borrows from some or all of the traditional fee arrangements. A combination of two or more types of fee arrangements, in an effort to create a compromise that would satisfy both lawyer and client, may serve the lawyer's need for an assured and sufficient fee, while preserving the client's prudent requirement of incentives to achieve desired results in a speedy and efficient manner.

Alternative fee arrangements vary almost infinitely. You might combine a contingent fee with a substantial advance retainer; a fixed fee or flat fee with a low hourly rate fee; an hourly rate fee with a bonus or a fixed fee based on results; a contingent fee with a minimal fixed fee in the event of loss; a nonrefundable advance retainer with a reduced contingent fee; a minimal hourly rate fee with a bonus for certain results; or an hourly rate fee capped through the inclusion of a detailed budget provision, with a bonus or contingent fee based on results. Any combination is possible, as long as these two goals are achieved: motivating the lawyer to get results and to work quickly and efficiently, and cutting down on expenses.

Use the same provisions given above to draft an appropriate provision into the fee agreement, to cover a combination fee arrangement. As a client, your primary concern should be to preserve, as much as possible, a monetary incentive for the lawyer to complete the representation speedily, efficiently, and with minimum expenses. Any substantial advance fee, high hourly rate, or any other assured fee not dependent on results would constitute a disincentive to the lawyer. As a rule a combination fee should only be created to give the lawyer an initial minimal fee to cover some expenses and cash-flow needs. However, the fee arrangement should never shift the payment of fee to an earlier date without attaching it to successful results.

Sample Provision: Combination Fee

8.6. Combination Fee

The combination of: Advance Retainer; Hourly Rate Fee; Contingent Fee; Fixed Fee; and, _____, as described above in the relevant provisions, shall cover all services provided by the Lawyer in connection with the Representation. If any of the relevant provisions create a discrepancy in any way, and Lawyer and Client fail to resolve the issue amicably, the provision of this Engagement Letter on Dispute Resolution shall apply.

EXPENSES AND DISBURSEMENTS

What Expenses Should You Pay?

In principle, expenses should be paid by a client or reimbursed by the client only if such expenses were incurred by the lawyer in addition to the lawyer's usual office expenses and were incurred exclusively in connection with the service to the specific client.

As a client, you should attempt to include all expenses in the contingent or fixed fee. If you hire a lawyer to represent you in purchasing a new home and agree on a fixed fee of $1,000, which includes all the elements of the representation, including drafting of contracts, reviewing of all related documents, and representation during the closing on the purchase of the house and the mortgage, such a fixed fee should also include all expenses and disbursements related to the lawyer's representation of you, with the exception of any filing fees, land survey, home inspection, and other such expenses that are customarily paid directly by the buyer of a new home. You should not pay any other office or transportation expenses or any expenses that the lawyer incurred in the usual line of maintaining an office and representing clients like you.

When all expenses are included in the predetermined fixed fee or contingent fee, the lawyer has great incentive to minimize such expenses. The opposite goes for a situation in which you undertake to reimburse the lawyer for any expenses incurred while representing you.

In contingent-fee cases relating to personal injury, the contingency is customarily calculated only after the expenses have been deducted from the judgment as paid by the defendant, and after the lawyer has received reimbursement for such expenses. It is, however, legitimate for the client to demand a cap on the amount of such expense, and the relevant provision in the fee agreement should then list what expenses are to be paid by the client.

In a contingent-fee or in a fixed-fee arrangement, try to negotiate a cap on the amount of expenses that may accrue in connection with your case. Such a cap would require the lawyer to make a good-faith assessment of all anticipated expenses and prevent a situation in which the lawyer might enhance his legal fees by incurring extra expenses. Caps can also be placed on certain types of expenses, for example, placing a cap on all photocopying, telephone, and travel expenses, but leaving the deposition expenses free of any caps (because of the difficulty in assessing in advance the length and cost of depositions and the cost of transcribing such proceedings).

Sample Provision: Expenses and Reimbursements in Hourly Rate Fee Arrangements

9. Expenses and Reimbursements in Hourly Rate Arrangement.

Client shall pay and reimburse Lawyer for any Expenses incurred in connection with this Representation. Lawyer shall itemize such expenses in each Bill submitted to Client as provided in this Engagement Letter, and Client will be liable to pay such Bill unless certain items are disputed by Client, in such case the provisions below relating to Dispute Resolution shall apply. Any reference in this Engagement Letter to expenses (the "Expenses") means all expenses incurred by Lawyer in connection with this Representation, such as filing fees, Marshal's fees, special service of process fees, photocopying, depositions, transcription, long-distance telephone and fax, special delivery and express mail, long-distance transportation and travel costs. Such Expenses include only expenses necessary and unavoidable, which are incurred solely in connection with Representation. Any specific Expense in excess of $100 will require advance approval by Client. Without the approval in writing of Client, no other expenditures by Lawyer shall be considered as Expenses under this Engagement Letter.

Sample Provision: Expenses and Reimbursements in Contingent-Fee Arrangements

9. Expenses and Reimbursements in Contingent-Fee Arrangement.

Upon conclusion of the Representation, and the collection of any judgment or settlement, Lawyer may charge and deduct the expenses relating to this Representation from the amount paid, before calculating the Contingent Fee amount as provided above. Otherwise, Client would have no obligation to reimburse Lawyer for any expenses other than as part of the Contingent Fee. At no event will the Expenses exceed $_____ in total. Any reference in this Engagement Letter to expenses (the "Expenses") means all expenses incurred by Lawyer in connection with this Representation, such as filing fees, Marshall's fees, special service of process fees, photocopying, depositions, transcription, long-distance telephone and fax, special delivery and express mail, long-distance transportation and travel costs. Such Expenses include only expenses necessary and unavoidable, which are incurred solely in connection with Representation. Any Expense in excess of $100 will require advance approval by Client. Without the approval in writing of Client, no other expenditures by Lawyer shall be considered as Expenses under this Engagement Letter.

Sample Provision: Expenses and Reimbursements in Fixed Fee Arrangements:

9. Expenses and Reimbursements in Fixed-Fee Arranement.

Client will not be liable to Lawyer for any Expenses or other reimbursement, except as provided by this Engagement Letter with respect to and as part of the payment of the Fixed Fee. Lawyer may not charge Client for any additional amount over the Fixed Fee.

METHOD OF BILLING AND PAYMENTS

The Contents of the Periodic Bill

In such fee arrangements as monthly retainer, hourly rate fee, or combination fee, the fee arrangement may require periodical payments of fees and expenses to the lawyer. In these cases, it is important to agree as to the format and contents of the bill, so that it includes enough information to facilitate an intelligent review by the client before payment is made.

Sample Provision: Method of Billing and Payments

10. Method of Billing and Payments.

Fees and Expenses, when due under the applicable provisions of this Engagement Letter, will be billed to Client every ___ month(s) at the completion of this Representation, in the form of a written bill (the "Bill"). Payment will be due within 30 days, except with respect to specific charges disputed by Client. A Bill shall include a breakdown of each charge of fee, in the form of a chart describing the task performed, time spent on task, and comments. Similarly, the Bill shall provide detailed breakdown of expense and disbursement. Disagreements over bills will be resolved amicably and in the method prescribed in the provisions applying to dispute resolution.

Names of Lawyers:	Description of Task:	Date Performed:	Time Spent:	Hourly Rate:	Cost in $:

[This table should indicate a breakdown of each time entry by each of the lawyers in the firm who performed legal work on the client's behalf, with a specific description of the work performed, number of hours spent on the specific task, the hourly rate that applied to this lawyer's work, and the coat for each task]

UNAUTHORIZED ACTIONS BY LAWYER: OFFSET AGAINST FEES

What Can the Lawyer Do in Your Name?

[T]he authority to make decisions is exclusively that of the client and, if made within the framework of the law, such decisions are binding on the lawyer. . . . It is for the client to decide whether to accept a settlement offer or whether to waive the right to plead an affirmative defense. . . . In the final analysis, however, the lawyer should always remember that the decision whether to forego legally available objectives or methods because of non-legal factors is ultimately for the client and not for the lawyer." (New York State Code of Professional Responsibility, Canon 7, EC 7–7 & EC 7–8)

Your lawyer is to some extent your agent, because by hiring a lawyer and signing an Engagement Letter you grant authority to a lawyer to represent you in the matters for which the representation was created. Whether it is a representation in a lawsuit, criminal indictment and trial, or business negotiations with other parties, the lawyer has power, as your agent, to bind you legally. Even though his power as agent is limited (see Chapter 12: "The Power of Attorney"), and even though ethics codes in most states include similar language to the quoted section of the New York State Code of Professional Responsibility, the risk of actions without consultation by a lawyer exists in every representation.

Therefore, notwithstanding loosely drafted legal ethics rules on the "ultimate" discretion that lies with you as the client, a contractual obligation on the lawyer's part to consult with you and to follow your instructions on every matter and action is necessary to tie down that obligation and set up a corresponding penalty for violations.

The Engagement Letter includes clear language that creates a contractual obligation on the part of the lawyer to consult with the client before taking any action. To ensure compliance by the lawyer, the Engagement Letter prescribes monetary sanctions for unauthorized actions, including offset against fees and payment of damages.

Sample Provision: Unauthorized Actions by Lawyer: Offset Against Fees

11. Unauthorized Actions by Lawyer: Offset Against Fees.

In the case of any damages caused to Client as a result of Lawyer's failure to consult with Client before taking any action on Client's behalf, Lawyer's action outside the Scope of Representation, or any other action taken by lawyer in violation of this Engagement Letter, or of any applicable ethics rules, Client may offset such damages suffered by Client against any fees and expenses owed to Lawyer at any time in connection with the Representation. This provision does not limit Client's right to pursue any available sanctions, remedies, or compensation under any applicable law or regulations.

CHAPTER 11

KRAMER V. KRAMER: HOW TO PROTECT YOUR INTERESTS WHEN BREAKING UP WITH YOUR LAWYER

The following discussion applies to those provisions of the Engagement Letter that regulate the ending of the relationship between you and your lawyer such as who has the right to terminate the relationship; when and in what manner the separation takes place; the contents of the final bill; the measures the lawyer may take to collect outstanding fees from you; and the tools available for resolving disputes between you and your lawyer. As in marriage, the best time to discuss matters relating to future separation is when you don't think such a separation is likely. When a dispute is already brewing, the chance for amicable resolution is slim.

TERMINATION OF THE REPRESENTATION: THE NEWLYWED SYNDROME—WHY TALK ABOUT IT NOW?

Never underestimate the power to terminate. Nothing could make your lawyer more devoted to you than knowing that if you are unhappy with her service, you have the right to terminate the relationship and find another lawyer to work with.

No fee arrangement works well without a corresponding "termination provision," giving you the option to terminate the representation, have your files returned (and your property, if the lawyer has any of it), get a refund of any unearned fee, and not owe anything to the lawyer who failed to keep you happy. In such a case, any dispute over outstanding fees owed to the lawyer should be subject to objective arbitration or court of law, without giving the lawyer any "temporary" liens over your files or property. Only after such a dispute is resolved in favor of the lawyer in accordance with the Engagement Letter's provision on dispute resolution, the lawyer may resort to normal collection methods, like any other creditor.

The following pages contain a chronological discussion of the issues involved in terminating the representation. An Engagement Letter should contain a clear provision allowing you to terminate the relationship at any time, without being held hostage by a bad lawyer. Just as newlyweds who try to discuss the terms of a possible future separation, you risk the convergence of clouds and possible rain on your optimistic parade. However, it is a risk well worth taking when negotiating the terms of your relationship with a lawyer, which, if it goes sour later could not only prevent you from taking your case to another, better lawyer, but could also ruin you financially. Therefore, do not shy away from raising the issue of termination and insisting on the inclusion of the provisions prescribed in the Engagement Letter, so that you are protected, in case of dispute, from being billed for excessive and unreasonable fees, being subjected to harsh collection measures by the lawyer, or even being sued by the lawyer for fees allegedly owed.

TERMINATION BY CLIENT

Clients Don't Leave Good Lawyers

If you are represented by a lawyer you no longer trust, you have every right to terminate the relationship with this lawyer and find better representation. Similarly, you have every right to ask that an appropriate provision be included in the Engagement Letter to deal with such a situation if it arises. The basic rules are: the client may fire the lawyer; the client may hire another lawyer; the ex-lawyer must communicate with the new lawyer and transfer all documents and information relevant to the client's case; and, finally, the ex-lawyer must be paid for the work she has done, unless her mistakes and bad service caused financial damages to the client, for which the ex-lawyer is responsible.

Sample Provision: Termination by Client

12.1. Termination by Client.

Client may terminate the Representation at any time. In such event, Lawyer shall communicate with Client or with another lawyer hired by Client to represent Client, and shall surrender and deliver all documents, materials, and information which came into Lawyer's possession in connection with the Representation. Termination of Representation by Client will be done in writing, and may include instructions pertaining to such termination and to the transition. Lawyer may not hold any documents or information relevant to this Representation after such termination, and shall transfer such documents and information according to Client's instructions. Within 30 days after such termination, Lawyer shall send Client a Final Bill, as provided in this Engagement Letter. Client shall have the right to claim, and deduct from any outstanding Bills, any financial damages sustained by Client as a result of mistakes or other negligence by Lawyer. Any disputes between Lawyer and Client with respect to outstanding Bills shall be resolved in accordance with the Dispute Resolution provision of this Engagement Letter.

TERMINATION BY LAWYER

Lawyer's Obligation to Protect Client's Interests

In taking you on as a client, the lawyer agreed to put your interests before hers and to serve you with honesty, integrity, and complete devotion, even at the expense of her own financial interests. This obligation continues even if the relationship fails and the lawyer wants out. The lawyer is professionally and ethically obligated to ensure that any separation from a client does not cause any damage to that client's interests. In accordance with the above principles, termination of the representation by the lawyer, for any reason, should only be done in a manner that ensures the client a continuity of legal representation without any additional costs or expenses.

Sample Provision: Termination by Lawyer

12.2. Termination by Lawyer.

Lawyer may withdraw from the Representation at any time, provided that another, qualified lawyer has been retained by Client, at Client's choice and complete satisfaction, and after such other lawyer has agreed to the Representation based on a review of all relevant documents and information required for such other lawyer to provide effective legal representation. Lawyer's withdrawal shall become effective only after Client has consented to such withdrawal in writing. Lawyer shall be responsible for the smooth transition of the Representation and all documents and information relevant to the Representation. Within 30 days after such withdrawal, Lawyer shall send Client a Final Bill as provided in this Engagement Letter. Any dispute over any item in such Final Bill shall be resolved in accordance with the provision on Dispute Resolution provided in this Engagement Letter. Lawyer shall not have the right to hold any documents or information after Lawyer has informed Client of Lawyer's intention to withdraw from the Representation.

THE FINAL BILL

A Bottom Line Summary of Charges

A final bill will be delivered by the lawyer to the client after the representation has ended for whatever reason—premature termination of the representation by either client or lawyer or ending of the representation after the desired results have been achieved. The content of the final bill depends, of course, on the fee structure agreed upon, but should include a detailed description of any outstanding charge and of any money or property held by the lawyer for the client. A final bill might include unexpected, improper, and excessive charges, depending on the circumstances of the termination, the relationship between the lawyer and the client, and the character, integrity, and honesty of the lawyer. To minimize the possibility of misunderstandings over the remaining mutual obligations of the lawyer and the client, the lawyer's obligation is to provide client with a final bill that is as detailed as possible. The client's corresponding obligation is to review the final bill carefully and verify that it is agreeable and consistent with the provisions of the Engagement Letter.

Sample Provision: Final Bill

13. The Final Bill.

Within 30 days after the completion, termination or withdrawal from the Representation, Lawyer shall provide Client with a Final Bill (the "Final Bill") setting forth all outstanding respective obligations. Any charges for fees, expenses or reimbursements shall be accompanied by a detailed explanation. Any dispute over any charge item in such Final Bill shall be resolved in accordance with the Dispute Resolution provision provided in this Engagement Letter. In the event of recovery of any amount as judgment or settlement on behalf of Client, Lawyer shall include in the Final Bill a statement explaining the method by which any Contingent Fee (if such has been agreed to in this Engagement Letter) is calculated, including the percentage pertaining to such settlement, judgment, or other sum recovered, and details of any expenses deducted by Lawyer from such amount paid, and whether such expenses were deducted before or after the calculation of contingency. Lawyer shall also state the outcome of the Representation, the amount of any recovery, the remittance to the client, and all calculations done in connection with such amounts.

RESTRICTIONS ON FEE-COLLECTION MEASURES

Beware of Below-the-Belt Collection Tactics

You hired your lawyer because of her great qualities: she is smart, aggressive, and completely devoted to your case. However, if a dispute arises between you and your lawyer over her fees, all those great qualities will likely turn against you, to be viciously utilized until the last drop of fee is extracted from you.

The fact is that lawyers almost always succeed in collecting disputed fees from their clients, not through negotiation, arbitration, or filing a claim with the court, but through the quick and efficient use of harsh fee-collection measures, such as retaining the client's files, property, or money, foreclosing a mortgage on the house of a client who was naive enough to let the lawyer record a mortgage on the client's home at the inception of the representation. Lawyers' intimate knowledge of their clients' affairs also enables them to obtain liens on the client's bank accounts or property that another creditor may not know about. Especially in divorce cases, but also in many other types of legal representation, the lawyer acquires extensive knowledge of the client's finances, and unless restricted by clear provisions in a signed Engagement Letter, the lawyer could very easily twist the former client's arm so painfully that the client pays whatever fee the lawyer demands.

Do Not Mortgage Your Home to Secure Legal Fees

Sounds like an obvious rule, doesn't it? Well, you'd be surprised. Many clients—especially in divorce cases—succumb to their lawyer's pressure and grant the lawyer a mortgage on the client's home, as security for future payments of the lawyer's fees.

Most states deal with the problem by restricting, to some extent, the process by which a lawyer may obtain a mortgage on the client's residence. Commonly, those conditions require that the fee not be excessive, that the client grant the mortgage free of any undue influence by the lawyer, that the lawyer is not granted the right to foreclose or press for quick sale of the property before giving the client the opportunity to pay the fee within a reasonable time, that the sale takes place in a way that ensures a fair price, that the lawyer is not the buyer of the property unless sold under supervision of other lawyers, and that the fee amount was determined at the time the mortgage was initially granted (New York State Bar Association, Opinion No. 550 (1983).

Matrimonial lawyers are subject to even stricter rules, requiring that the mortgage is granted under a retainer agreement that clearly provides that the other spouse was informed of the granting of a mortgage, that the court that has jurisdiction over the proceedings has approved the granting of a mortgage, and that foreclosure does not take place on "the marital residence while the spouse who consents to the mortgage remains the titleholder of the residence." The last condition, simply said, requires that one spouse should not lose his or her half of the home because the other spouse, who is staying in the home, has granted a mortgage to secure lawyer's fees (Rule 22, New York Court Rules and Regulations, 1993).

Retaining Liens, Attachments, and Summary Proceedings

In most states, ethics rules allow lawyers to exercise their right for a "retaining lien," which gives lawyers the right to retain, until all fees are paid, the client's money, property, documents, securities, or any other items belonging to the client which the lawyer possesses in connection with the representation.

Retaining liens take effect automatically whenever a demand for payment of the fee is not fulfilled by the client, regardless of whether or not the representation has been completed, the lawyer has been discharged by the client or otherwise withdrew from the representation, or even when the demand for the fee is unjustified. One unpaid bill is sufficient to give the lawyer an automatic "retaining lien."

Exempted from such retaining liens are items or money that the lawyer holds in escrow on behalf of the client or a third party, and property that did not come into the lawyer's possession by actions taken in the course of legal representation of the client. For example, client's property that came into the lawyer's possession under an escrow agreement, a trust agreement, or another fiduciary responsibility would not be subject to a retaining lien. Regretfully, the line separating such "escrow" properties from "properties received through representing the client" is a fine one and lengthy proceedings may be required to determine whether a particular piece of the client's property may be subject to a retaining lien. The practical consequence of this legal ambiguity is that a lawyer can seize virtually any of her client's property, under the argument that it is not escrow property, but property available for a retaining lien.

Last, a lawyer may proceed quickly through summary proceedings in court to fix a lien on any other property belonging to the client. Such proceedings not only require the client to retain a new lawyer, but may also result in the creation of a lien "ex parte" without the client having a chance to prevent the lien by appearing in court and arguing against it.

Your best chance to prevent your lawyer from ever seizing any of your property on account of fees is by making the lawyer waive any use of draconian fee-collection methods. Your lawyer should have collection power not greater than any other person who demands payment of a purported debt from you. If the lawyer can prove in arbitration or in court that indeed the demanded fee is justified, a host of collection measures is provided for by the law for the benefit of any creditor. As long as the disputed bill is still being adjudicated, you should not be held hostage by your lawyer.

Sample Provision: Restriction on Fee-Collection Measures

14. Restriction on Fee-Collection Measures.

Should Client in any way dispute a charge in the Final Bill or any other Bill, Client may refuse to pay such charge and the provision on Dispute Resolution provided in this Engagement Letter shall apply. Until such dispute has been resolved amicably, through binding arbitration, or by a final judgment of the court of appropriate jurisdiction, Lawyer may not place a lien of any type, or otherwise use any mortgage, summary proceedings, or any other collection measures against Client. Under no circumstances will Lawyer have the right to retain Client's property, documents, or money, pending resolution of any dispute between Lawyer and Client.

DISPUTE RESOLUTION

What Do Lawyers and Clients Fight About?

Money is the paramount reason for lawyer-client disputes, and such disputes occur more often than one would hope. The typical dispute involves excessive fees, unjustified charges for expenses, or disagreements over fee-calculation methods. In some cases, the dispute grows out of the client's general dissatisfaction with the lawyer's service. If the client decides to hire a new lawyer, a dispute with the former lawyer over outstanding fees is not unlikely.

In addition to the provisions of the Engagement Letter setting forth the way the lawyer's fee is to be calculated, you should also prepare to protect yourself against the potentially disastrous ramifications of a fee dispute with a combative lawyer. The qualities for which you hired the lawyer may now turn against you in a fight over fees that you consider excessive. By setting forth (in the Engagement Letter) a clear method for resolving future disputes, both you and the lawyer commit yourselves to a civilized, prearranged method of resolving any disagreements, and also rule out the use of uncivilized collection tools by the lawyer.

In most states, consumer groups have pushed bar associations and state legislatures in the direction of establishing protective measures to assist clients in disputes with lawyers. In general, especially with respect to divorce lawyers, guidelines have been set to allow clients access to independent and objective arbitration proceedings, at the client's choice, while limiting a lawyer's right to engage in aggressive fee-collection measures.

The following sample provision is based on rules published in 1993 by the courts of the State of New York, aimed at regulating lawyers' conduct in matrimonial actions but equally applicable in all types of legal representation.

Sample Provision: Dispute Resolution

15. Dispute Resolution.

In the event of a dispute between Lawyer and Client regarding any matter relating to the Representation, Client shall have the right to commence arbitration proceedings, which will be binding upon both Lawyer and Client. In the event of such dispute, Lawyer shall assist and advise Client on the appropriate way to commence arbitration, and shall cooperate fully with such proceedings. If Client chooses not to commence binding arbitration, Lawyer may file a claim with a court of appropriate jurisdiction. Under no circumstances will Lawyer retain any documents, information, or property of Client, whether or not relating to the Representation, pending resolution of any dispute. In the course of resolving any disputes between Lawyer and Client, Lawyer will not disclose any otherwise confidential information except to the extent directly necessary to the just resolution of the dispute.

CHAPTER 12

THE POWER OF ATTORNEY: A BEAST WITHOUT A MUZZLE

A power of attorney is a document that empowers another person to act on your behalf as your legal agent. Once you have signed a power of attorney, a force is unleashed that is comparable to a beast without a muzzle. Unless properly restricted, it gives the empowered person vast authority to act on your behalf and to commit you legally to anything, anytime, anywhere.

Should you sign a power of attorney? Can you make changes to a preprinted-form power of attorney? These questions and others are discussed in this chapter to help you decide if and when to sign a power of attorney, whether in favor of your new lawyer or of another person. However, the underlying truth is that a power of attorney is a document more powerful (and potentially disastrous) than anything else you might ever sign.

WHEN IS A POWER OF ATTORNEY NECESSARY?

Almost never. The sample power of attorney reproduced in Appendix B, which is based on a widely used form, gives the attorney unrestricted powers to do anything with the property and other rights of the person who signed it. In most cases, your lawyer does not need such power of attorney.

Only when your lawyer, your spouse, or another person whom you trust with all that you own (and all that you will ever own), has to make a purchase or a disposition or take any other legal action on your behalf, only then should you sign a power of attorney. In such a case, the power of attorney should be very restricted (as explained below) so it may only be used to perform the actions directly related to the intended purpose.

PREVENTING UNAUTHORIZED USE OF THE POWER OF ATTORNEY

The sample power of attorney printed in Appendix B is so inclusive that the person empowered as the "Attorney" will be able to do anything he wishes with the property and rights of the Principal. No action requires approval, no conflict of interest is monitored, and nothing prevents the Attorney from taking advantage of the powers granted to him. Therefore, such a document should never be signed unless circumstances absolutely necessitate it.

As a rule, a power of attorney should only be signed when you know that you are not going to be available to perform a certain legal action yourself, and that such legal action is absolutely necessary during your absence or period of incompetence. And even under such extreme circumstances that necessitate you sign a power of attorney authorizing your lawyer or any other person to take one or more legal actions on your behalf, you should limit the power of attorney to the specific matter, and limit the time during which it can be used. The following provision should be added to the power of attorney:

Scope of this Power of Attorney.

Notwithstanding any other provision of this Power of Attorney, this Power of Attorney is limited and restricted to matters and actions directly related to the following matter: [defined purpose]: _____. No provision of this Power of Attorney shall be interpreted to grant said Attorney any powers, authority, or discretion with respect to any other matters or actions, and any such actions shall have no binding effect on Principal. Furthermore, this Power of Attorney is limited in time, and will automatically expire on the 60th day from the day of signing of this Power of Attorney, unless extended in writing.

REVOKING THE POWER OF ATTORNEY

Power of attorney should only remain in force as long as necessary. Immediately after the power of attorney is no longer needed, revoke it.

The need no longer exists when the intended purpose has been fulfilled or when you do not wish the person to represent you in that matter anymore.

Do not leave a power of attorney with a lawyer, or with any other person, unless it is essential and is meant to be used for an immediate and specific purpose that you cannot perform yourself.

Revoking a power of attorney is done by physically repossessing the document itself. Taking back the power of attorney from the person you have given it to is the only way to fully protect yourself from an unauthorized use of the power of attorney. Remember that, on its face, the power of attorney appears to be valid and the person holding it may present it to a third party and pretend to act on your behalf, incurring debt, purchasing or selling property, or making other legally binding contracts. In the case of an unscrupulous lawyer, his professional status may buttress the signed power of attorney and enable that lawyer to cause you even more damage.

When you ask for the return of the signed power of attorney, even an honest lawyer may contend that he has to keep the revoked power of attorney in his files as a proof that he had the authority during the period prior to the revocation, in case of a future dispute. In such a case, you should ask his permission to physically revoke the original power of attorney by placing a diagonal line across the document, and by writing "Revoked and Canceled on [date]."

If you cannot repossess the power of attorney itself, or mark the original as canceled, your next step is to send the following letter to the lawyer (send it Certified Mail with return receipt):

Date [   ]

To: Lawyer [Name]

[Address]

Re: Revocation of Power of Attorney

Dear Lawyer [Name]:

I hereby revoke and cancel the Power of Attorney dated_____, signed by me. As of the date of this letter, you have no authority to act on my behalf in any matter whatsoever. Please acknowledge this letter, and return the original Power of Attorney to me as soon as possible.

[Signature]

_____ (Client's name)

Simultaneously with sending the revocation to the lawyer for signature, send a notice of it to all the persons who could mistakenly rely on the power of attorney.

DEALING WITH UNAUTHORIZED ACTIONS

After trying to sell your house for almost a year, you withdrew your house from the market as it became apparent to you that there was no chance to get the selling price you hoped for. The last offer, which was too low, had been flatly rejected by you. You paid a small bill sent to you by the real estate lawyer you hired to advise you on the prospective sale, and resigned yourself to wait another few years before trying again to sell the house. Now, six months later, you are holding in your hand a letter from Smith & Lansky, a local law firm, informing you that, under a sale contract signed on your behalf by your lawyer, you should vacate your house within fifteen days, and deliver it to the buyer "broom clean" and in livable condition. Your astonishment soon turns to panic, and you call your lawyer on the phone, ready to scream.

"The number you have dialed has been disconnected," and a monotonous voice informs you, "Please call the operator." You slam down the phone and drive to your lawyer's office. You find the door locked, with a sheriff's notice of eviction stuck on it.

Your next stop is at Smith & Lansky, where a very polite young associate leads you to a mahogany-paneled conference room. An older partner appears within minutes to show you a copy of the sale contract, which your lawyer signed on your behalf under a power of attorney, a copy of which is attached to the sale contract. There is also a receipt for a down payment of $20,000, which your lawyer has pocketed. What can you do?

Your first step should be to hire a new lawyer, preferably someone with expertise in real estate disputes and litigation. Do not sign anything or agree to any arrangements before consulting with a lawyer. Your only hope lies in proving that, at the time your former lawyer signed the sales contract, he no longer had the authority to do so on your behalf.

You are in this unfortunate position because:

- There was no need to have given your lawyer a power of attorney. In the context of a house sale, you could have signed all necessary documents yourself, and the lawyer's role should have been limited to dispensing advice, reviewing documents, and negotiating agreements. Only if you were planning to be away on an extended trip, hospitalized for a long time, or otherwise unavailable to sign the documents yourself should you have given your lawyer a power of attorney.

- If you had to give your lawyer a power of attorney, you should have limited it in time by including a section stating: "This Power of Attorney is valid for the period of sixty days from this date, unless revoked earlier."

- Assuming you had good reasons to give your lawyer a power of attorney, such reasons no longer existed when you decided not to sell your house. At that time, you should have demanded that the power of attorney be returned to you immediately, or, if impossible, taken the steps described above in "Revoking the Power of Attorney."

If you have made any of these mistakes, your only hope is to convince a court that, by informing your lawyer that you wished no longer to sell your house, you had revoked (verbally) the power of attorney, and, as soon as the power of attorney was revoked, the "umbilical cord" connecting you (as a principal) with your lawyer (as your agent) was severed, and with it, the lawyer's power to effect a sale on your behalf.

Your chances in such a case vary from state to state, depending on state agency laws and state court precedents. After all, from the buyer's point of view, the purchase was made in reliance on a valid power of attorney presented by your lawyer, therefore producing a legally binding contract for sale.

PART IV

STICK AND CARROT:
THE FEED AND CARE OF
YOUR HARDWORKING LAWYER

CHAPTER 13

ALL IN THE FAMILY: THE LAWYER'S DUTY TO KEEP SECRETS

An essential element of the lawyer-client relationship is the lawyer's obligation to maintain strict confidentiality with respect to any verbal or written communications with the client, and with respect to any information gained in the course of the representation. Under ethics rules, the client has a proprietary right over all materials, documents, and information that the lawyer received from the client, or on behalf of the client, during the representation. The lawyer is not allowed to disclose such confidential information to anybody, including the opposite party in business transactions or litigation cases, police officers, government authorities investigating the client's conduct, or even a judge sitting in a court of law. Concurrent with the lawyer's obligation to keep clients' secrets, a lawyer cannot be punished by the authorities for not divulging such information, with only a few exceptions.

THE ATTORNEY-CLIENT PRIVILEGE

The attorney-client privilege (the "Privilege") prohibits lawyers from disclosing clients' secrets and protects lawyers from being forced to disclose clients' secrets. The Privilege has existed for centuries. It covers all materials and information received from the client in connection with the legal representation by the lawyer of the client, and, together with the "work-product privilege," protects all the documents, memoranda, research notes, and strategy papers produced by the lawyer as part of the representation.

The Origins of the Attorney-Client Privilege

> Inasmuch as the testimony of witnesses (in the modern sense) did not come to be common source of proof in jury trial until the early 1500's, and as testimonial compulsion does not appear to have been generally authorized until the early part of Elizabeth's reign, it would seem that the Privilege could hardly have come much earlier into existence, for there could have been but little material for its application. It thus appears to have commended itself at the very outset as a natural exception to the then novel right of testimonial compulsion. (Wigmore, Evidence, Vol. 8, § 2290 at 542-543, McNaughton Rev., 1961.)

Wigmore's historic concept of protecting lawyers against compulsory testimony during civil or criminal trials, with respect to documents and information they receive from their clients, has developed over the years to include almost every form of communication between lawyers and clients. The purpose of the Privilege, as Wigmore points out is to facilitate legal services:

> The policy of the Privilege has been plainly grounded since the latter part of the 1700's as subjective considerations. In order to promote freedom of consultation of legal advisors by clients, the apprehension of compelled disclosure by the legal advisors must be removed; hence the law must prohibit such disclosure except on the client's consent. (Wigmore, at § 2291.)

In the United States, the Privilege now covers every field of legal representation, including criminal representation, grand jury proceedings, representation in government audits and other administrative cases, representation in business transactions, and any other contact between the lawyer, as a legal adviser, and a client. The U.S. Supreme Court in 1981 stated:

> [The purpose of the attorney-client privilege] is to encourage full and frank communication between attorneys and their clients [and to] promote broader public interests in their observance of law and administration of justice. The privilege recognizes that sound legal advice or advocacy serves public ends and that such advice or advocacy depends on the lawyer being fully informed by the client. (*Upjohn v. United States*, 1981.)

In other cases, the Supreme Court reasoned that the U.S. Constitution protects a lawyer against being compelled to disclose confidential information, under the Fifth Amendment, which protects against self-incrimination, and the Sixth Amendment, which grants all those accused of criminal offenses a right to the effective assistance of a lawyer. Legal experts recognize that such constitutional rights could not be effective without granting a client assurance that any discussions with a lawyer would remain strictly confidential and that no court could force the lawyer to reveal the content of such confidential communications (see, for example, "The Attorney-Client Privilege: Fixed Rules, Balancing and Constitutional Entitlement," 91 *Harvard Law Review*, p. 464 [1977]).

How Is a Privilege Created?

The Privilege, that is, the lawyer's duty to keep information in confidence and the protection against a lawyer being forced to disclose information about her client, covers all communications between the client and the lawyer made in confidence for the purpose of legal advice or representation.

The Privilege covers only communications between the lawyer and the client, not communications with others, and not communications between the lawyer and a third party on behalf of the client. In some states, the Privilege is limited to only those communications made in response to a specific request by the client. The communication covered by the Privilege must be between the client and the lawyer (or employees of the lawyer) in direct connection with the legal representation. The fact that any employee or assistant of the lawyer was present during the communication does not harm the Privilege, as long as such other person or persons were present as part of the representation or the formulation of legal advice. The Privilege also covers communications with clients that are corporations or partnerships, and in some cases, even communications between the employees of a corporation and the corporation's in-house lawyer.

Only information disclosed to the lawyer "in confidence" is covered by the Privilege. The intention to keep the information confidential should be demonstrated. For example, if someone else was present during a meeting between the lawyer and the client, or if a document was also disclosed to other parties, the information may not be protected by the Privilege because the intent to keep it confidential was not demonstrated.

The Privilege covers only communications that took place in connection with legal representation, and not other information, or routine correspondence between the lawyer and the client for purposes of general updates on business developments. The Privilege also does not cover nonlegal services by the lawyer. For example, if you hire a lawyer to do research on your behalf or to prepare your taxes, the information gathered by the lawyer while performing such "nonlawyerly" tasks is not protected by the Privilege because it was not obtained in connection with legal representation.

THE PRIVILEGE UNDER THE WORK-PRODUCT DOCTRINE

The Basis for the Work-Product Privilege

The work-product privilege is another, more specific component of the Privilege that protects information in the lawyer's possession from compulsory disclosure to other parties. The U.S. Supreme Court case *Hickman v. Taylor* (1947) is credited with creating the work-product privilege. In general, the work-product privilege protects all the materials, memoranda, and notes created or collected by the lawyer in preparation for litigation.

The work-product privilege is not as strict as the general attorney-client privilege because materials covered only under the work-product privilege may be subject to forced disclosure to other parties if such other parties prove compelling need for that material. However, the Supreme Court granted greater protection to documents that could expose the lawyer's analysis and mental impressions relevant to the lawyer's representation of the client.

The work-product privilege has been incorporated into federal and state laws, with respect to both civil and criminal matters. (For example, the Federal Rules of Civil Procedure [Rule 26(b)(3)] and the Federal Rules of Criminal Procedure [Rule 16(b)(2)].) Under these rules, the work-product privilege applies to pretrial discovery and protects all documents prepared by the lawyer or by the client in preparation for litigation.

In criminal proceedings the work-product privilege prohibits disclosure of any document that reveals the lawyer's mental impression, without regard to the government's need for such information, and in civil litigation it protects disclosure of documents or other tangible items, but not verbal communication. Most states have similar rules, in some ways even more inclusive than the federal rules, in that they prohibit disclosure without regard to the other party's need for the material.

What Is Covered by the Work-Product Privilege?

The work-product privilege covers all documents and tangible items that would otherwise be subject to forced disclosure during litigation, either in pretrial discovery or in trial testimony. Under the work-product privilege, your lawyer may not be forced to disclose documents generated by you, as a client, by your employees on your behalf, or by the lawyer or the lawyer's employees, in preparation or anticipation of a lawsuit.

In order to establish the work-product privilege, it is not necessary to prove that a lawsuit has actually been commenced or even threatened. It is only required that it was fairly probable that a lawsuit will take place.

The rationale behind the work-product privilege is to prevent an opposing party from taking a "free ride" on your trial preparation, whether the materials were prepared for trial (or any other adversary proceedings), by you, as a client, or your lawyer. It is only necessary to establish that the motivation for preparing these materials was the anticipation of litigation.

A court may order disclosure of documents protected by the work-product privilege if the opposing party can show that it is impossible to obtain the information in any other way or that it would be an "undue hardship" to obtain such documents in another way. However, it is almost impossible to use the "undue hardship" argument to force production of documents prepared by the lawyer as strategy or analysis, or other opinion memoranda. On the other hand, documents prepared by experts who are scheduled to appear during the trial, documents pertaining to the lawyer's own conduct, if it is a subject in the trial, and materials prepared to assist in a crime or fraud, may not be covered by the work-product privilege.

CRIMINAL ACTIVITY MAY PIERCE THE LAWYER'S DUTY OF SECRECY

Your lawyer's duty to secrecy, and the protection afforded to your lawyer against forced disclosure of information pertaining to the representation, may be voided if the government can prove that either you or the lawyer had intentions to defraud others.

In a recent case (described by Daniel Wise in "Lawyer Ordered Deposed Despite Privilege," *New York Law Journal*, September 21, 1994), a client attempted to create a misleading record of documents to be used as evidence in a lawsuit against the Hilton International Company. The court found that the client may have had an intent to present the concocted letters as if they were genuine. The lawsuit involved a claim by a female employee that she was discriminated against by her employer on the basis of gender and national origin when the employer fired her and appointed a male employee to replace her. During pretrial discovery, the court ordered the lawyers, a major New York law firm, to answer, under oath, questions about their conversations with their client. The court's decision, written by Judge Sotomayor, stated that "the facts of this case demonstrate if not an actual fraud, at least an intent on the part of the defendant to defraud the plaintiff." The court further explained that, in order to force a lawyer to reveal the content of consultations with the client, thereby creating an exception to the privilege, the party wishing to force such disclosure has to show prima facie evidence that the communication between the client and the lawyer was in "furtherance of an ongoing or planned wrongdoing," such as fraud or other crimes. There is no need to prove that the lawyer was aware of the client's illegal intentions, the court ruled, but only that the client "knew or reasonably should have known" of such illegality.

In another case, *U.S. v. Edwin H. Rivera* (1993), the court ordered that legal files be turned over to the prosecutors in a federal criminal case. In that case, a man, who was not a lawyer, falsely presented himself as an immigration lawyer and represented many clients in immigration proceedings before the U.S. Immigration and Naturalization Service. Even though the court noted that the attorney-client privilege arises out of the client's belief that he is dealing with a legitimate lawyer, not on the actual professional status of the person claiming to be a lawyer, the court concluded that, under the circumstances, the attorney-client privilege should be pierced. The communications in question, which included phony amnesty applications containing fake invoices, forged documents pertaining to age, and forged airline boarding passes and flight tickets, were intended to be filed with the Immigration and Naturalization Service, the court noted, and the clients were aware that the documents included in the files were forged, thereby making the client privy to the fraudulent intentions of the "lawyer." Such intentions by a client to defraud others pierces the attorney-client privilege.

THE LAWYER'S LEGAL OBLIGATION TO REPORT
CRIMINAL CONSPIRACIES

In some circumstances, ethics rules actually require lawyers to report the content of confidential communications with their clients to the authorities, if such disclosure may prevent a future crime.

A Nassau County (New York) Bar Association Ethics Committee opinion (Opinion No. 94-21, 1994, as reported in *New York Law Journal*, June 29, 1994), states that a lawyer has the duty to report fraudulent conduct by a client when the lawyer has actual knowledge or a clear belief that the conduct has occurred; the conduct is sufficiently material as to constitute fraud; and the lawyer's information does not constitute a client confidence or secret. If, due to the confidential or secret nature of the information, the lawyer is prevented from reporting the fraudulent conduct, the lawyer nevertheless is prohibited from assisting the client in perpetuating the fraud.

Another ethics opinion (New York Bar Association Ethics Committee Opinion No. 1994-8), specifically states that, even when it is clear to the lawyer that the client's action constitutes a fraud perpetrated by the client, the lawyer may still not reveal the information if the lawyer received the information "in confidence" or "in secret." This opinion was rendered in connection with a case in which a real estate lawyer was told by his client that the client, in buying certain real estate, intended to pay the seller an additional amount of money, undisclosed in the purchase contract and all the tax forms to be filed with relevant authorities. The payment of such "under-the-table" amount, together with the avoidance of city and state real estate transfer tax, clearly constituted fraud. However, the Bar Association determined that the lawyer had only the obligation to withdraw from the representation immediately, because continuing the representation would have assisted the client in perpetuating the fraud, but was not allowed to disclose the fraud to the authorities.

The only exception to this rule is that: the lawyer is permitted *but not obligated* to disclose "the intention of the client to commit a crime [if] the information is necessary to prevent the crime" [New York Code of Professional Responsibility, D.R. 101 (C)(3)].

As a rule, when you share information with your lawyer under circumstances that make it clear that the information is given to the lawyer in "confidence" and therefore is protected by the attorney-client privilege, the lawyer is not allowed to disclose such information unless it reveals your intention to commit a crime and by revealing the information, it could prevent the crime from taking place. However, the lawyer does not have an obligation to reveal such information.

For example, suppose all you want is an opinion from your lawyer on whether a certain transfer of money or property to your children would constitute a taxable event. You ask your lawyer whether, if you give your children "cash" or deposit money for them overseas, the government has any way of learning about such transactions. At this point, your questions are only intended to get acquainted with every possible means of transferring money to your children without getting taxed. You may have no intention of defrauding the government, but are only seeking legal ways to avoid payment of taxes. However, your questions might be interpreted by the lawyer as revealing an intention to defraud the government. Would the lawyer be free to disclose such information to the government? Does the lawyer have the obligation to disclose such information?

To avoid such a close call, always phrase your questions in a way that makes it clear that you have no intention to defraud a third party or to commit any crime. In order to avoid a crime, you have to know what legally constitutes a crime, and, therefore, a discussion of potentially illegal acts might be necessary to rule out taking any actions which, in your lawyer's opinion, are illegal. So long as you make it clear that you have no criminal intentions, your lawyer is ethically and legally prohibited from disclosing any part of your communication to a third party.

HOW TO AVOID ACCIDENTAL WAIVER OF THE ATTORNEY-CLIENT PRIVILEGE

The attorney-client Privilege does not take effect automatically. As a client, you must affirmatively raise and assert the Privilege with respect to communications with your lawyer. Worse yet, the Privilege may be inadvertently waived, by mistake, through actions that negate the confidential nature of the communication.

Waiver by Presence of Another Person

One spring day in 1992, a seventy-six-year-old woman lost control of her car and sped into Washington Square Park in New York City. She killed five people and injured twenty-six. During the woman's trial, the prosecution questioned the woman's lawyer about a conversation the lawyer had with the defendant in the lawyer's office. The woman's daughter was present during those meetings. The trial court, in *Stroh v. General Motors Corp.*, (*New York Law Journal,* June 9, 1994, p. 7, col. 1), held that the attorney-client privilege had been pierced by the presence of the daughter, and therefore the lawyer had to reveal the content of the conversations with his client. The court based its decision on the theory that the presence of a third person during a meeting between a lawyer and the client constitutes a de facto waiver of the Privilege, which protects the communication between the lawyer and the client. However, the New York Appellate Division, First Department, which reviewed the case on appeal, unanimously reversed the trial court decision, ruling that the conversations were protected by the Privilege (*New York Law Journal,* March 22, 1995, p.1, col. 1). The appellate court said:

> We are here presented with an aged woman required to recall and perhaps relive, what was probably the most traumatic experience of her life. Her daughter selected the law firm to represent her, transported her to the law office, and put her sufficiently at ease to communicate effectively with counsel. [The daughter] was clearly acting as her mother's agent [and therefore her presence did not change the confidential nature of the communication.]

This case draws a useful line between the kind of third-person presence that would violate the confidential nature of a meeting with a lawyer and the presence of someone who is really an agent of the client and therefore does not constitute a "stranger." So, when meeting with a lawyer, only the client and the client's agent, interpreter, or a fellow-client may be present. Otherwise, even the presence of a close family member may constitute a de facto waiver of the Privilege. The lawyer, however, has the duty to advise the client of that risk and require that all confidential communications take place in private.

Please note that these New York cases, although they provide useful examples of general issues concerning the Privilege, apply only to New York, and that other states may have drawn the lines somewhat differently.

Waiver by Disclosure to Outsiders

Some courts have gone as far as holding that inadvertent disclosure of confidential information constitutes a complete waiver of the Privilege (for example, *O'Leary v. Purcell* [1985]). Other courts thought that if the disclosure is a result of the lawyer's negligence, the client should not be punished by removing the protection of Privilege (for example, *Mendenhall v. Barber-Green Company* [1982]).

However, controversy exists as to disclosure of confidential information during government audits or government investigations. For example, some corporations occasionally cooperate with such government agencies as the Securities and Exchange Commission, the Justice Department, the Federal Trade Commission, or the Internal Revenue Service, and in the course of this cooperation share confidential documents (which would otherwise be protected by the attorney-client privilege), in order to prove that the corporation's conduct was lawful. Though such cooperation with government investigators often helps to avoid extensive audits and legal proceedings, many of those corporations later find themselves in civil litigation, for example, shareholders' lawsuits, in which plaintiffs may argue that, by disclosing the information to the government, the attorney-client privilege had been waived and therefore the information was no longer protected by the Privilege. In *In re Steinhardt Partners L.P.* (1994) the Federal Court of Appeals for the Second Circuit held that a corporation, when voluntarily disclosing information to the Securities and Exchange Commission, waived the Privilege with respect to any subsequent civil litigation. However, other courts have stated that, in certain circumstances, the Privilege may be preserved even if the information is disclosed to the government. In practical terms, therefore, disclosure of confidential information to anyone, including the government, may prove harmful when the same information is sought by your opponent in future litigation.

Waiver by Reliance on a Lawyer's Opinion

You may be audited by the IRS, and be told that certain entries in your tax returns were not only untrue, but also misleading and potentially fraudulent, for example, with respect to taking business deductions for private expenses. You immediately raise, as a defense, the fact that you have consulted with your lawyer and received legal advice that such expenses were deductible as business expenses. In such a case, any communication you had with your lawyer is no longer confidential or protected by the Privilege. The IRS may then subpoena all correspondence between you and your lawyer relating to this matter, force the lawyer to testify with respect to verbal communications between you, and also look at the lawyer's notes taken at the time. The reason is that, when the content of the lawyer-client communication is raised affirmatively by the client as a defense, there is no reason to preserve the Privilege with respect to such communication, because the client herself disclosed the content of the communications. Note that the rule dictates that, after a waiver of the Privilege takes place, all lawyer-client communications relating to the same matter are now unprotected by the privilege and may be disclosed to other parties.

THE LAWYER'S LIABILITY FOR DISCLOSURE OF CLIENT'S SECRETS

Lawyer's Failure Is Difficult To Cure

Under the attorney-client Privilege, all your communication with your lawyer, and all the lawyer's notes, memoranda, research materials, appointment book (the pages detailing meetings related to your matter), and any documents discussing or relating to your case are protected from disclosure to third parties. However, even though the government or the opposite party in litigation cannot force your lawyer to disclose such documents or information, your lawyer may inadvertently let such information or documents find their way into someone else's hands. In such a case, the Privilege may be lost.

Your lawyer's failure to keep your secrets and maintain the safety of documents relating to your matters is a violation of ethics rules and a basis for a malpractice suit. But even though your lawyer may be liable for negligence, if the information disclosed by his negligence is extremely harmful to either your business or your chances of prevailing in your legal dispute, the lawyer's pockets may not be deep enough to compensate you for your losses resulting from the unlawful disclosure.

How to Prevent Breach of Confidence

Prevention is your best defense against a lawyer's negligence in keeping your secrets. Starting with the initial meetings, insist that your lawyer meet you in an office or a conference room away from the reception area, and that no secretary or paralegal attend the meeting unless they are part of the staff involved in the representation. If you do not wish the fact of the representation itself to be known, insist that the receptionist not announce your name on speakers heard by anyone other than the lawyer and directly involved staff. Ask your lawyer to instruct her staff not to discuss your case in the elevator, at lunch, or otherwise outside the office. Make sure that your files are kept out of visitors' view and that no one has access to them. Ask your lawyer whether strangers have access to her computer files and whether other employees of the law firm could access your information online. You should also feel free to inquire whether documents relating to your case may find their way to unprotected trash disposal or recycling boxes, and ask that all disposable documents be shredded.

All these precautions are customary in any upstanding lawyer's office, and your inquiries in this respect may assist you in assessing how professional and responsible this lawyer is, not only with respect to maintaining client confidence, but also in general.

WHAT TO DO WHEN YOUR PROTECTED DOCUMENTS FALL INTO THE WRONG HANDS

In *U.S. v. Mittleman* (1993), the Court of Appeals for the Ninth Circuit considered the admissibility of confidential information obtained by the prosecution. In that case, government agents searched the residence of a man suspected of bank and bankruptcy fraud. Later, the agents convinced a magistrate that there was probable cause to believe that the suspect's lawyer's files contained evidence of that lawyer's participation in the crime. The magistrate allowed a search of the lawyer's office, which the agents were supposed to perform in accordance with the relevant rules prescribed by the American Law Institute (ALI) Model Code of Pre-Arraignment Procedure.

Pursuant to the magistrate's warrant, the agents searched the lawyer's office but the search was allegedly too broad and abusive. The Court of Appeals found that the agents failed to follow (and had never even read) the ALI procedures. The agents apparently searched the entire office, looked at all the files, failed to follow proper sealing regulations, and broke into computer files and computer disks. Furthermore, the agents' original affidavit, which was the basis for the magistrate's warrant, included false statements and omissions.

Despite all that, the court found that "the agents' false statements did not relate at all to the issue of probable cause; nor, by analogy did they relate to the issue of necessity," and therefore, because "there are no rules for searching law offices . . . the lower court's remedy—blanket suppression—is appropriate only if violations of the warrant's requirements were so extreme that the search was essentially transformed into an impermissible search." Therefore, the court held that "although we agree that special care should be taken when conducting a search of law offices, separate legal rules are not necessary for remedying such searches when they exceed the scope of the warrant." The court refused to uphold the suppression order and returned the case to the lower court for continued proceedings, instructing that if the "violations of the search warrant were not so extreme as to justify this extraordinary remedy, the district court should determine what evidence, if any, was seized in violation of the warrant and order the suppression of that evidence only."

This case shows that, for you as a client, there is no effective protection from being incriminated based on evidence found during an unwarranted government search of your lawyer's office. As the Court of Appeals stated in *Mittleman*, in order for the evidence gathered by searching a lawyer's office to be suppressed—unavailable for the prosecution for use in the trial—the violation of the warrant allowing the search has to be "extreme."

Therefore, if confidentiality is sufficiently important to you, instruct your lawyer to keep as little as possible on file and discard any unnecessary notes, letters, or other materials that she does not expect to use in the future. Your instructions should be forceful enough to overcome the lawyer's professional, obsessive tendency to place every piece of paper in a file.

In civil litigation, courts have been more receptive to the idea that information disclosed by a lawyer in violation of the attorney-client Privilege cannot be used against the client. For example, in *Ackerman v. National Property Analysts* (1992), Judge Louis J. Freeh (who later became director of the FBI) ruled that a group of investors in partnerships owning a series of shopping centers could not bring a lawsuit against the partnerships' management based on documents protected by the Privilege. The documents were supplied to the investors by a lawyer who used to work for the defendants. Judge Freeh dismissed the lawsuits without prejudice (which means the lawsuits may be brought again based on new evidence), because the lawsuits "relied almost exclusively on [the lawyer's] improper disclosures." By relying on such "inside information" and confidential information disclosed in violation of the Privilege, the plaintiffs "tainted" their lawsuit.

Judge Freeh also noted the rule that ethics violations are assumed when a lawyer, who at one time had access to files containing client's secrets, is involved in a lawsuit against the former client or is assisting another lawyer in the representation of a party adversary to the former client. In that respect, you should keep a record of the names of all lawyers and lawyers' staff that had access to your files and information. These people, who are obligated to maintain the confidentiality of your information under the Privilege, are not allowed to later assist a party opposing you in other proceedings, and their presence creates an assumption that the protected information is being used against you. If you can establish such a connection, you may have a basis to ask the court for dismissal of the lawsuit against you in which privileged information is used.

CHAPTER 14

HOUSE TRAINING AND FEEDING HABITS: HOW TO GET THE MOST OUT OF YOUR LAWYER WITHOUT RAISING YOUR VOICE

WHO'S IN CHARGE?

Douglas Rosenthal, in his well-known work *The Lawyer and the Client: Who's in Charge* (1974), offered a comprehensive study of the relationship between lawyers and clients in personal injury cases. Rosenthal's conclusions were clear: The active client, who participates in the process of litigating the personal injury lawsuit, who demands to remain involved in the process, who maintains constant communications with his lawyer, achieves better results than the passive client who lets the lawyer run free.

Rosenthal's conclusions point at the inherent weakness of the traditional relationship between lawyers and clients, in which the lawyer completely dominates the relationship, makes all the decisions, and does not consult the client on strategy, direction, or even settlement negotiations. Rosenthal concludes that an involved and dominant client receives infinitely better service from his lawyer, because "a quick settlement is often in the lawyer's financial interest, while waiting the insurer out is often in the client's financial interest." Rosenthal further warns clients that the lawyer may be under financial or personal restraints, which could lead the lawyer to be negligent in the preparation of the lawsuit; be aggressive in "padding" time and expenses; pressure the client to agree to a quick settlement, and in general fail to discuss with the client all the facts and considerations necessary to reach the decision that best serves the client's interests.

ANYTHING FOR A BLOODY BONE

Remember that great dog-training book you bought when your daughter made you bring home a four-week-old golden retriever? The basic principles are:

- Your dog won't have a bowel movement unless she can walk away from the smelly crime scene.
- Your dog will do anything for a bloody bone (but good luck trying to make her do tricks after she's got it!)

Well, the same principles apply to your lawyer:

- Your lawyer won't screw up your case unless he can walk away from his screw-up without having to explain his mistakes and pay for the consequences.
- Your lawyer will do anything for a good fee (but try to make him spend any energy on your case after he's got it!).

Whether you hire the lawyer to represent you in a lawsuit, negotiate a business transaction, or give you legal advice, the relationship with your lawyer will succeed only if the rules are defined clearly and your lawyer recognizes your ability to assert your rights as a client and demand quality legal service for your money. Because you pay the lawyer's bills, you are the boss.

Being the boss is not about power, but rather about making a relationship with a lawyer work as it should. Being a good boss requires that you:

- Make your expectations clear so that your lawyer knows what goals are set for him to achieve in performing the legal services.
- Set rules for continuous communication between you and the lawyer, and the content of such communications, so that you are well-informed as to developments in your case and the relevant law.
- Make clear that you expect to be present at meetings and conferences relevant to your case, participate in and consulted on forming the strategy of the representation, and immediately informed of unexpected increases in your legal costs.

A CLIENT AND A GENTLEMAN (OR LADY)

Demanding loyalty from your lawyer will only succeed if you show equal loyalty toward the lawyer. In *Faison v. Thornton* (1993), the Federal District Court in Nevada determined that two lawyers committed "flagrant" violation of ethics rules by holding a five-hour meeting with a person, while knowing that person was represented by another lawyer (who was not present at the meeting). Such "ex parte" meetings by lawyers with persons represented by other lawyers constitute ethical violations. Lawyers are not permitted to go behind their peers' backs. Likewise, though not sanctioned by the law, clients should show the same courtesy to their lawyers.

As a client you owe your lawyer the same measure of loyalty, not only by avoiding meetings with lawyers for the opposing party in a lawsuit, which could be extremely harmful to your chances of winning a case, but also by not taking any steps relevant to the matter for which you hired your lawyer without consulting with him first. You should show your lawyer as much respect as you expect him to show you.

That is not to say that you should always obey your lawyer when it comes to legal issues. On the contrary, there should be no confusion between respect and submission. You should educate yourself as much as possible on the relevant laws and regulations, always question your lawyer, and make sure it is you, the client, who makes the final determination on any action taken on your behalf.

THE TOYOTA SUPPLY SYSTEM

Toyota's leadership position in the automobile industry has long been attributable to its superb "just-in-time" supply system. The Toyota supply system brought the relationship between a manufacturer and its outside suppliers to perfection by going beyond written specifications for parts ordered. Through the ongoing, mutual exchange of information on problems and solutions between Toyota and its suppliers, and the exchange of experts and engineers, Toyota's relationship with its auto-parts suppliers reached a point where the suppliers' role became integral to Toyota's own operation.

In addition to getting higher-quality parts that were perfectly suited for the cars in which they were to be installed, Toyota was able to minimize inventory, by getting its supplies "in real time" and by preventing a buildup of not-yet-needed parts. The key factor in the unusual success of the Toyota supply system is the quality of uninterrupted communication, which made Toyota's suppliers continuously aware of Toyota's needs and expectations.

The Toyota supply system can also easily be implemented in the "supply" of legal services. As a client, you should insist on continuous communication with your lawyer. When legal representation is initiated, whether for representation in a lawsuit or a business transaction, the picture is not yet clear with respect to all the details of the legal service that needs to be "supplied." It may take you a while to form an opinion about what it is that you really want your lawyer to do for you. The formation of your expectations may also be a continuing process that may also be assisted by ongoing advice from your lawyer. Continuous adjustments to the strategy of your case, or your business negotiation, is essential to get the best legal services your money can buy. By creating a flow of communication between you and your lawyer, you will save on legal fees (because your lawyer does not spend time on unnecessary matters), you can quickly adjust the lawyer's focus and, subject to particular developments in the case or the business transaction, you can redefine the goals of the representation.

Legal service, even more than automobile parts, requires a constant flow of information along the ever-turning path of a lawsuit or a business transaction. There is no end to surprises and unexpected turns of events, as it is impossible to accurately predict all the decisions and moves made by the opposing parties. In order to get the best quality legal service, it is not enough to find the best lawyer. You must also be a thoughtful, involved, and well-informed client.

CURBING YOUR LAWYER'S MILITANCY

Win Your Battles Without Losing the War

The longer the war the higher the legal fees—especially if you are paying your lawyer an hourly rate. Every additional legal battle, every complication in the negotiation of the fine points of a contract, can cost you thousands of dollars in legal fees. How can you avoid such a buildup of legal costs?

Always remain involved. Be involved in each stage of the representation, and train your lawyer to consult with you and get your permission before taking a new turn in the way he represents you. Remember the story about the $100,000 legal bill for litigating $909 worth of window bars? That could happen to you. To avoid it, make sure your lawyer does not file a new motion in the lawsuit, does not raise negligible issues that unnecessarily prolong the business negotiations, and does not take any important step in the representation unless you are convinced it is necessary.

Cooperating With Government Investigations

Your company is being investigated by the Securities and Exchange Commission for suspected violations of securities laws with respect to last year's initial public offering of the company's stock. You hire the best securities lawyer in town to represent you in the investigation. The lawyer, together with a staff of five other lawyers and ten legal assistants, spends the weekend learning the case. On Monday morning, the lawyer comes up with an aggressive, militant strategy to combat the Securities and Exchange Commission by filing an immediate motion in federal court for a protective order, by claiming inadequacies and prejudice in the government's actions, and by claiming that all materials requested by the government are privileged materials protected by various confidentiality claims.

Do not confuse the lawyer's aggressiveness with devotion to your cause. A *Business Week* article (Linda Himelstein, "When the Company Becomes a Cop," June 6, 1994), argues that cooperating with the government, rather than fighting it, may save your company from disaster. The article compares the fates of E.F. Hutton & Co. and Drexel Burnham Lambert, Inc., both of which collapsed after securities scandals, with that of Salomon Brothers Inc., which was investigated for questionable treasury options and government securities trading practices in 1992 and survived.

According to the article, Salomon Brothers gave government agents free access to its files, computers, records of internal investigations, and ordered its employees to cooperate and give all requested information to the government. Furthermore, Salomon waived the protection of confidentiality under the attorney-client privilege and shared legal documents with the government. Other such companies as Kidder,

Peabody & Co., followed Salomon's example and cooperated with government investigations. These companies hired lawyers with expertise in securities laws—but instructed their lawyers to cooperate, not fight with the government.

This strategy of cooperation is intended to convince government officials that the corporation is sincere and that any wrongdoing will be corrected. Later on, more companies, for example, Prudential Securities Inc., Sequoia Corporation, and Arochem International Inc., all avoided criminal indictments and trials by cooperating with the government and, if necessary, by paying a fine.

In the case of large financial institutions, avoiding high legal bills may not be a primary goal, because the risks to their freedom to engage in securities transactions may have enormous financial ramifications. Therefore, an important lesson can be learned from their choice of amicable resolution over militancy.

If you need to hire a lawyer to represent you in a government investigation or in any other adversarial legal matter, beware that your lawyer is mostly interested in accumulating many billable hours of legal work, possibly bringing the case to the front pages of newspapers and onto TV screens, and winning a great victory. The lawyer's interests, therefore, directly conflict with your own goals, such as speedy resolution and minimizing the risks of disaster. Your goal is survival—unharmed and without great financial loss. Public victory is irrelevant, and high legal bills do not necessarily entail quality legal service. If you believe that no wrongdoing took place, cooperating with government investigations, even in the case of an IRS audit, may prove to be the most cost-effective route to take.

The Benefits of a Settlement

If you are involved in a lawsuit, whether as a plaintiff or as a defendant, you should always have an interest in reducing legal costs. Even in contingent-fee arrangements, compensation received through settlement will be subject to a smaller contingent fee, therefore enlarging the amount you receive. Theoretically, settlement negotiations, which take place after lawyers for both parties have educated themselves on the law and the facts, should reach an economically and legally just result, saving the high expense of taking the case through trial. For both defendant and plaintiff, a settlement minimizes the risk of a "wacky" jury verdict, whether in the form of an excessive award for the plaintiff or in complete rejection of the plaintiff's legitimate claim.

In addition, lengthy litigation always places high demands on the litigant's time, which indirectly bites into otherwise productive hours. Settlements not only save time, but also keep the dispute itself and related matters confidential, prevent unwanted publicity, and may also enable both parties to achieve secondary goals in the form of adding certain conditions and provisions to the settlement agreement, even though those issues are not directly related to the main subject matter of the litigation. So, even though your search for the best lawyer was based on the assumption that your lawyer would have to fight throughout all the stages of a litigation battle, you and your lawyer should dedicate same time to explore the possibility of settlement.

Settlement negotiations should not start too early, as it is impossible to form an adequate assessment of a settlement proposal without knowing the facts and the law pertaining to the case. Therefore, your lawyer should not only be a good strategist, a clear and forceful writer, and an excellent witness-examiner, but should also be a skilled investigator. A thorough use of discovery rules enables lawyers to investigate all the relevant facts of the case. After a thorough investigation of all the relevant documents and witnesses, and further research of all the relevant laws, your lawyer should be able to form an opinion about your chances of winning the case and also assess what would be a just settlement under the circumstances.

Your lawyer should prepare to fight the case to the bitter end, primarily because it is impossible to know whether or not the adversary will be receptive to settlement negotiations. Additionally, your adversary will be more willing to settle fairly if your lawyer communicates his preparedness and competence to win at trial.

Last, do not accept your lawyer's statement that "I'm a litigator, not a settlement lawyer." The following title of one *New York Law Journal* article says it all: "Settlement Skills: An Essential Item in a Litigator's Bag of Tricks" (Jonathan M. Wagner, *New York Law Journal*, July 11, 1994). A good litigation lawyer must be able to complete a thorough investigation of the case, conclude what would be a fair compromise, command negotiation skills good enough to start the negotiation with a high, yet not outrageous, demand, argue a good case during the settlement negotiations, prove to the adversary that the settlement is just and that you are making an honest sacrifice, and even offer to get a good-faith appraisal by involving a mutual referee or mediator to assist in the settlement efforts. A good lawyer is able to communicate to the other side his confidence that he would win the case if no settlement is achieved, but he must also be sensible and amicable during such settlement negotiations. A good settlement may save you legal fees, wasted time, and some of the high emotional price that always accompanies involvement in a lawsuit.

Overkill May Kill Your Deal

You hired a real estate lawyer to represent you in the purchase of your dream home. The sellers, an elderly couple eager to move on to their retirement community in Florida, are equally eager to protect their nest egg, or retirement fund. You make an offer of $150,000 for the house in which they spent fifty years and raised four children. They accept. You all shake hands. In your heart you know that the house is worth at least $20,000 more, and you are extremely happy.

When the lawyers start talking, your lawyer insists on including, in the sale contract, a provision in which the sellers guarantee that all the home appliances left behind, including stove, refrigerator, and central air system, are all in perfect order and will be trouble-free for the next three years. Such a "warranty" may result in the sellers' obligation to fix or replace the central air system, for example, if it breaks down during the next three years. Also, your lawyer demands that the sellers give similar warranties with respect to the structural integrity of the walls, ceilings, roof, electrical system, and plumbing of the house. Even though the sellers' lawyer argues that such demands are not customary, your lawyer insists that you should be fully protected because the house is old and breakdowns are probable. During a final showdown between your lawyer and the sellers' lawyer, in which all of you are present, the elderly couple becomes highly agitated, and suddenly announce that they no longer wish to sell their house to you.

Such "overkill" by an aggressive lawyer, even though it is a good-faith effort to protect you and achieve the best terms on your behalf, may prove to be a deal killer. It is your responsibility to make sure your lawyer understands your expectations. In the context of any business transaction, you should instruct your lawyer to be reasonable. It is also legitimate for you to handle much of the business negotiations yourself and to pull your lawyer back when you realize his teeth are about to sink into the adversary's flesh.

In the above example, you should consult with a real estate broker as to the true value of the house and the added value of repairs, should you chose to make them. Also, consult an engineer and try to attach a dollar number to each of the points raised by your lawyer; that is, what would be the cost of repairing such breakdowns if they occurred. Any engineer experienced in home inspection would be able to predict, with a fair amount of accuracy, what the chances are of any of the appliances or structural component of the house needing repair. If the engineer finds, for example, that all systems should function well except for the central air system, which is bound to give you trouble within the following year, such information can be used to narrow the disagreement and convince the sellers to give you some kind of partial warranty with respect to that specific system or make an allowance in the sale price to cover for such risk.

Therefore, when your lawyer's demands with respect to certain issues in the business transaction are not met by the other side and you suspect that such demands may kill the deal, be sure to know the facts, and furthermore, make sure your lawyer avoids "overkill" because of ignorance or tardiness in the pursuit of accurate facts.

CHAPTER 15

WHAT DO LAWYERS LIE ABOUT?

TRUST ME, I'M A LAWYER!

To his client [the lawyer] owes absolute candor, unswerving fidelity, and undivided allegiance, furthering [the client's] cause with entire devotion, warm zeal, and . . . ability and learning. . . . Countenancing no form of fraud, trickery, or deceit, which if brought to life, would shame [the lawyer's] conscience or bring discredit to his profession. (H. Drinker, *Legal Ethics* 6, 1953.)

Many lawyers practice Drinker's ideal of candor and loyalty to their client. Many lawyers view truthfulness to their clients as a matter of professional pride. But in general the public views lawyers, at best, with skepticism.

Legal scholars who write about lawyers' dishonesty tend to center on the theoretical questions of whether lawyers should be ethically allowed to deceive the adversary on behalf of their clients, whether lawyers should report their client's intention to lie on the witness stand, or whether lawyers may use "poker" (that is, deceitful) tactics in negotiating a favorable settlement for their clients. Conspicuously absent from such legal scholars' discussions is the question of whether, and to what extent, it is ethical for lawyers to deceive their own clients.

Lawyers' ethics rules in most states go only as far as stating that, in general, lawyers should fulfill their role with honesty. The question of being candid specifically with the client is not addressed. Judge Marvin Frankel and others have argued that, in practice, lawyers' duties to their clients are greater than their duty of candor toward the courts or other tribunals, which are therefore subject to subtle or outright deceit by lawyers on behalf of their clients (Frankel, "The Search for Truth: An Umpireal View," *University of Pennsylvania Law Review*, 1975).

A murky line separates lawyers' deceit of others on behalf of their clients from lawyers' deceit of their own clients. Leading scholars have concluded that lawyers' deceit has become painfully common:

> For years we have "winked, blinked, and nodded" at blatant, if not outrageous, lying and deception in pleading, negotiating, investigating, testifying, and bargaining. In almost any aspect of our professional practice, we have come to accept, in fact to expect, a certain amount of lying and deception.... Whether predicated on the seemingly sacrosanct grounds of lawyer-client privilege, client confidentiality, or zealous advocacy, or on the less hallowed grounds of "puffing," "bluffing," and accepted conventions, lawyer lying and deception cannot be squared with a principal statement of the purposes and goals of the profession. (Burke, "Truth in Lawyering: An Essay on Lying and Deceit in the Practice of Law," *Arkansas Law Review*, 1984.)

The problem of lawyers' lack of honesty is best summarized in Professor Lisa G. Lerman's words:

> The traditional model of lawyer-client relations might be viewed as a smokescreen that obscures the pecuniary interests of lawyers. The model of lawyer solely devoted to client interests reassures clients that their lawyers are not exploiting them. The smokescreen may be somewhat effective, but a large percentage of clients harbor unspoken mistrusts for their lawyers. (Lisa G. Lerman, "Lying to Clients," *University of Pennsylvania Law Review*, 1990.)

In her daring article, Professor Lerman discusses instances where lawyers were caught lying to their clients about such matters as charging baseless legal fees, billing clients at a higher hourly rate than the rate agreed upon, billing the client for tasks supposedly performed for the client when no such actions took place, or embezzlement of money entrusted with the lawyer by a client.

LAWYERS' LIES MAY NOT GIVE BASIS TO A MALPRACTICE CLAIM

In malpractice cases, many examples show that some lawyers do not shy from outright deceit, such as the lawyer who continually reported to his client of the development in the client's personal injury lawsuit as it supposedly progressed along, even discussing an imaginary settlement offer, while in truth no claim had ever even been filed in court and the statute of limitations (the time limit during which a claim must be made), had run out. Another lawyer charged his client an excessive contingent fee, taking the money out of a settlement without revealing the true amounts to the client.

In a case bordening on absurdity, *Hill v. Montgomery* (Illinois, 1899), a woman was falsely informed by her lawyer that he had represented her in divorce proceedings and that the court had decreed in her favor, so that she was legally divorced from her husband, while no such proceedings ever took place. The woman then went on to marry another man, unaware that she was still married to her first husband.

Another lawyer, in the case *Lupo v. Lupo* (Louisiana, 1985), allegedly convinced his client to sign appeal bonds under the false pretense that no legal obligations were created by the signature. Consequently, the client found himself owing large amounts of money.

The above cases are examples of malpractice lawsuits filed by clients claiming deceit by their lawyers and asking for payment of damages, including punitive damages. Lawyers should, and often do, pay for their misdeeds. However, Professor Lerman notes that insurance companies often limit the coverage under legal malpractice policies so that the lawyer's "dishonest or fraudulent conduct" is not covered by the malpractice policy. Also, some courts have refused to recognize such cases of lawyers' deceit of clients as malpractice, viewing the lawyers' deeds as fraud rather than professional negligence.

HOW TO AVOID LAWYERS' LIES

Prevention and supervision are your only weapons of defense against a dishonest lawyer. In practice, correcting the wrong done by a lawyer lying to her client may prove difficult, whether by means of ethics disciplinary proceedings or through malpractice actions. It is hard to prove and may take years to correct through disciplinary sanctions or payment of damages. As a client, your choice of a lawyer has to be wise so that the lawyer you hire will treat you with loyalty and honesty, in addition to providing top-quality legal services. However, being aware of the cases in which lawyers were caught lying to their clients and the high probability of many other cases in which lawyers lied to their clients, but were not caught, you would do well to err on the side of caution.

Professor Lerman interviewed twenty lawyers, most of them in private practice, the minority in government and public-service institutions. In addition to the full interviews, she also spoke with many other lawyers in different law firms, with different types of practices. She defined the purpose of her study as "not to expose egregious deception, but to probe the fabric of daily law practice to identify common types of deception." Professor Lerman believes that her study represents "not flagrant or unusual examples of deception, but rather . . . a sampling of [those lawyers'] recent experiences."

The following examples illustrate various instances in which lawyers are most likely to misrepresent the facts or flat out lie to their clients. These examples are based primarily on Professor Lerman's research. She found that most cases in which clients felt that their lawyers were dishonest involved excessive demands for fees, excuses for delays in performing their services, low quality of the services rendered, failure to admit conflicts of interest, or failure to keep clients' confidence.

INFLATED BILLS: PADDING TIME AND EXPENSES

As discussed earlier in this book, hiring a lawyer on an hourly rate basis, without a corresponding cap on the number of hours to be spent on the matter or on specific tasks, exposes the client to the risk of overcharging by the lawyer.

When a lawyer bills a client on a monthly basis (whereby the number of hours spent on the client's matter is multiplied by the agreed hourly rate), the lawyer is supposed to record in her calendar the exact time she spends on the client's matter each day. However, because the lawyer's income grows by "running the meter," the incentive to "pad" one's time is high.

For example, the lawyer you hired to represent you in the purchase of a restaurant franchise might charge you five hours for researching the law on the franchisor's right of termination. The lawyer might also charge you three hours, or twenty-five hours, for the same task. A lawyer might negotiate agreements and complete the transaction on your behalf within days or might progress glacially through the transaction by researching each subject, leave no stone unturned, and argue every fine point of the law with the lawyer for the other side. In the absence of a cap on the hours the lawyer might spend on specific tasks or on the matter in general, her only consideration (except integrity) in billing hours is whether you will be willing to pay. Professor Lerman reported that the lawyers she interviewed indicated that their decision whether or not to engage in "padding" their timesheet depended to a large extent on their assessment of the likelihood that the client would pay without questioning the bill.

When you hire a specialty lawyer—for example, an expert on franchise transactions—you should not be charged for educating the lawyer on franchise law nor for receiving written materials from the lawyer about franchise law. However, many lawyers will try to charge you anyway. Similarly, your lawyer might produce a thirty-page memo explaining the various aspects of purchasing a franchise from a national chain, including your rights and obligations under federal and state laws, and then bill you for dozens of hours for putting the memo together. Your lawyer might not tell you, however, that the same memo has been presented to numerous clients and was initially prepared (and paid for) by another client months or even years ago. The practice of charging clients for the reproduction of the same product is a common form of padding. Likewise, the first drafts of virtually every franchise agreement, lease agreement, or forms for incorporation were based on similar documents used in other transactions. Nonetheless, lawyers routinely bill clients at least a few hours for putting together the first draft of an agreement, failing to inform the client that the draft was pulled up out of a computer and adapted within thirty minutes.

There is a joke about a thirty-four-year-old lawyer who died and went to Hell. As he saw the gates of Hell, he told Satan, "There must be some mistake. I'm too young to have died." To which Satan replied, "I'm sorry, but according to your timesheets, you must be at least 144 years old."

Especially in large law firms, junior associates are under tremendous pressure to bill as many hours as possible, commonly 2,000 to 2,500 hours per year. In order to do so, associates may bill up to twenty hours per day on different matters, although in truth they worked no more than half that number of hours. The practice, which is plainly deceitful, is based on billing the same hour of work to several clients by padding the time spent on each matter. For instance, a markup of a lease agreement, which in truth took one hour to complete, might be billed to the client as five hours of work.

Even lawyers who would not lie outright about their billable time tend to be "flexible" with their time entries. Because lawyers are under tremendous pressure to serve many clients at the same time, they often fail to make daily entries on their timesheets, but instead take an hour at the end of the month and fill out daily time sheets for the whole month by making a rough estimate of time spent on each client. That practice is not only inaccurate but opens the door to other such considerations as cutting down on time supposedly spent on behalf of a client who is "hard-up" and padding the time spent on matters for a client who is "wealthy."

One of Professor Lerman's interviewees recalled a massive overcharge for "research time" in a bill sent to a rich Asian client. When discussing the reasons for padding wealthy clients' bills, the interviewee explained that rich clients "can afford it," that they probably lose track of the hours because so much work is done for them, that "padding is unlikely to be noticed because the bills are so large," and that "small clients have no money, and to keep hours up lawyers must bill their time to someone" (which seems fair from a "Robin Hood" perspective).

In some cases, a lawyer may feel that the service given is of such unique quality, and the results achieved are of such extraordinary success, that her work is worth more than the straightforward hourly multiple. This is a sad, yet common, example of a false sense of entitlement, which often leads lawyers to excessive padding of their billable hours and other alleged expenses.

Another way of extracting more money from a client is to tell the client that a certain task is not included in the "Representation" as it was defined in the Engagement Letter, and therefore requires a separate payment of fees. For example, you are an entrepreneur running your own small business. You hired a business lawyer to give you legal services on an ongoing basis in return for payment by you of a monthly retainer. One day you call your lawyer to ask a question regarding your decision to fire one of your employees. The lawyer promises to get back to you, and indeed, three days later, the lawyer sends you by fax a five-page memo discussing the legal issues involved in the termination of the employee and outlining the recommended procedure. The memo is obviously the product of extensive research and deliberation by the lawyer, who calls you the next day to say that the question was so complicated that it couldn't be answered verbally (hence the written memo). He also tells you that, by the way, the memo was beyond the scope of the monthly retainer. Therefore, a special bill was on the way.

What the lawyer may not have told you is that the question has been presented to him many times in the past, that he knew the answer off-hand, that the memo was produced in one minute from the computer data bank, and that the unusually high expenses his office had in the past month created a severe cash-flow problem, which required an immediate infusion of cash. Hence the fictitious "extraordinary" effort to deal with your "complicated" legal issue, and the additional bill.

Whether or not you know these facts, an extra bill is an extra expense that you had not anticipated. You are right to be upset and should not hesitate to express your disappointment. A lawyer who presented him-self as an expert in your line of industry and as capable of giving you ongoing legal advice for your business should be able to give you quick answers—at most requiring brief research. If not, his education should not come at your expense. And, most important, a written memo was not requested by you. All you asked for was a bottom-line answer to a simple question: "What is required to terminate that employee in a lawful manner?" A verbal communication would have been enough, and an extra bill should only be paid if the work involved had taken place after—not before—you have approved the extra effort.

The charging of expenses or "wasted" time is another way for dishon-est lawyers to increase their income. Unless the Engagement Letter is specific about what services a lawyer may legitimately bill you for, you may end up paying for the time the lawyer spent on an airplane on the way to a meeting relevant to your matter, even though the lawyer spent the time reading a John Grisham novel and napping. Similarly, costs of transportation home at a late hour, take-out meals, cleaning the lawyer's office, creating files, disposing of recyclable paper, or other expenses resulting from inefficiency, may find their way into the "Expenses" entry in your legal bill. In Chapter 18 you will find a road map to auditing your lawyer's bills and learn ways to discuss suspicious entries with the lawyer. It is important to be aware of the practices available to dishonest lawyers, even if you hope that your own lawyer does not exercise them.

BREAST-BEATING AND RAINMAKING

In the professional jargon, "breast-beating" refers to bragging about one's standing as a lawyer. A lawyer, while "pitching" for your case, may resort to exaggeration of high-powered political contacts, bragging of free access to important judges, or even claim close affiliation with a prestigious law firm in another city. In an article in the *Wall Street Journal* ("Lawyers Who Boast of Faraway Contacts Catch ABA Panel's Ear," Amy Stevens, December 30, 1994), a member of an ABA committee on the subject was quoted as saying: "Law firms shouldn't puff about their capabilities. Some are trying to sound more important than they are."

Lawyers need clients to either make a living or to get rich, as the case may be. To convince a client to sign up, the lawyer does a lot of breast-beating, making a strong sale of her unique and fabulous skills that ensure a great victory and the achievement of whatever results the client desires. The lawyer must prove expertise, experience, and a record of victories. Contacts and friends in high places are also a plus. In some instances, breast-beating is performed by a lawyer for the benefit of an existing client, in an effort to convince the client to hire the lawyer to handle a new matter.

Several of Professor Lerman's interviewees point to the "macho germ" that afflicts some lawyers, producing a symptomatic bravado in the form of "I can learn anything in a week." These lawyers are afflicted by arrogance, coupled with dishonesty. They claim expertise in every needed area of the law, relying on their quick-learning skills and their confidence that, even if presently they know nothing about the legal issue, they will become experts as soon as they are hired to handle the case.

Lawyers who falsely claim expertise are usually vague about their lack of experience in the field, or at worst, invent such experience. They may boast about personal contact with certain judges, government officials, or others with authority on the matter at hand, and may exaggerate technical skills related to legal matters such as patent law, antitrust laws, or communications. One of Professor Lerman's interviewees admitted that a client whom he represented in a lawsuit had the impression that he was an experienced trial lawyer. Even though that lawyer had no experience in actual trials, he admitted to Professor Lerman that he did nothing to correct the client's wrong impression.

In many cases of breast-beating, the lawyer may not admit even to herself that her behavior is flagrantly deceptive, because the lawyer believes that, if hired, she would be able to handle the matter successfully. Most lawyers also expect you, the client, to have done your market research and expect you to blame yourself for making a wrong assessment of their experience. This represents a somewhat distorted version of the old British law principle: *caveat emptor* ("buyer beware").

The phrase "rainmaking" was coined to describe the lawyers' art of producing legal work out of thin air. A good rainmaker can convince an existing client of the firm that the client's legal needs are greater than previously assumed. This form of rainmaking is practiced by pointing out to the client that some of his legal problems require immediate legal defense. The rainmaker urges the client to consider the need to lobby against pending government legislation, analyze and prepare for new regulations relevant to the client's business, and how the law firm can assist the client in facing all these issues by doing research and writing memos that the client can use in preparing for and dealing with new laws and regulations.

Another form of rainmaking involves convincing the client to commence a lawsuit against someone who has wronged the client in some way, even though such a lawsuit would be an expensive venture with questionable chances of bearing any fruit. After convincing the client that the new matter has to be dealt with legally, the lawyer will proceed to convince the client that she is the best lawyer to handle that new and urgent matter. Remember the case of the $909 window bars?

HIDING ERRORS AND OTHER MISHAPS

The lease for the land and warehouse in which you operate your nursery business is about to expire. Through friends you have located a new lot, which is ideal for your business. It is located near a major intersection, visible from the main road, and is in proximity to several affluent residential neighborhoods. The lot is owned by a local bank which invites offers by a certain date. You hire a lawyer to represent you in the transaction, and instruct him to make an offer to lease the lot for five years for $10,000 per year. The bank official negotiates directly with your lawyer, and your lawyer informs you that your offer was accepted and that he will draft all the necessary documents. However, your lawyer fails to inform you that the bank set a deadline of ten days for the signing of a binding lease, after which it will be taking new bids from other interested parties. You sign two copies of the lease, which your lawyer prepares to send over to the bank.

Unknown to you, due to a heavy caseload and bad memory, your lawyer fails to send in the executed lease in time, and the bank is able to solicit another, higher bid from someone else, which it now prepares to accept—unless your bid is increased. You have no idea what is taking place, and your lawyer lies to you about what happened. He says that, even though you "got the deal," the bank is refusing to sign. He says that "these guys are playing hardball, asking for more money or else they'll cancel the deal." He convinces you to raise your bid, reasoning that the bank can always come up with some legal excuse for rejecting your already-accepted bid, and that "you can't win against a bank, anyway." Your lawyer never tells you that your lower bid expired because of her tardiness.

Professor Lerman's interviewees all concurred that one of the most common reasons for lawyers to deceive their clients is to avoid disclosing their mistakes, and that because of fear of losing future business, lawyers always hide their neglectful mistakes. They give false excuses for failing to return calls, for missing deadlines, for producing mediocre legal products, or they blame a secretary or a junior lawyer for their own mistakes.

One of Professor Lerman's interviewees recounted an incident in which a lawyer sent a client a package that contained the wrong document, a document belonging to another client. The natural excuse was "It's so hard to get good help these days." The interviewee commented, "Blaming the secretary happens all the time. Every lawyer I have ever worked with does it. It's obnoxious, undermines the relationship with the support staff, and is lame. Who directs the secretary? Who is ultimately responsible?"

A lawyer will never tell a client that the client's case is not top priority. Instead the lawyer will try to excuse his errors by lying. The lawyer might avoid sending the client documents that show mistakes, or a document of top quality prepared by the adversary which, in comparison, would shame the lawyer's own work-product. In general, the bigger the mishap, the bigger the lie.

In litigation, technical errors are common, including missing deadlines, arriving late to conferences with the judge, making errors in briefs as to the law or the facts of the case, failing to file a certain document on time, or mistakenly revealing client's secrets that are protected by attorney-client privilege. All these mistakes could be excusable as human errors, but they are religiously hidden from clients. Normally judges do not dismiss cases because of technical mistakes, but even so, a lawyer would never reveal such a mistake to his client, reasoning that there is no need for the client to worry about things that turn out to be nothing.

Your lawyer might hide his mistakes not only for fear of your wrath, but also for fear of undermining her efforts to win your respect, trust, and security in his competence. In some cases, the lawyer's misrepresentation is unwise because, when you uncover the mistake, you have also uncovered the lie, which is much worse. In some cases, the lawyer will admit the problem but blame the judge for being wrong on the law in misinterpreting deadline rules and blame the adversary for misleading the judge.

The way to protect yourself from deception by your lawyer (and protecting him from his deceitful self) is for you to be personally involved in every stage of your case. As explained in Chapter 16, in the sections "Being There," "The Art of Nonadversarial Supervision," and in Chapter 18, "How to Control Your Legal Costs and Keep Your Lawyer Happy," your presence at every meeting, and your insistence on getting copies of correspondence and documents exchanged in the matter, will keep you abreast of every development. In the example concerning the leasing of a lot for your nursery business, leaving the matter completely in your lawyer's hands is a mistake. You should remain involved in every step of the transaction, especially when it is crucial for your business. Always be informed, read the correspondence, and make sure you know all the deadlines that need to be met and the tasks that need to be accomplished by your lawyer. Do not expect your lawyer to worry about your case or business more than you do.

LAW FIRMS' INTERNAL POLITICS

In large law firms, where hundreds of lawyers work together in a system that comprises senior partners, junior partners, senior associates, junior associates, legal support staff, secretaries, and other nonlegal staff, the internal politics resembles that of any large company. Junior associates are expected to bill a minimum number of hours per year, on average 2,000 to 2,500 hours per year. That number applies only to hours that are billable to a client. The time an associate spends on general work, such as keeping abreast of developments in the law, office duties, recruiting, and management of personal affairs, is not counted as billable time. As a result, associates are under enormous pressure to bill as many hours per day as possible. A partner's power within a firm also depends principally on the total number of hours billed to clients brought to the firm by that partner. Professor Lerman's interviewees repeatedly pointed to internal firm pressure for more billable hours as a reason for various lies told to clients. For the same reason, fear of the partner's wrath may cause an associate to hide a client's complaint from the partner.

Professor Lerman concluded that the typical law firm's atmosphere contributes to lawyers' "white lies," such as giving false reasons for not returning client's phone calls, lying about the reasons for not completing a draft on time, lying about the status of documents or court proceedings, misrepresenting the importance of other clients' work, or exaggerating their own caseload to justify delays. Conversely, an associate may try to manipulate a client into complimenting the associate's work in front of a partner to gain points with the partner. Professor Lerman concluded that these white lies are excused by lawyers as harmless, and that "the very structure of law firms fosters deception of clients," because "the firms indoctrinate lawyers to accept and engage in some deceptive behavior."

As a client of a large law firm you must be aware of the double-tier structure of the firm—the division between associates, who earn a fixed salary and are expected to work as many billable hours as possible, and partners, who primarily dedicate their time to generating business and share in the profits produced by associates' hours. The management of a large firm is handled by the partners without the involvement of associates, which, according to Professor Lerman, "leads many associates to feel alienated and anxious about what goes on behind closed doors."

If all or part of your case is handled by an associate in a large law firm, be sensitive to the bind in which the associate operates, but try also to ascertain the associate's candor in communicating with you by insisting on frequent contacts with the partner. Your own candor and show of confidence in the associate's work and the quality of her service will likely be rewarded by better communication and greater dedication to your case. But always remember that even though a big-firm associate is a full-fledged lawyer and a member of the bar, she is also an employee anxious about her job security and her chance of becoming a partner.

CHAPTER 16

THE SAVVY CLIENT'S TOOL KIT

TRAIN YOUR LAWYER TO COMMUNICATE

Hiring a lawyer and negotiating an Engagement Letter is only the first step on a long journey. For example, when you hire a lawyer to represent you in a civil lawsuit, either as plaintiff or defendant, the litigation is likely to last up to five years, during which there will be long periods of inaction as well as times of intensive activity. (The process will be somewhat different in a criminal case.) First, there will be discovery, a lengthy process involving the exchange of copies of all relevant documents in the possession of either party and the taking of depositions (testimonies out of court, taken by the lawyers, of potential witnesses in the case). After discovery comes extensive legal research, formation of trial strategy, drafting, filing, and arguing pretrial motions in court, selecting the jury, and, finally, the trial itself, which can last a long time. After a trial and verdict, in many cases, one or both parties appeal to a higher court, a process that may take a few more years.

Whether you hire a business lawyer to represent you in a business transaction, a divorce lawyer to represent you in a separation from your spouse, or a real estate lawyer to represent you in the purchase or sale of your home, it is up to you to make sure that you know everything the lawyer does on your behalf. Your ongoing communication with your lawyer may be verbal (in person or by phone), through fax messages, or in written correspondence accompanying the various drafts of legal documents. Your only hope to stay in control, not only of your lawyer, but of your fate as a party to a lawsuit or to business negotiations, is to communicate with your lawyer as often as possible while maintaining accurate and complete records of the contents of your continual communications with your lawyer, including notes from verbal communications and copies of all relevant documents. To achieve this, follow the steps described below.

Set Up Your Control Files

At a minimum, your control files should include:

- *Notes and verbal communication.* This file includes notes (which you should take regularly) of all meetings and telephone conversations you have with your lawyer, with your lawyer's staff, or with any other person regarding the legal matter. Each note should include the date on which the conversation took place, the form of the conversation (a meeting, telephone conversation, or message received from the lawyer on your answering machine or through a family member), and the content of such communication. If you had an argument with your lawyer, include the content of such argument and the conclusion. Especially when your lawyer calls to consult with you about taking certain actions, your notes should specify what the lawyer's suggestions and advice were, and what instructions you gave the lawyer.

- *Correspondence with your lawyer.* Every letter, fax message, and memorandum from your lawyer should be in this file. Note that fax paper tends to fade after three to six months. Copy such messages on plain paper and file them.

- *Court papers/business documents.* Place all copies of court documents, whether produced by your lawyer or received from the adversary, in this file. Similarly, include copies of business documents negotiated on your behalf by your lawyer, including important drafts of such documents.

- *Fees and expenses.* In this file you should place all of your lawyer's bills, including any fees or expenses, and also records of payments made by you on account of fees and expenses. This file should include copies of correspondence between you and the lawyer relating to fees or expenses, and also copies of the Engagement Letter signed by you and the lawyer at the inception of the representation.

Demand Information in Real Time

Every stage in the process of litigating a lawsuit is subject to deadlines. The court's rules of civil and criminal procedure are riddled with deadlines. Every court document filed by one party to the litigation entitles the adversary to file a reply within a specified period of time, be it seven days, fourteen days, or more. You should insist that your lawyer report to you immediately as soon as anything happens in your case (or in the business negotiations in which the lawyer represents you). Not only will this deter your lawyer from missing deadlines, but will also ensure that you have enough time to understand the developments in your case and have a chance to ponder them, consult with your lawyer about all the possible ramifications, and form a strategy of response to each development. Of course, the immediacy of your lawyer's communication with you should depend on the importance of the particular development, but any event that requires action by your lawyer should be communicated to you as soon as it is known to the lawyer.

Request Copies of Every Document

Many lawyers tend to be extremely possessive of their clients' files—so possessive that they sometime fail to share documents with the client if they can avoid it. The reason is not so much a mental disorder, but rather relates to the old "retaining" lien, which allows the lawyer to keep a client's file until all outstanding fees and expenses are paid by the client.

You should, therefore, make it clear from the outset that you wish to receive copies of every document relating to your case, whether it is correspondence from the adversary, court documents, memoranda of law describing your lawyer's research, or any other documents relevant to your case. You should review these documents as soon as you receive them, and insist on your right to understand the documents and their ramifications for your case. This will ensure your involvement in the case and prevent your lawyer from being neglectful.

Request Notices of Developments in the Law

Your lawyer should know that you expect to be informed of any developments in the law that have bearing on your legal status. For example, if you are in the process of purchasing a house, the lawyer who represents you in the transaction should inform you immediately of any changes in real estate laws, zoning laws, or regulations that require certain safety equipment or aesthetic maintenance that would have a financial impact on you as the owner of the house you are in the process of purchasing. Similarly, developments in tax law may have substantial impact on a business transaction you are contemplating. It is the duty of your lawyer to keep you abreast of any developments in the law that would have an impact on your chances of achieving the goals for which you hired the lawyer.

THE SUM OF ALL FEARS: HOW TO AVOID UNEXPECTED COST INCREASES

This is the sum of all clients' fears: Your lawyer calls you with the bad news that your case will require additional work, which was previously unforeseeable, and which will increase your legal costs by thousands of dollars. When that happens, do not automatically agree to the cost increase, but rather treat it with great suspicion. Your first step should be to reread the Engagement Letter which you and the lawyer have executed at the inception of your relationship.

If your Engagement Letter allows (or does not forbid) this midlife-cost crisis, you should now examine why it is that additional work needs to be done. The only acceptable justification for additional work is the occurrence of events that were unforeseeable earlier. For example, after suing your employer for age discrimination, you are now being countersued by your former employer for allegedly embezzling money from the employer and sexually harassing fellow employees. These allegations, though baseless, require legal defense. The lawyer you hired to prosecute your lawsuit against your employer for age discrimination agreed to do so for a certain fee (either a contingent, fixed, or hourly rate fee) but did not expect such counterclaim at the time his fee was negotiated. Defending such a counterclaim is outside the scope of your lawyer's responsibilities to you, would indeed require additional work, and therefore constitutes a justified request for additional fees.

On the other hand, some lawyers engage in the unethical practice of signing up a client for a low fee, only to turn around later during the representation and tell the client additional payment is required. At this point in time, after the client has invested substantial time and money in the relationship with this lawyer and the lawyer is familiar with the case, taking the case to another lawyer would cost the client too much, both in money and time. In a way, the client is now a hostage of the lawyer's unscrupulous fee-generating tactics.

If your Engagement Letter does not include provisions against such contingencies, you can still fight it by confronting your lawyer with the unreasonableness of these demands and forcing him to retract them. If amicable discussion fails, it may be necessary to demand that the bar association appoint a mediator to assess the situation. You may also have the right to terminate the relationship with the lawyer and sue for malpractice to recover damages brought on by the lawyer's unreasonable demands and the need to switch to another lawyer and start the process anew.

BEING THERE

Key to successful use of a lawyer:

Status Conferences

To keep abreast of any developments in your case and, at the same time, to ensure that your lawyer is aware of your involvement and concern, it is a good practice to request a periodic status conference with your lawyer. A status conference can take place by phone or, preferably, in person, and gives the lawyer a chance to update you on any developments in your case, discuss important questions or concerns, and decide together on the strategy of the representation.

Always remind yourself of Professor Rosenthal's statement (quoted in Chapter 14) that clients who remain actively involved in their cases get better legal service than passive, uninvolved clients. Periodic status conferences remind the lawyer that you pay the bills, the service is intended to benefit you, and you are the ultimate decision maker. Hence, you are the most important party in the case. Such status conferences should be scheduled in advance, even if nothing is expected to happen in the case during the interim, and are extremely beneficial even if they take place on the phone and are brief.

Meetings With Adversaries

You cannot have full knowledge of the developments in your case, whether it is a lawsuit or a business transaction, without actually being present during meetings in which your lawyer represents you.

Do not confuse representation by a lawyer with, for example, delegation of authority to a subordinate in the workplace. Your lawyer represents you, but does not, and should not, take your place. Representation by a lawyer is beneficial because the lawyer is trained and experienced to deal with a high level of legalese. However, you are the party to the lawsuit (or the business transaction), and you should be present when the fate of your important interests is decided.

A mistake made by many clients is that they submit themselves completely to the lawyer, leaving to his discretion all aspects of their lawsuit or business transaction. Such an attitude is a grave mistake, based on misconception of the lawyer's role. The best and most effective use of a lawyer is achieved by leaving the lawyer in the traditional role of counselor and advocate. Conversely, a client should be in the driver's seat, namely, after a client brings a legal claim, a business transaction, or any other legal problem to a lawyer, the lawyer forms a legal opinion on the various elements involved in the case, and advises the client of the law. The client makes the ultimate decision as to the best route to take, and then the client, represented by the lawyer, confronts the adversary.

Confronting the adversary in a lawsuit, or negotiating with a potential party to a complicated business transaction, is much easier if you have a competent lawyer to advocate your case and protect your interests. However, your presence makes it clear that it is you whose interests are being discussed. Your presence allows you to observe firsthand the exchange of opinions and positions. Most important, you are able to direct your lawyer in real time to adjust or emphasize this or that point, by taking a break to discuss a major change in strategy or by slipping him a written note explaining your suggestion or instruction.

Some lawyers may object to your presence at such meetings with other parties to a lawsuit or a business transaction. The reasons for this attitude may vary. The lawyer may fear that his performance, as compared with the adversary's lawyer, may disappoint you. He may be concerned that you may get too emotional or interfere with his role during the meetings, or he simply wants you "out of his hair." Even if you suspect that the meeting may prove to be uncomfortable for you, whether as a result of your own lawyer's displeasure or because of the presence of other people with whom you do not feel comfortable, your presence is of the utmost importance.

Chambers Conferences, Hearings, and Trials

As discussed at length in Chapter 4, "Planning the Hunt: What Type of Lawyer Do You Need?" litigation includes of many complex stages of discovery, including pretrial motions, trials, and appeals—a long and complicated process that is usually not worthwhile to get involved in unless the stakes are high. And because the stakes are high, you should be present at every hearing and conference concerning the case. In lawsuits, when pretrial discovery is completed, the judge normally invites all parties to chambers for an initial "chambers conference." During such a conference with the judge, many of the pending legal and factual issues will be discussed, and often the judge will make an effort to bring the parties closer to a settlement. Many judges try to provoke a settlement in every hearing, and even after the trial begins.

As a party to a lawsuit, it is of utmost importance that you view firsthand every discovery hearing, every pretrial hearing, the process of jury selection, and obviously the trial itself. Your presence will not only motivate your lawyer, but will also intimidate the adversary and, hopefully, make the jury and the judge sympathetic to you as a person whose face they know. It will also give you the chance to get your own impressions at every stage of the process.

Especially in a trial situation, your constant presence in the courtroom makes the judge and jury see you as a human being, and realize how concerned you are about the outcome of this case, which consequently creates an underlying sense of responsibility toward you as the person whose financial or personal fate will be determined by this trial. In addition, it offers you a way to participate in the process, through your lawyer, by making suggestions and being available as a source of information for your lawyer with respect to issues that may come up during hearings or trial.

THE ART OF NONADVERSARIAL SUPERVISION

Working with your lawyer to achieve the best possible results in a lawsuit or a business transaction requires that you maintain a delicate balance of trust and mistrust, of loyalty and self-interest, of respect and suspicion, of reliance and self-education, and most important, of being demanding but also realistic.

Be especially realistic about your lawyer's private agenda. Your lawyer is in business to make money. He has to deal with his own financial, professional, and personal pressures, while making your case his first priority. Not that you should allow your lawyer to make your case second priority: In the relationship between you and your lawyer, the risks are all yours, you are the one facing an important legal matter, you will ultimately pay the lawyer's bill, and therefore you have the right to make decisions and demand competence. At the same time, given the fundamental fiduciary aspects of the lawyer-client relationship and the realization that only amicable cooperation between you and your lawyer can bring you closer to achieving the desired results of the representation, your supervision of your lawyer's work should be characterized by a nonadversarial, amicable attitude.

Be appreciative of the efforts your lawyer makes. Most lawyers shed sweat, blood, and even tears during long days of hard work on behalf of their clients. The taxing effort to balance the needs of different clients, the needs of the lawyer's superiors, if any, and the need to make a good living may force some lawyers to lower their standards of integrity and loyalty toward their clients, whether in the form of misrepresenting information, overcharging fees, or providing less than competent service. Cooperation through amicable supervision of your lawyer's work will help you in directing your lawyer toward producing the best possible legal service.

Respect Thy Lawyer

Training as a lawyer and building a practice successful enough to draw you as a client demands intellectual abilities and strength of character. The best form of respect is mutual respect. To gain your lawyer's respect (not just shallow flattery), you should treat your lawyer the way you wish to be treated, while giving some consideration to his time constraints and his need to juggle other clients' needs. If your insistence on timely and competent service is both respectful and considerate, the lawyer will be more willing to share with you his thoughts about your case and his concerns about various strengths and weaknesses in your legal status or in the way your case fits into his caseload.

It Takes One to Know One: Second-Seating Your Lawyer

Educating yourself about the laws relevant to your situation may prove extremely beneficial in empowering you as a client and giving you tools to derive the most effective service from your lawyer. In her excellent book *Smart Questions to Ask Your Lawyer*, Dorothy Leeds (with Sue Belevich Schilling, 1992), offers a great source for basic understanding of the legal issues in a variety of areas, such as marriage, divorce, child custody, transactions related to your home, contracts, business law, lawsuits in general, criminal law, civil rights litigation, bankruptcy, and wills and estates. Other such books as the *West Nutshell Series*, offer a synopsized survey of different areas of the law.

Your goal is not to become a lawyer yourself, but rather to "second seat" your lawyer by trying to understand the nature of the legal issues and the reasons for various proceedings, documents, and forms. You want to be able to have substantial input in the process of bringing your case to a favorable conclusion. In addition, teaching yourself the basics of relevant law may save your lawyer time otherwise spent trying to explain the law to you.

The purpose of educating yourself on the law is not to catch your lawyer making mistakes, but rather to enable you to make better use of your lawyer, to have a better understanding of the problems your lawyer is trying to solve on your behalf, to understand your lawyer's advice, and to make better decisions on how to handle your case or business transaction.

Discussing Strategy: Macro and Micro

Lawsuits are often won through attention to small details. For example, you hire a lawyer to handle a lawsuit against your former employer for replacing you with a younger employee. You feel that you were wrongfully terminated for being too old. A well-qualified lawyer agrees to take your case. The lawyer interviews you, notes all the facts and documents you collected, and sends you home with an assurance that you will be notified when your presence is needed for discovery depositions. At this point, you must resist that subtle patronization.

Explain to the lawyer that you insist on being involved in every stage of the case. Not only are you interested in the macro (the legal theory of your case and the general way in which your lawyer is going to proceed), but also in the micro, namely, the elements of fact, the names of the witnesses whose testimony should be taken in depositions, which documents your lawyer should demand to see, what questions should be asked of the company's executives or your coworkers during depositions, and, later on, what type of jury members will be receptive to your claim. It is your lawsuit, and the process of litigating it will take years to move through various stages. Your personal involvement in every stage—not as a passive participant, but as a partner in decision-making and as a member of the strategy-forming team, together with your lawyer—will give your case a far better chance of success.

Does Your Lawyer Have a Hidden Agenda?

You hire a lawyer to give you advice and to represent you in a business transaction or in a dispute. Under ethics rules and under the fundamentals of the Engagement Letter you both sign, your lawyer should represent you in "good faith," which means your lawyer should have your interests and wellbeing as the one and only motive for his actions. Furthermore, the lawyer should disclose to you any conflicting interests or motives, and keep no secrets from you that are relevant to your affairs. Most lawyers treat the issue of "conflict of interest" religiously, and will inform you of any problem. However, some lawyers may fail to do this, and you should bear in mind that your lawyer may have a "private agenda" that conflicts with your own interests.

In a sensational opinion, the New York County Lawyers' Association Ethics Committee (Question No. 696, 1993) stated that lawyers may secretly tape phone calls to which a client is a party, without notifying the client that the call is being recorded. In its decision, the committee stated: "We believe that the secret recording of a telephone conversation, where one party to the conversation has consented, cannot be deceitful per se. . . . A party to a telephone conversation should reasonably expect the possibility that his or her conversation may be recorded."

Representing two clients with directly conflicting interests is another method of breaching the client's most basic expectation. In 1993, a judge in Fairfax County, Virginia, hit a prestigious Washington, D.C. law firm with a $500,000 malpractice judgment. The judge's decision stemmed from a situation in which the firm, which specialized in lobbying, represented two clients whose interests were completely and unquestionably conflicting. The law firm assisted one client (a retired admiral and former chief of staff to Vice President Bush) in establishing his new lobbying business, which would directly compete with another client of the law firm, also a lobbying business of which the retired admiral had previously been a partner. The law firm's treatment of the issue was criticized by the judge as "seriously deficient."

In yet another case, a New York jury issued a $250,000 verdict in favor of a client in a malpractice lawsuit against her former lawyer. The client, who had suffered extensive burn injuries in a fire at her home, proved that her lawyer, while representing her in a personal injury case against her landlord and an insurance company, had convinced her to reach a small settlement before trial, despite the fact that her case was strong, her injuries extensive, and the insurance company's ability to pay unlimited. As the malpractice trial facts showed, the lawyer was strapped for cash and had a strong self-interest in reaching an immediate settlement (so he could immediately collect his contingent fee). Because he was under financial pressure, the lawyer neglected the client's best interest to await trial and obtain a jury judgment in her personal injury case.

These examples show that, in many cases, your lawyer may have a private agenda of which you may not be aware. There is very little you can do to prevent your lawyer from having other, often conflicting interests. Furthermore, in today's competitive atmosphere, lawyers are subject to the pull of various forces beyond their control. Your only effective defense is to remain as involved as possible in your case. Insist on understanding the reasoning for any recommendation your lawyer makes, and on being informed in real time as to every development in your case.

CHAPTER 17

SEX, LIES, AND VIDEOTAPE: YOUR LAWYER AS A MATE, DATE, OR BUSINESS PARTNER

The secret of maintaining an effective lawyer-client relationship is simple: You pay a fee; your lawyer provides legal services. The further you depart from this simple truth, the bigger the risk of disappointment, and the likelier the relationship will have a sour ending.

BE A PROFESSIONAL CLIENT

Your relationship with your lawyer is a fee-for-service arrangement. You pay your lawyer for expert services, but while the lawyer represents you, the continuous interaction between you requires your active participation. In your role as a client, you should exercise the same measure of professionalism that you demand from your lawyer.

Being a "professional client" requires you to be clear about your expectations from your lawyer; continue communications with your lawyer to discuss the type and quality of service you wish to receive; curb your lawyer's militancy; watch out for inaccuracies in your lawyer's presentations; maintain complete files that contain all verbal and written communication with your lawyer and retain copies of all documents exchanged between you and the adversary during the representation; and attend all meetings, chambers conferences, hearings, and trials. As a professional client, you should exercise a continuous, nonadversarial supervision over your lawyer's actions. Be respectful but retain the ultimate decision-making power.

241

Being an "unprofessional client" means inserting improper and destructive elements into the professional relationship with your lawyer, such as friendship, physical intimacy, or joint business dealings. Being an unprofessional client will ultimately diminish the quality of legal service you receive. Furthermore, your review of the relationship as "more" than a lawyer-client relationship may later collide with the harsh reality that, for the lawyer, you are nothing more, nothing less, than a fee-generating client.

SEXUAL INVOLVEMENT WITH YOUR LAWYER

In a 1994 case in Rhode Island, a female client was awarded $225,000 after proving that her lawyer "harassed" her into a sexual relationship. The case was considered by experts to be highly unusual, because the relationship between the lawyer and the client lasted more than eighteen months, included at least 200 nights spent together, and the possibility of marriage was discussed. Nevertheless, the court ruled that, even if the lawyer's intentions were sincere and the client was in command of her senses, the lawyer was in a "position of power" to force his female client into a sexual relationship.

The Rhode Island case is instructive in the sense that a client may feel that, in order to achieve the lawyer's complete loyalty and devotion to the case, more than the payment of a fee is required. The client is making a crucial mistake, because not only is a fair fee all that a good lawyer needs to generate the highest motivation to win the case, but also because a healthy lawyer-client relationship loses its professionalism whenever intimacy invades it or whenever other misplaced overtures get in the way of a simple fee-for-service relationship.

A recent trend among courts and bar associations has led to strict rules forbidding sexual relations between matrimonial lawyers and their clients. Pointing to the uniqueness of matrimonial cases—a lawyer in a position of power and a client in a state of emotional and financial vulnerability—lawyers have staged strong opposition to legislative attempts to implement a general ban on sexual relationships between lawyers and their clients that would cover not only matrimonial, but all other types of legal representation.

DOING BUSINESS WITH YOUR LAWYER

In *Niccum v. Meyer* (Federal District Court, Northern Illinois, 1994), a lawyer bought certain real estate property from a client while allegedly representing the client in other matters. The payments to the client for the land were made by the lawyer on checks bearing the client's name—but instead of giving the checks to the client, the lawyer allegedly falsified the client's endorsement and deposited those checks in another account that the lawyer controlled through a business entity. The client was not represented by another lawyer during the real property transaction, and was not given proper legal advice and disclosure of the lawyer's own, conflicting interests. Also, there was no explanation as to how the checks found their way into the lawyer's business account. The court held that the transaction was the result of "undue influence" by the lawyer, and was therefore, void.

Niccum should serve as a lesson to every client who thinks about doing business with her lawyer. Lawyers, by virtue of their education, experience, and practice, normally possess vast business knowledge, superior understanding of the laws pertaining to various transactions, and the ability to exert professional authority in negotiating the terms of the transaction. Ethics rules, however, do not forbid business transactions between lawyers and clients. However, lawyers have fiduciary duties toward their clients, and their professional obligation is to promote clients' interests rather than their own. Therefore, in a business transaction between a lawyer and a client, the lawyer faces an unavoidable conflict between his own and his client's interests. Will the lawyer advise you to demand certain conditions in the contract that are necessary to protect you, while these very conditions create obligations on the part of the other party to the contract—in this case, the lawyer himself?

Measuring the "fairness" of a business transaction may be easy if the transaction is simple and you have control over it. For example, if you own an electronics store, you may sell your lawyer a stereo set at a reduced or increased price, as the case may be. However, if you retain a lawyer to represent you in the sale of your restaurant, and the lawyer proposes to buy it herself, you should immediately retain another lawyer to represent you in the transaction. Even the most righteous lawyer (if such an oxymoron exists) will find it impossible to represent you effectively and protect your interests fairly at the expense of her own pocket.

Even if your lawyer has been advising you for years on a variety of business transactions, and you have full faith in her integrity, the inherent conflict in having a lawyer who is also the opposite party in a transaction should compel you to hire another, independent lawyer to represent your interests. Furthermore, it is your lawyer's duty to insist that you be represented by an independent lawyer and that all documents be reviewed and approved by that independent lawyer before you sign them.

CHAPTER 18

CATS AND MILK, LAWYERS AND MONEY

A good lawyer can protect your freedom, your financial interests, and your right to assert a claim against another person. A good lawyer can save, or salvage, your personal and financial future. For the same reasons, a bad lawyer can ruin your life beyond repair. And, as some clients forget, the same lawyer may be good for one purpose and ruinous for another purpose. Your lawyer may be the best in his ability to win a harsh legal battle for you, but once the fortunes are won, you may find out that the brave legal warrior is not the best gatekeeper, that the lawyer who has fought on your behalf for justice is corruptible himself. To minimize that risk you need to minimize the temptation. The following will help you do so.

YOUR LAWYER IS NOT A GOVERNMENT-INSURED BANK

Don't leave your money in the lawyer's coffers. Lawyers provide legal services. Because most legal matters involve pecuniary interests, most lawyers possess a high level of business skills and a keen interest in money. A host of ethics rules and legal malpractice cases have laid a solid foundation for the lawyer's fiduciary duties, primarily the lawyer's duty to preserve a client's money and property for the benefit of the representation of the client. Nevertheless, you should not confuse your lawyer with a bank, which will normally be insured by the federal government.

"Safekeeping" of worthy property by your lawyer should take place only when it is necessary to accomplish the purpose of the representation. For example, it is common to leave to real estate lawyers the safekeeping (in "escrow") of a down payment on a purchase of property, pending the closing of a real estate transaction. In other situations, the lawyer's role may require that a certain amount of money be held by the lawyer pending certain developments in a lawsuit or a business transaction. Otherwise, if there is no clear necessity to leave money or property with a lawyer, don't do so, as the temptation may prove too great for your lawyer.

Unfortunately, clients often make the mistake of entrusting large amounts of money to their lawyers, even though such amounts should be under the client's complete domain, deposited in an appropriate bank or investment account independent of the lawyer's control. As the following discussion illustrates, such a mistake may prove to be very costly.

ETHICS RULES GOVERNING CLIENTS' MONEY

Every lawyer practicing in the United States is subject to specific rules (such as the New York State Code of Professional Responsibility, Disciplinary Rule 9-102) regarding safekeeping of money and property that belongs to a client or others.

Ethics rules dictate that clients' funds (or other property) that are held by the lawyer in connection with legal representation are subject to the lawyer's fiduciary duties and therefore should not commingle with the lawyer's own money or property.

To prevent commingling of clients' money with the lawyer's own money, the lawyer is required to maintain a separate account (for each client) in a bank or a trust company. In the lawyer's capacity as executor, guardian, trustee, receiver, or any similar fiduciary capacity, the lawyer is required to keep such separate accounts and maintain complete records of all deposits and withdrawals from each of these accounts, including the reasons for any withdrawals for fees, expenses, or disbursements to the client.

The lawyer is also required to notify the client of receipt of any money or property, on the client's behalf or on behalf of another person, relevant to the client's representation. In case of property, the lawyer is required to identify and label the property (such as securities, furniture, or other valuables), and keep it in a safe place, such as a safe-deposit box. A client's file should include a complete record of the status and transactions relating to such money or property, including evidence of disposal and the reason for such disposal. Finally, if there is no reason for the lawyer to keep the money or property that belongs to the client, the lawyer is required to deliver it to the client as soon as practicable.

In summary, with respect to client's money or property, ethic rules require that the lawyer keep each client's money and property separate and distinct from other clients' (and the lawyer's own) money or property; keep complete bookkeeping records that track the money or property, including receipt and disposal of such; and promptly pay or deliver to the client any money or property received on the client's behalf when the client's representation does not require that the lawyer remain in possession of that money or property.

SCREWED-UP ESCROW ACCOUNTS

Most lawyers religiously observe the ethics rules that require them to keep clients' money in separate accounts. Most lawyers do not lure their clients into investments by using false promises of profit. But the combination of a lawyer in dire need of cash and a client who is too trusting may prove fatal to the client's financial interests.

A New York court (Disciplinary Proceeding, Appellate Division, First Department, as reported in *The New York Law Journal,* July 6, 1993), opened to the public a window into the secret deeds of one veteran lawyer, admitted to the bar almost thirty years earlier, whose clients' misconceptions of his role, together with misplaced trust in him, led them to devastating financial losses. The lawyer in that case was found guilty of twenty-one incidents of deceit, misappropriation of client property, commingling of clients' money with his own, conversion of assets, failure to maintain proper records, and engaging in business with his clients.

One client, represented by her laywer in the early 1980s in her divorce case against her husband, was awarded sole ownership of the family residence. The residence was sold for approximately $700,000, which was paid directly to the woman's lawyer. The lawyer placed the money in an "escrow" account (an account intended to keep clients' money in trust pending the completion of certain legal tasks) for his client and her husband. In fact, the lawyer commingled the money with his own personal and business account, withdrew $77,000, and then an additional $135,000, and then later $194,000, all to cover his various personal and business needs. The client received only $204,000 from the sale, with no explanation of what had happened to the rest of the money (almost $500,000)! When the client's divorce case was resolved in 1989, only a small portion of the proceeds from the sale of her residence remained.

In another divorce case, the same lawyer received a total of $164,000 in payment of regular maintenance and child support on behalf of his client. The lawyer failed to deposit the payments into an interest-bearing escrow account, as required by law, but instead put the money in his own savings account, out of which he occasionally made payments to his client. At the same time, the lawyer used the same account to pay his own personal expenses and other business disbursements unrelated to the client. The client was not informed of these unwarranted withdrawals from her "escrow" account, but instead received false reports that the money was being safely kept for her in an escrow account.

Dipping into clients' escrow accounts may be more common among lawyers than assumed. In most cases, the lawyer is later able to straighten out his own cash-flow problems and return such money to the client's account. However, in many cases, the client's own neglect may contribute to the lawyer's failure to abide by the fiduciary duties that require keeping clients' money in a separate escrow account.

In such cases as the sale of a couple's residence during divorce proceedings, it is customary to have the proceeds of the sale kept by one of the lawyers involved in the divorce proceedings until the proceedings are concluded and a decision is made by the court as to the fair division of the money between the husband and wife. However, even when this arrangement is unavoidable, there are ways to minimize the risk of embezzlement of escrow accounts by the lawyer. These cautionary steps should be taken:

- Require that the money be kept in an escrow account controlled by lawyers for both sides, such as lawyers for both the husband and the wife in a divorce proceeding. The escrow account conditions should stipulate that no money can be withdrawn from the account without the signatures of both lawyers or pursuant to a specific court order.

- If the matter is such that no adversary lawyer is available to share the guardian role, it is a good practice to demand that the account also bear your name, that periodic statements be sent by the bank to both you and your lawyer, and that any withdrawals be made only after the bank receives consent from you or from the court.

When your money is placed in an escrow account, as a client you should ask to receive a bi-weekly (or at least a monthly) statement from the bank and a similar report from the lawyer explaining any deposit or withdrawal from the account. In case of withdrawals, the lawyer's explanation should be comprehensive enough to determine the reason for each withdrawal and whether it was on account of fees, expenses, or payments made to you or on your behalf.

If these precautionary steps are taken, you can quickly detect any problem with the maintenance of your escrow accounts. If there are problems, you should confront your lawyer immediately and make certain that you either receive a satisfactory explanation or that any unjustifiable withdrawal is paid back into the account immediately.

LAWYERS AS PART-TIME MONEY MANAGERS (AND OTHER BEDTIME HORROR STORIES)

The Winning Client Who Went to Sleep and Woke Up a Losing Investor

The same New York lawyer who dipped into clients' escrow accounts was also successful in convincing other clients that he could serve as their "money manager" and invest their money for them to achieve great profits. On one occasion, the lawyer negotiated a settlement in a divorce proceeding in 1986 on behalf of a client. The settlement led to a payment of an amount greater than $1 million. Thereafter, for more than three years, the lawyer was able to convince his client to "invest" in a business venture controlled by the lawyer himself. Gradually, the client's "investment" grew to more than $800,000, while the lawyer was giving the client assurances that the investment was successful, and making periodic payments to the client of relatively small amounts as "profits" from the investment. When the client and her ex-husband became suspicious, they received only partial accounting of the "investment" and later were informed in a letter that the money was kept by the lawyer under "prior understanding and agreement wherein you have agreed to invest, via loan to me [the lawyer] varying sums of moneys less certain repayments, which I agreed that you will be receiving 18 percent per annum."

During those years, the lawyer used the money for his personal needs and unsuccessful investments, in which the client had no interest. When confronted by a disciplinary panel, the lawyer claimed that, because there was no agreement between the client and himself as to what should be done with the money, the lawyer was under no restriction prohibiting personal use of the money. The lawyer further argued that the investment of his client's money was a "legitimate" business transaction with another party who coincidentally was also a client. The explanation was rejected by the panel, together with the lawyer's contention that the lawyer-client relationship had ended immediately after the 1986 settlement, converting into a regular business relationship.

In another instance, the lawyer had a long relationship with a client until, in 1989, the lawyer convinced the client to invest in a "highly profitable real estate transaction." The client invested $50,000, based on the lawyer's guarantee of a return of 19 percent interest per annum. The client was provided with a promissory note and a loan agreement. Shortly after the first loan, and after making several small interest payments, the lawyer convinced his client to make an additional $50,000 loan, while failing to disclose to the client that he was in severe financial trouble. Soon after, the lawyer could not repay the loans or the interest. There was no proof that any "lucrative" real estate transaction had ever actually taken place, and the money was used for the lawyer's personal needs.

In yet another instance, in 1990 the same New York lawyer was able to solicit a $250,000 loan from a client for an "extraordinarily lucrative real estate investment." The client was promised 12 percent percent per annum, with repayment in two years. The lawyer promised to secure the loan by assignment of the lawyer's life insurance policies and granting of a mortgage on two properties owned by the lawyer. In fact, the lawyer was in dire need for money to cover other debts, and had very little interest in the property offered as security. The lawyer failed to repay a substantial part of the loan.

After You Win a Lawsuit: Take Your Money and Run!

The disasters described above all stem from mistaking a good divorce lawyer for a good money manager. Such fraudulent practices by lawyers are the exception rather than the rule. Most lawyers deal with their clients' money with utmost care and do not risk their reputation and their license to practice law by stealing from their clients. However, even if you are convinced that your lawyer is honest and diligent, you should nevertheless leave management of investments, including real estate investments, interest-bearing investments, and even the simple task of safekeeping your money, to the institutions licensed to do just that. The safekeeping of your money is best done in a universe of banks, investment companies, mutual funds, and professional money managers. Your lawyer, as good as he may be as a lawyer, is not an investment bank. Furthermore, your lawyer will always have an advantage over you when negotiating with you and convincing you to engage in one or another investment. Your lawyer should provide you with top-quality legal service for a fair fee. But as soon as a case is won, take your money to a reputable institution capable of managing your investments.

The New York lawyer, whose successes as a divorce lawyer led to those horrible acts of embezzlement and deceit, of which his clients were the victims, was disbarred by the New York Bar Association, and his name was stricken from the roll of attorneys and counselors-at-law in the state of New York. The New York courts ordered him to make full restitution to his clients. It is unknown whether such restitution ever took place.

HOW TO CONTROL YOUR LEGAL COSTS AND KEEP YOUR LAWYER HAPPY

Keeping down the costs of legal service, while maintaining the quality of service you receive, requires involvement and persistence. First, define the specific service you need, so that the lawyer does not need to spend time on unnecessary matters. Furthermore, review and audit the lawyer's bills, make sure the fees are in accordance with the fee agreement, assess the reasonableness of the expenses charged to your account, discuss amicably any questionable charges with the lawyer, and avoid piecemeal increases in your legal costs.

Give your lawyer a "shoulder," not the pound of flesh Shakespeare suggested, by assisting your lawyer in his honest effort to provide you with high-quality, speedy service. Your goal should be to make the most of your lawyer's time by preparing for every meeting, giving a lot of thought to an issue before raising it with the lawyer, and having your house in order.

For example, before you meet with your lawyer for a periodic consultation regarding the legal aspects of your small business, don't shy away from doing the necessary legwork to prepare for the meeting. Collect any drafts of contracts used in similar deals in the past. Prepare all the documents relevant to the discussion, and tag them so that you can find a specific document easily during the meeting, take with you any material—names and telephone numbers, sample products, photographs, and so on—that your lawyer may need. In some cases, you may want to fax written materials and documents to your lawyer in advance, so that he can prepare for the meeting as well. Most important, though, is your effort to consider issues carefully before raising them with your lawyer, to foresee legal problems well in advance, and to discuss these issues with your lawyer while making all pertinent information accessible to him for review.

Even though controlling the cost of legal services begins with negotiating a detailed and fair Engagement Letter, keeping those costs down involves continual effort on your part, such as giving your lawyer a "shoulder" whenever there are tasks that can be done by you, thus saving the lawyer's time.

HOW TO AUDIT YOUR LAWYER'S BILL

Auditing your lawyer's bill may not be as painful a task as it may sound. It involves understanding how a lawyer's bill should look and what information should be included in it, verifying the fairness of the charges in light of the applicable provisions of the Engagement Letter, and conducting an amicable discussion of any misplaced charges.

Instructive Examples of Abuse

In "The Empress Strikes Back" (*National Law Journal*, July 11, 1994) Andrew Bloom reports on a lawsuit filed by the New York millionaire Leona Helmsley against her New York lawyers for $35 million for charging excessive legal fees, unjustifiable expenses, and otherwise conspiring to defraud her. Helmsley, who herself served time in jail for tax evasion, claimed in her lawsuit that her lawyers, who handled various real estate

Sample Lawyer's Bill for Fees and Expenses

For professional services rendered to Client in connection with the sale and purchase of franchise rights from the Tackie Belle Corporation of America, and related matters: general due diligence review; preparation and revision of the Franchise Agreement; review of and advice with respect to the Franchise Circular; review of and advice on the Lease Agreement and the Temporary Employment Agreement; telephone conferences with representatives of, and counsel and independent accountants for, the Tackie Belle Corporation of America; mortgage preparations, including negotiations with representatives of the Green Bills Bank; preparation of the Memorandum of Closing and other documents relating to the purchase and financing; attendance at the closing and review of documents delivered; and, advice generally as to the foregoing and related matters:

(Agreed fixed fee:) *$5,000.00*

Or total of hourly charges (Appendix:) .... *$ _____*

Nonprofessional Charges and Disbursements

Word Processing and Secretarial Expense .... *$ 288.60*

Telephone, Fax, and Telex Expense *181.08*

Duplication Expense *124.95*

Staff Overtime Expense *30.00*

Meals and Entertainment *52.81*

Postage Courier & Freight Expense *19.20*

Messenger Expense *10.00*

Total Nonprofessional Charges and Disbursements *695.64*

TOTAL *$5,695.64*

APPENDIX TO BILL
The following is a summary of Hours Billed to Client:

Names of Lawyer:	Description of Task:	Date Performed:	Time Spent:	Hourly Rate:	Cost in $:

[This table should include a breakdown of each time entry by each of the lawyers in the firm who performed legal work on the client's behalf, with a specific description of the work performed, number of hours spent on the specific task, the hourly rate that applies to this lawyer's work, and the cost for each task.]

transactions for Helmsley and her companies between 1990 and 1992, billed her excessively for fees and expenses.

For example, Mrs. Helmsley claimed that her lawyers charged her in one bill for 43 hours of paralegal work during the day of January 10, 1991; a charge for a round-trip taxi fare to the airport for one lawyer who was not working on any of Mrs. Helmsley's matters that day but was, rather, on his way back from a vacation in Europe; a charge of $193.73 for an unrelated dinner; $148.92 for books on wine, computers, science fiction, and *Chutzpah* by Alan Dershowitz; $238.16 for clothing purchased at Saks Fifth Avenue; $85.00 for a meal; and other excessive hourly fee charges that, allegedly, justified recovery of $10 million in monetary damages and $25 million in punitive damages.

Mrs. Helmsley's allegations, if true, present an example of the ways in which lawyer-client relationships are open to lawyers' unethical billing practices. Your Engagement Letter should require the lawyer to submit detailed bills (as shown on the sample form provided on the next page) so that you have the opportunity to audit these bills and detect questionable charges.

Detecting Excessive Fee Charges

Your first step in auditing your lawyer's bill should be to compare it to the Engagement Letter. If you have agreed on a fixed fee, including expenses, to be paid at the completion of the representation, the lawyer's bill should not exceed that fixed fee. If you agreed on a contingent fee, the lawyer's bill should include a full disclosure of the way his fee was calculated, and how it is adequate pursuant to the Engagement Letter. However, if your Engagement Letter provides for an hourly rate fee, to be charged by the lawyer as the representation proceeds, your task is more complicated.

Especially in case of hourly rate fee, the chart included as an appendix to the sample lawyer's bill should be an essential part of the bill you receive from your lawyer. It will enable you to see exactly who worked on your case, including the lawyer himself and any associates and support staff.

Detecting an overcharge similar to those indicated by Mrs. Helmsley, where one lawyer charged more than 24 hours of work in one day, should be easy to detect on the chart, which includes entries for each lawyer, each date, and each task. You should insist that the lawyer break down the charges to the smallest unit, that is, each entry of time charged to your account should appear separately with all the required information.

Second, in the entry describing the nature of the task performed by the lawyer, look for vague entries, such as "research," "drafting memo," "telephone conference," "reviewing documents," and other entries that describe the nature of the work, but fail to indicate what exactly was the subject matter of the work performed. A correct entry would say, "research on New York State franchise law with respect to rights of terminating franchisee's contract." Similarly, any other entry should be specific enough for you to understand what exactly was done during the time charged by the lawyer.

Accurate descriptions enable you to estimate whether the time spent was reasonable. For example, "reviewing the franchise agreement and producing second draft" should not take more than 1.5 hours if the franchise agreement is ten pages long. If the lawyer entered eight hours of work for that task, his charge is excessive. In addition, your insistence on the inclusion of such accurate and full descriptions in a separate chart would prevent excessive entries in the first place, because the lawyer would hesitate to include excessive entries knowing you will review the chart with a fine-tooth comb.

The descriptions should also enable you to detect excessive staffing, such as when the same task is performed by three junior associates, even though one would have been enough, or when several lawyers are present in the same meeting though not all of them are useful. Similarly, an entry such as "copying franchise agreement and distribution to client and other parties," if entered by the lawyer himself is unjustified, because a secretary or an assistant could have done the same task without charging an expensive hourly rate to your account.

A common phenomenon in large law firms is the rotation of numerous associates in and out of a matter, where each one of them has to read all the relevant documents in order to acquaint themselves with the matter. Such mismanagement should not be billed to the client. To detect this practice on your bill, look for charges by lawyers whose name you are not familiar with, for "review documents" or "conference with [another lawyer in the same office]." If the law firm's management fails to staff your case with lawyers who take it from start to finish, the cost of "changing horses" should be borne by the law firm and not charged to you.

The auditing of time entries in a lawyer's bill can be done by you even without extensive knowledge of the legal profession. Common sense is your best tool. However, if you feel that professional assistance may help you, some accounting firms offer "legal auditing services." Such auditors specialize in reviewing lawyers' bills and may have the skills to detect overcharging and present a better case in arguing for reduction of the bills. Note, though, that the cost of such audits may exceed the legal bill itself, and you should turn to such services only if it would be cost-effective.

Fees in Disguise

The detection of false charging may be easier when it comes to false expenses. Your Engagement Letter lists the specific items of expenses for which you would be charged. Beyond that, a sense of what is reasonable and what is not can assist you in the process. Your lawyer should include in the bill a breakdown for each charge made to your account and not just a general category such as "messenger service."

Expenses of a kind not agreed upon in advance should be rejected at the outset. A good example is Mrs. Helmsley's lawyers' alleged charge for $238.16 for clothing items (including shirts, socks, and underwear) from Saks Fifth Avenue, billed by her lawyers as a business expense. Lawyer's clothing should not be included as a business expense, except in extreme situations. Some major New York law firms, whose clients may expect to have a lawyer stay on a transaction for 36 or 48 hours without leaving the office, commonly allow their lawyers to charge for certain clothing items in circumstances in which the lawyer could not have anticipated so long a stay at the office.

Another example provided by Mrs. Helmsley's lawsuit is a $6.09 entry for a meal that was charged by a lawyer who had worked less than two hours on Mrs. Helmsley's matters that day. Other unusual charges complained of by Mrs. Helmsley were parking, tolls, gasoline, and other meals, none of which was clearly connected to tasks done on Mrs. Helmsley's behalf. All of these dubious charges came to light by cross-checking expenses against lawyers' time entries for the date the expense was incurred.

Other charges that may appear on your bill may relate to the use of the law firm's conference rooms, catering service, air conditioning or heating after hours, and other "overhead" expenses. The billing of a law firm's overhead expenses to clients serves the law firm twice: first, overhead costs are reduced by shifting them to the clients and, second, the practice creates additional "profit centers" that are added on top of legal fees. In such a manner, the traditional product lawyers sell—legal services—is supplemented by secondary products, such as, for example, fax charges. Suppose the cost to the firm of sending a one-page fax to a local number is 25¢ cents (including the cost of a telephone call, paper and ink, and the wear and tear on the machine itself), but the charge to the client is 50¢, which leaves a 25¢ per page profit to the firm. Accumulating such profits over one year of operation when the firm charged clients for a total of 100,000 pages gives the firm an additional $25,000 profit. If this is applied to other "products," such as telephone calls, copying, local travel, secretarial time, etc., these additional profit centers increase the law firm revenues substantially without increasing legal fees. However, as a client you have the right (and the obligation) to object to charges that reflect costs higher than the true cost of the "product."

AMICABLE DISCUSSIONS OF EXCESSIVE CHARGES

One of the interviewees in Professor Lerman's article stated that "when a client challenges a bill that is not entirely accurate" the lawyer often buttresses one lie with another. The interviewee added that "when a client questioned a bill, the lawyer who had billed the hours would review the bill with [the] client and explain it." The explanation, however, would often be deceitful.

Your first tool in confronting your lawyer regarding a possibly excessive charge is to use amicable language, avoiding an attack that would make the lawyer defensive. Under no circumstances should you accuse the lawyer of lying at the outset.

Second, your inquiry should be characterized as an effort to understand the charge, rather than a disputation of the charge. You might also consider accepting the fact that, even if you are not successful in convincing the lawyer to reduce the charges included in the bill, you have probably been successful in ensuring that future bills will be prepared by the lawyer more carefully and will less likely include entries that are not easily justifiable. Additionally, you should always leave the door open for the lawyer to admit a "clerical" mistake.

In preparing for a meeting with the lawyer to discuss vague entries in the lawyer's last bill, take time to consider each charge as suspect, try to think what excuses the lawyer would raise with respect to that charge, and come up with good responses. In case the excessive charge is of a magnitude that is not acceptable to you, it is perfectly legitimate to consult with another lawyer who is familiar with the subject matter of the representation and who could offer you insight into the nature of the tasks for which you were billed and shed light on acceptable practices among lawyers with respect to such matters.

AVOIDING "PIECEMEAL" COST INCREASES

Remember the New York co-op board that sued one of the tenants for the $909 cost of installing child-guard window bars on the tenant's apartment windows? The co-op board ended up spending more than $100,000 for years of litigation in four different courts, which issued numerous opinions, reversals, and affirmations. When you are involved in a dispute that has unfortunately turned into a lawsuit, your lawyer may often be able to convince you to continue the battle even though you have already lost the war. That technique, called "piecemeal litigation," is based on the argument that because you have already invested so much in the matter, it is worthwhile to invest a little more. That same rationale often works for different types of legal matters.

The healthiest way of using a lawyer is by defining, in advance, what is the end result you wish to achieve with the assistance of the lawyer. After you define the desired results in your Engagement Letter, stick to it, and do not listen when the lawyer tries to provoke you into embarking on new legal battles that did not appear in your initial game plan.

In a New York case, *Liddle et al.* (Federal District Court, Southern District of New York, 1994), a jury awarded only $1,000 in damages in favor of the lawyers' lawsuit against a client who failed to pay legal fees in the amount of $105,523. Apparently, the client had initially hired the lawyer to prosecute a claim against a former employer for $50,000 in unpaid severance benefits. Initially, the lawyer and the client agreed to a fixed fee of $10,000. Later on, during the prosecution of the case, the lawyers allegedly convinced the client to pursue other claims, making the arbitration proceedings lengthier and more complicated but with no better results. The client ended up paying the lawyer $26,710, in addition to expenses of $16,574. When he refused to pay more, his lawyers sued him, winning only a $1,000 judgment against him.

This is a good example of a client who became a "Daisy," herded obediently into the dairy farm and milked for the last drop of fee. Though the client eventually rebelled, he had spent more than $42,000, well over the agreed-upon fee, before refusing to pay more. Whether your fee arrangement with the lawyer is based on a fixed fee or a contingent fee, or on the riskier hourly rate fee, the Engagement Letter should include a cap, setting a maximum fee that may be charged to you. During the representation, resist any attempt by your lawyer to engage in new matters not included in the initial "Representation," as it is defined in the Engagement Letter between you and the lawyer. Stick to your game plan—or end up the village fool, as did that New York co-op board that paid $100,000 in legal fees for $909 worth of window bars.

CONCLUSION

A FINAL WORD ON LAWYERS AND USED-CAR DEALERS

FINAL NOTE:
LAWYERS AND USED
CAR DEALERS

You embark on a Saturday-morning venture: finding a used car for your daughter, who is heading for college. You have collected and reviewed a pile of car-pricing directories including consumer quality surveys and charts showing wholesale and retail prices for each model. Pages torn from the *Automobile* section of the Sunday newspapers—which you have meticulously collected over the past year—are in a thick envelope on your lap. You have chosen the model, the year, the optional equipment, the sound system, and the color (orange, for best visibility—only the best for your daughter!). Knowing that kicking the tires isn't enough, you have written down a long checklist of items to look for: oil stains under the car, depth of the grooves in the tires, rust on the undercarriage, punctures in the brake-fluid pipes, suspicious welds on the chassis, cracks in the bumpers, looseness in the steering-column housing, rattling in the springs or leaks from the shock absorbers. . . . As you drive into the first of seven used-car lots on your list, you feel the cash in your pocket—$2,500!—and remind yourself for the hundredth time: *Don't trust the dealer! Check the car for yourself!*

There are honest used-car dealers. The problem is you will only find out how honest the dealer was after driving the car for a few months. Therefore, it is wise to check the car thoroughly and bargain hard for a fair price. The same rules apply to the purchase of legal services. There are honest lawyers who are competent and industrious in their chosen specialty. Regrettably, there are dishonest lawyers who will sell you legal services of low quality, costing you a fortune and exposing you to risks—risks much greater than the legal risks involved in buying a "lemon."

The short time you have spent with this guide will save you thousands in ill-spent legal fees. Instead of leaving you at the mercy of an unscrupulous or incompetent lawyer, this guide will accompany you from the moment your legal need arises: It will help you determine what type of lawyer you need, how to go about finding a reputable lawyer in that specialty, what questions to ask when you interview the lawyer (and what to ask the clients offered as references), and how to negotiate a fair and motivational fee arrangement that fits your needs and financial ability. After you have purchased a lawyer's services, this book will provide you with the tools needed to supervise the lawyer as he works *for you*, enable you to judge the quality of the legal service provided and protect you from excessive charges of fees or expenses by guiding you through an easy review of the lawyer's bill. Remember, dangerous pitfalls dot the legal landscape. *You Lawyer on a Short Leash* will be your loyal companion as you travel safely and succesfully through the winding legal process to your ultimate destination. Good luck!

APPENDIX A

SAMPLE ENGAGEMENT LETTER

Table of Contents:

1. General.

2. Obligations and Warranties.

3. Service to Entrepreneurs and Business Owners (when applicable).

4. Scope of Representation and Desired Results.

5. Estimated Budget.

6. Division of Fees with Other Lawyers.

7. Payment of Advance Retainer.

8. Method of Calculating the Fee (choose only one option).

    8.1. Monthly Retainer.

    8.2. Hourly Rate.

    8.3. Contingent Fee in a Lawsuit.

    8.4. Contingent Fee in Business Transactions.

    8.5. Fixed Fee.

    8.6. Combination Fee.

9. Expenses and Disbursements.

10. Method of Billing and Payments.

11. Unauthorized Actions by Lawyer: Offset Against Fees.

12. Termination and Withdrawal from the Representation.

    12.1, Termination by Client.

12.2 Termination by Lawyer.

13. The Final Bill.

14. Restriction on Fee-Collection Measures.

15. Dispute Resolution.

1.   General.

This Engagement Letter is hereby entered into by_____(the "Client") in connection with the representation by_____(the "Lawyer") in the matter described below. This Engagement Letter constitutes a binding contract between Client and Lawyer, and defines their respective rights and obligations with respect to each other; provided, however, that this Engagement Letter is intended to supplement, rather than replace or detract from, Lawyer's obligations under any applicable rules of ethics and/or professional responsibility, which are hereby incorporated herein.

2.   Obligations and Warranties.

(1) Lawyer will be readily available to represent Client's best interests. Lawyer may not refuse to represent Client, or withdraw from the Representation (as this term is defined below), because of Client's personal beliefs, faith, color, sex, national origin, or disability.

(2) Lawyer has the professional qualifications and experience to handle the Representation. Lawyer shall engage in the Representation with good-faith intention to serve Client with courtesy, zeal, loyalty, and confidentiality, and will preserve Client's secrets revealed to Lawyer in the course of the Representation.

(3) Lawyer has negotiated in good faith this Engagement Letter, setting forth the nature of the Representation and the fee and expenses to be paid by the Client.

(4) Client will receive from Lawyer clarifications in writing of any terms or provisions of this Engagement Letter which Client finds confusing, and any amendment to this Engagement Letter will be in writing, signed by both Lawyer and Client after good-faith negotiations between Lawyer and Client.

(5) Lawyer hereby acknowledges that Lawyer reviewed this Engagement Letter with Client, and that Lawyer is satisfied that Client fully understands the provisions included in this Engagement Letter.

(6) No fee, bonus, expense reimbursement, or any other payment, will be required by Lawyer, unless specifically agreed to in this Engagement Letter. No advance retainer is "nonrefundable" unless this Engagement Letter specifically so states. Any unearned fee will be refunded to Client if Representation is terminated for any reason.

(7) The Representation, and all related work, will be done by Lawyer personally, unless the identity of other lawyers or support staff has been specified in this Engagement Letter, and the cost for such additional persons' work has been so specified and agreed upon.

(8) If this Engagement Letter includes a provision of budget for the cost of the Representation, lawyer shall provide all the Representation in accordance with such budget.

(9) Client will be provided with written, itemized bills on a monthly basis, unless no additional costs have incurred during such month.

(10) The monthly bills will be reviewed by Client, and Client will notify the Lawyer of any disputed entries. Lawyer will not charge Client for time spent in discussions of such bills, related dispute-resolution proceedings, or any other discussions relating to this Engagement Letter or the relationship between Lawyer and Client.

(11) Lawyer will inform Client immediately of any developments in the Representation, and of any communication or event otherwise relevant to Client's affairs or to the Representation.

(12) Lawyer will provide Client with copies of all documents exchanged with other parties during the Representation, including, but not limited to, briefs prepared by Lawyer or received from other parties, correspondence, and court documents.

(13) Lawyer will consult with Client regarding any development in the Representation. Lawyer will discuss strategy of the Representation, and will not act on any matter without Client's consent. Lawyer will consult with Client before scheduling any meeting, conference, or a trial in the case. Client will have the opportunity to be present at any such event.

(14) Lawyer will notify Client of any material change in the law that is applicable in any way to the Representation.

(15) Client will have the sole discretion regarding any settlement.

(16) Lawyer will notify Client in advance of any unexpected costs or expenses in connection with the Representation.

(17) Client will provide Lawyer with all necessary information, documents, and any other assistance required to enable Lawyer to provide competent Representation.

(18) In case of termination of Representation by either Lawyer or Client, outstanding fees or expenses owed to Lawyer shall be paid by Client promptly. If any such fees or expenses are disputed by Client, such dispute shall be resolved in accordance with the relevant provisions of this Engagement Letter. Lawyer will not take any collection actions other than in accordance with the relevant provisions of this Engagement Letter. All of Client's files and documents relating to the Representation, and all other property or money in which Client has proprietary rights, will be returned to Client promptly after termination of the Representation, and will not be held pending payment of fees or expenses.

(19) Lawyer will devote best efforts to achieving the desired results of the Representation as defined below.

(20) At any time, Client may report to the clerk of the court [or any other authority overseeing lawyers' conduct and discipline] with respect to any suspected unethical conduct by Lawyer.

(21) In case of any disagreement between Lawyer and Client, Lawyer will advise Client of the availability of fee-arbitration procedures, as defined below, bar association ethics committee procedure, and malpractice legal action, as the case may be. Lawyer will assist Client in obtaining legal representation by another lawyer in such matters.

3.   Service to Entrepreneurs and Business Owners *(when applicable).*

(1) Lawyer is familiar with Client's line of business, and has knowledge of the laws and regulations applicable to Client's business activities.

(2) Lawyer will be available to service Client through telephonic conferences and meetings on short notice, to facilitate Client's needs for ongoing, day-to-day legal advice.

(3) Lawyer will notify Client of any scheduled business trips or vacations that will keep Lawyer out of town for more than two days. Lawyer will provide Client with forwarding telephone numbers and other ways of communication. If such communications are impractical, Lawyer will provide Client with a substitute lawyer with equal qualifications to be available for Client's legal needs.

Such substitute lawyer's services will be billed to Client by Lawyer (not by the substitute lawyer) and will be paid in the same manner and rates as Lawyer's services are paid for according to this Engagement Letter.

(4) Lawyer will notify Client when Client's legal needs are not within Lawyer's areas of expertise, or exceed Lawyer's professional capabilities. Lawyer will, at Client's consent, make the necessary arrangements to obtain the services of another lawyer with the needed competence as required. If Lawyer concludes that it would be economically beneficial for Client if Lawyer devotes time to gaining expertise in such new matter, Client will not be billed for such additional time.

(5) Client will submit to Lawyer's review business contracts and other documents, including government forms and statements. Lawyer will review such documents and provide Client with legal advice in a prompt and speedy manner. When needed, Lawyer will communicate with Client's accountant or other professional advisors.

4.   Scope of Representation and Desired Results.[1]

Lawyers will not negotiate independently on behalf of Client, will not sign any agreement on behalf of Client, and will not represent Client in any business transaction unless specifically authorized by Client to do so.

5.   Estimated Budget.

Lawyer estimates the cost of the Representation, including all of lawyer's services in this matter, to be as follows:

---

[1] See Chapter 8 for sample provisions to be used in various types of representation such as ongoing business advice, personal injury cases, commercial litigation, divorce, etc.

	Matter/component of representation;	Amount:
(i)	[Monthly retainer, all included................................	$_____
(ii)	....	$_____
(iii)	....	$_____
(iv)	....	$_____
(v)	....	$_____
(vi)	Estimated expenses and reimbursements.................	$_____
	TOTAL	$_____

Estimated Total Budget: Lawyer estimates the total cost of the Representation at no more than $_____, covering all matters required to complete the Representation.

6. Division of Fees With Other Lawyers.

No referral fee, finder's fee, or other commission is paid by Lawyer to any person in connection with this Engagement Letter or with the Representation. No person will have the right to receive or collect from Lawyer any portion of the fees paid to Lawyer by Client without the written consent of Client.

7. Payment of Advance Retainer.

Client shall pay Lawyer an advance retainer (the "Advance Retainer") of $_____, payable upon the signing of this Engagement Letter. Such Advance Retainer shall constitute an advance payment on account of future fees and expenses, as accumulated periodically, and shall be credited to client through a deduction from the first amount of fee billed to Client hereafter. Should the Representation be terminated for any reason, Lawyer shall refund promptly any portion of the Advance Retainer that has not been actually earned prior to such termination or been applied to specific expenses. At such time Lawyer will provide Client with a Final Bill, as provided by this Engagement Letter.

8. Method of Calculating Fee.[2]

8.1. Monthly Retainer.

Client will pay Lawyer a monthly retainer (the "Monthly Retainer") of $_____ every month on the first day of the month. Lawyer will not charge Client any additional fee for legal services, except for work not included in the Representation (as such term is defined in Section 4 of this Engagement Letter: Scope of Representation and Desired Results) and only

---

[2] Choose only the applicable provisions of Section 8. Strike out those methods of payment that do not apply.

after such additional fee has been agreed upon between Lawyer and Client in writing. The amount of Monthly Retainer will be subject to renegotiation once every twelve months, and will be based on a tentative hourly rate of $____per hour. Any amount of Monthly Retainer actually paid would be nonrefundable, and would be considered earned as soon as it was paid.

8.2. Hourly Rate.[3]

Client will pay lawyer a fee which shall be calculated as follows: for time spent in connection with the Representation, including advice and conferences between Client and Lawyer, client will pay a fee at the rate of $____per hour for services actually rendered (with credit for the Advance Retainer paid at the signing of this Engagement Letter). Under no circumstances will Client be charged for time in excess of the maximum set forth in the Estimated Budget provision of this Engagement Letter.

8.3. Contingent Fee in a Lawsuit.

Client will pay Lawyer a fee (the "Contingent Fee") to be calculated as a contingent of the amount recovered on Client's behalf in this Representation (the "Sum Recovered"). Lawyer will not demand any additional fee for any work done in connection with this Representation or otherwise, unless such unrelated work and the payment of a fee therefor has been agreed to in writing. In the case of a settlement before the beginning of a trial, the Contingent Fee would be___% of the Sum Recovered; the Contingent Fee would be___% with respect to any Sum Recovered during or after a trial. The Contingent Fee will cover all the work done by Lawyer in connection with the claim against_____, and with this Representation. The Sum Recovered which is subject to this Contingent Fee shall not include any reimbursement paid to or on behalf of Client for any medical or other expense sustained by Client. Lawyer's expenses listed below will be deducted from the Sum Recovered and paid to Lawyer before the calculation of the above Contingent Fee.

In the event Client decides to terminate this Representation for any reason prior to the final resolution of the Representation, no Contingent Fee or other fee will be owed by Client to Lawyer. However, in such case, Lawyer will have the right to receive a reduced Contingent Fee, equivalent to the portion of the legal work performed by Lawyer of the total legal work required to bring the Representation to final conclusion.

---

[3] For an example of an hourly rate provision for a law firm, see Chapter 10.

Such reduced Contingent Fee will not become due unless such final resolution of the suit has taken place in favor of Client, and the Sum Recovered has actually been recovered. The measure of such reduced Contingent Fee will be determined by agreement, between Lawyer and Client, at the time of such termination or, in the event of disagreement, shall be subject to the provisions of this Engagement Letter relating to Dispute Resolution.

8.4.   Contingent Fee in Business Transactions.

Client will pay Lawyer a fee (the "Contingent Fee") to be calculated as a contingent of the amount received by Client in connection with this Representation (the "Sum Recovered"). Lawyer will not demand any additional fee for any work done in connection with this Representation or otherwise, unless such unrelated work and the payment of a fee therefor has been agreed to in writing. The Contingent Fee would be___% of the Sum Recovered, and be paid out of amounts received by or on behalf of client as each such amount is received. The Contingent Fee will cover all the work done by Lawyer in connection with the Representation. The Sum Recovered which is subject to this Contingent Fee shall not include any reimbursement paid to or on behalf of Client for any professional, medical, travel or other expense sustained by Client. Lawyer's expenses listed below will be deducted from any Sum Recovered and paid to Lawyer before the calculation of the Contingent Fee.

In the event Client decides to terminate this Representation for any reason prior to the final conclusion of the Representation, no Contingent Fee or other fee will be owed by Client to Lawyer. However, in such case, Lawyer will have the right to receive a reduced Contingent Fee, equivalent to the portion of the legal work performed by Lawyer of the total legal work that directly contributed to the successful conclusion of the Representation. Such reduced Contingent Fee will not become due until such final conclusion of the Representation, and until the Sum Recovered has actually been collected by Client. The measure of such reduced Contingent Fee will be determined by agreement, between Lawyer and Client, at the time of such termination or, in the event of disagreement, shall be subject to the provisions of this Engagement Letter relating to Dispute Resolution.

8.5.   Fixed Fee

Client will pay Lawyer $___as complete and total fee for all of Lawyer's services involved in the Representation. Such fee shall be paid at the completion of the Representation, and shall include any and all expenses, reimbursements, and fees involved in this Representation. Lawyer will not demand any additional fees or expenses for services to this Representation.

8.6. Combination Fee

The combination of: Advance Retainer; Hourly Rate Fee; Contingent Fee; Fixed Fee; and, _____,[4] as described above in the relevant provisions, shall cover all services provided by the lawyer in connection with the Representation. If any of the relevant provisions create a discrepancy in any way, and Lawyer and Client fail to resolve the issue amicably, the provision of this Engagement Letter on Dispute Resolution shall apply.

9. Expenses and Reimbusements (as applicable).

9.1. Expenses and Reimbursements in Hourly Rate Arrangement.

Client shall pay and reimburse Lawyer for any Expenses incurred in connection with this Representation. Lawyer shall itemize such expenses in each Bill submitted to Client as provided in this Engagement Letter, and Client will be liable to pay such Bill unless certain items are disputed by Client, in such case the provisions below relating to Dispute Resolution shall apply. Any reference in this Engagement Letter to expenses (the "Expenses") means all expenses incurred by Lawyer in connection with this Representation, such as filing fees, Marshall's fees, special service of process fees, photocopying, depositions, transcription, long-distance telephone and fax, special delivery and express mail, long-distance transportation and travel costs. Such Expenses include only expenses necessary and unavoidable, which are incurred solely in connection with Representation. Any specific Expense in excess of $100 will require advance approval by Client. Without the approval in writing of Client, no other expenditures by Lawyer shall be considered as Expenses under this Engagement Letter.

9.2. Expenses and Reimbursements in Contingent-Fee Arrangement.

Upon conclusion of the Representation, and the collection of any judgment or settlement, Lawyer may charge and deduct the expenses relating to this Representation from the amount paid, before calculating the Contingent Fee amount as provided above. Otherwise, Client would have no obligation to reimburse Lawyer for any expenses other than as

---

[4] Strike out non-applicable methods.

part of the Contingent Fee. At no event will the Expenses exceed $____ in total. Any reference in this Engagement Letter to expenses (the "Expenses") means all expenses incurred by Lawyer in connection with this Representation, such as filing fees, Marshall's fees, special service of process fees, photocopying, depositions, transcription, long-distance telephone and fax, special delivery and express mail, long-distance transportation and travel costs. Such Expenses include only expenses necessary and unavoidable, which are incurred solely in connection with Representation. Any Expense in excess of $100 will require advance approval by Client. Without the approval in writing of Client, no other expenditures by Lawyer shall be considered as Expenses under this Engagement Letter.

9.3. Expenses and Reimbursements in Fixed-Fee Arranement.

Client will not be liable to Lawyer for any Expenses or other reimbursement, except as provided by this Engagement Letter with respect to and as part of the payment of the Fixed Fee. Lawyer may not charge Client for any additional amount over the Fixed Fee.

10. Method of Billing and Payments.

Fees and Expenses, when due under the applicable provisions of this Engagement Letter, will be billed to Client every__ month(s)/at the completion of this Representation, in the form of a written bill (the "Bill"). Payment will be due within 30 days, except with respect to specific charges disputed by Client. A Bill shall include a breakdown of each charge of fee, in the form of a chart describing the task performed, time spent on task, and comments. Similarly, the Bill shall provide detailed breakdown of expense and disbursement. Disagreements over bills will be resolved amicably and in the method prescribed in the provisions applying to dispute resolution.

Names of Lawyer:	Description of Task:	Date Performed:	Time Spent:	Hourly Rate:	Cost in $:

[This table should indicate a breakdown of each time entry by each of the lawyers in the firm who performed legal work on the client's behalf, with a specific description of the work performed, number of hours spent on the specific task, the hourly rate that applies to this lawyer's work, and the cost for each task.]

11. Unauthorized Actions by Lawyer: Offset Against Fees.

In the case of any damages caused to Client as a result of Lawyer's failure to consult with Client before taking any action on Client's behalf,

Lawyer's action outside the Scope of Representation, or any other action taken by lawyer in violation of this Engagement Letter, or of any applicable ethics rules, Client may offset such damages suffered by Client against any fees and expenses owed to Lawyer at any time in connection with the Representation. This provision does not limit Client's right to pursue any available sanctions, remedies, or compensation under any applicable law or regulations.

12.1. Termination by Client.

Client may terminate the Representation at any time. In such event, Lawyer shall communicate with Client or with another lawyer hired by Client to represent Client, and shall surrender and deliver all documents, materials, and information which came into Lawyer's possession in connection with the Representation. Termination of Representation by Client will be done in writing, and may include instructions pertaining to such termination and to the transition. Lawyer may not hold any documents or information relevant to this Representation after such termination, and shall transfer such documents and information according to Client's instructions. Within 30 days after such termination, Lawyer shall send Client a Final Bill, as provided in this Engagement Letter. Client shall have the right to claim, and deduct from any outstanding Bills, any financial damages sustained by Client as a result of mistakes or other negligence by Lawyer. Any disputes between Lawyer and Client with respect to outstanding Bills shall be resolved in accordance with the Dispute Resolution provision of this Engagement Letter.

12.2. Termination by Lawyer.

Lawyer may withdraw from the Representation at any time, provided that another, qualified lawyer has been retained by Client, at Client's choice and complete satisfaction, and after such other lawyer has agreed to the Representation based on a review of all relevant documents and information required for such other lawyer to provide effective legal representation. Lawyer's withdrawal shall become effective only after Client has consented to such withdrawal in writing. Lawyer shall be responsible for the smooth transition of the Representation and all documents and information relevant to the Representation. Within 30 days after such withdrawal, Lawyer shall send Client a Final Bill as provided in this Engagement Letter. Any dispute over any item in such Final Bill shall be resolved in accordance with the provision on Dispute Resolution provided in this Engagement Letter. Lawyer shall not have the right to hold any documents or information after Lawyer has informed Client of Lawyer's intention to withdraw from the Representation.

13.   The Final Bill.

Within 30 days after the completion, termination, or withdrawal from the Representation, Lawyer shall provide Client with a Final Bill (the "Final Bill") setting forth all outstanding respective obligations. Any charges for fees, expenses, or reimbursements shall be accompanied by a detailed explanation. Any dispute over any charge item in such Final Bill shall be resolved in accordance with the Dispute Resolution provision provided in this Engagement Letter. In the event of recovery of any amount as judgment or settlement on behalf of Client, Lawyer shall include in the Final Bill a statement explaining the method by which any Contingent Fee (if such has been agreed to in this Engagement Letter) is calculated, including the percentage pertaining to such settlement, judgment, or other sum recovered, and details of any expenses deducted by Lawyer from such amount paid, and whether such expenses were deducted before or after the calculation of contingency. Lawyer shall also state the outcome of the Representation, the amount of any recovery, the remittance to the client, and all calculations done in connection with such amounts.

14.   Restriction on Fee-Collection Measures.

Should Client in any way dispute a charge in the Final Bill or any other Bill, Client may refuse to pay such charge and the provision on Dispute Resolution provided in this Engagement Letter shall apply. Until such dispute has been resolved amicably, through binding arbitration, or by a final judgment of the court of appropriate jurisdiction, Lawyer may not place a lien of any type, or otherwise use any mortgage, summary proceedings, or any other collection measures against Client. Under no circumstances will Lawyer have the right (which is hereby expressly waived) to retain Client's property, documents, or money, pending resolution of any dispute between Lawyer and Client.

15.   Dispute Resolution.

In the event of a dispute between Lawyer and Client regarding any matter relating to the Representation, Client shall have the right to commence arbitration proceedings, which will be binding upon both Lawyer and Client. In the event of such dispute, Lawyer shall assist and advise Client on the appropriate way to commence arbitration, and shall cooperate fully with such proceedings. If Client chooses not to commence binding arbitration, Lawyer may file a claim with a court of appropriate jurisdiction. Under no circumstances will Lawyer retain any documents, information, or property of Client, relating to the Representation, pending resolution of any dispute. In the course of resolving any disputes between Lawyer and Client, Lawyer will not disclose any otherwise confidential information except to the extent directly necessary to the just resolution of the dispute.

Client's Signature: Lawyer's Signature:

_____   _____

Name   Name

Date   Date

APPENDIX B

SAMPLE GENERAL POWER OF ATTORNEY

GENERAL POWER OF ATTORNEY*

KNOW ALL MEN BY THESE PRESENTS: That I,("Principal"), whose address is_____, hereby authorize and do hereby make, constitute and appoint _____, whose address is _____, ("Attorney") as my true and lawful attorney to act in my name, place and stead

(a) To ask, demand, sue for, recover, collect and receive each and every sum of money, debt, account, legacy, bequest, interest, dividend, annuity, and demand (which now or hereafter shall become due, owing or payable) belonging to or claimed by me, and to use and take any lawful means for the recovery thereof by legal process or otherwise, and to execute and deliver satisfaction or release therefore, together with the right and power to compromise or compound any claim or demand;

(b) To exercise any or all of the following powers as to my real and personal property, any interest therein and/or any building thereon: To contract for, purchase, receive and take possession thereof and of evidence of title thereto; to lease the same for any term or purpose, including leases for business, residence, and oil and/or mineral development; to sell,

---

*Do not sign this General Power of Attorney without first consulting your lawyer. See Chapter 12.

exchange, grant or convey the same with or without warranty; and to mortgage, transfer in trust, or otherwise encumber or hypothecate the same to secure payment of a negotiable or non-negotiable note or performance of any obligation or agreement;

(c) To exercise any or all of the following powers as to all kinds of personal property and goods, wares and merchandise, and other property in possession or in action to contract for, buy, sell, exchange, transfer in trust, or otherwise encumber or hypothecate the same to secure payment of a negotiable or non-negotiable note or performance of any obligation or agreement;

(d) To borrow money and to execute and deliver negotiable or non-negotiable notes therefore with or without security; and to loan money and receive negotiable or non-negotiable notes therefor with such security as he shall deem proper;

(e) To create, amend, supplement, and terminate any trust and to instruct and advise the trustee of any trust wherein I am or may be trust or beneficiary; to represent and vote stock, exercise stock rights, accept and deal with any dividend, distribution or bonus, join in any corporate financing, reorganization, merger, liquidation, consolidation or other action and the extension, compromise, conversion, adjustment, enforcement or foreclosure, singly or in conjunction with others of any corporate stock, bond, note, debenture or other security; to compound, compromise, adjust, settle and satisfy any obligation, secured or unsecured, owing by or to me and to give or accept any property and/or money whether or not equal to or less in value than the amount owing in payment, settlement or satisfaction thereof;

(f) To transact business of any kind or class and as my act and deed to sign, execute, acknowledge and deliver any deed, lease, assignment of lease, covenant, indenture, indemnity, agreement, mortgage, deed of trust, assignment of mortgage or of the beneficial interest under deed of trust, extension or renewal of any obligation, subordination or waiver of priority, hypothecation, bottomry, charter party, bill of lading, bill of sale, bill, bond, note, whether negotiable or nonnegotiable, receipt, evidence of debt, full or partial release or satisfaction of mortgage, judgment of other debt, request for partial or full reconveyance of deed of trust and such other instruments in writing of any kind or class as may be necessary or proper in the premises.

GIVING AND GRANTING unto my said Attorney full power and authority to do and perform all and every act and thing whatsoever requisite, necessary or appropriate to be done in and about the premises as fully to all intents and purposes as I might or could do if personally present, hereby ratifying all that my said Attorney shall lawfully do or cause to be done by virtue of these presents. The powers and authority hereby conferred upon my said Attorney shall be applicable to all real and personal property or interest therein now owned or hereafter acquired by me and wherever situate. This power of attorney shall not be affected by the disability of the principal.

My said Attorney is empowered hereby to determine in his sole discretion the time when, purpose for, and manner in which any power herein conferred upon him shall be exercised, and the conditions, provisions and covenants of any instrument or document which may be executed by him pursuant hereto; and in the acquisition or disposition of real or personal property, my said Attorney shall have exclusive power to fix the terms thereof for cash, credit and/or property, and if on credit with or without security.

IN TESTIMONY WHEREOF, I have hereunto set my hand and seal this___day of____, in the year 19__

_____

Signature of Principal

City of_____

)SS.

State of____)

I,_____, in and for the jurisdiction aforesaid, do hereby certify that the above persons,_____(as Principal) and_____(as Attorney) signing this document as parties to the foregoing Power of Attorney, personally appeared before me, being known to me as the person who executed said Power of Attorney, and then and there acknowledged the same to be his act and deed.

GIVEN under my hand and official seal, this___day of ___, hr ___19____

Notary Public (Seal)